Remote Control

Remote Control

Television in Prison

Victoria Knight

De Montfort University, UK

First published 2016 by
PALGRAVE MACMILLAN

The author has asserted her right to be identified as the author of this work in accordance with the Copyright, Designs and Patents Act 1988.

Palgrave Macmillan in the UK is an imprint of Macmillan Publishers Limited, registered in England, company number 785998, of Houndmills, Basingstoke, Hampshire, RG21 6XS.

Palgrave Macmillan in the US is a division of Nature America, Inc., One New York Plaza, Suite 4500, New York, NY 10004-1562.

Palgrave Macmillan is the global academic imprint of the above companies and has companies and representatives throughout the world.

Hardback ISBN: 978–1–137–44390–8
E-PUB ISBN: 978–1–137–44392–2
E-PDF ISBN: 978–1–137–44391–5
DOI: 10.1057/9781137443915

Distribution in the UK, Europe and the rest of the world is by Palgrave Macmillan®, a division of Macmillan Publishers Limited, registered in England, company number 785998, of Houndmills, Basingstoke, Hampshire RG21 6XS.

Library of Congress Cataloging-in-Publication Data

Knight, Victoria, 1971– author.
    Remote control : television in prison / Victoria Knight.
      pages   cm
    Includes bibliographical references.
    ISBN 978–1–137–44390–8 (hardback)
    1. Prisoners—Recreation—Great Britain.   2. Prisoners—Great Britain—Social conditions.   3. Television—Great Britain.
    4. Television viewers—Great Britain.   5. Mass media—Social aspects—Great Britain.   I. Title.
    HV8860.K65 2016
    365′.668—dc23   2015033226

A catalogue record for the book is available from the British Library.

For
Olive Florence Roberts (2006–)
Lois Helen Roberts (2012–)

Contents

Figures and Tables

Figures

Tables

Acknowledgements

I am especially grateful to the unnamed prison in this study for permitting me access to the establishment to conduct the research, and to the participants (prisoners and staff) who volunteered their time to share their own experiences. What is recorded here was galvanised by your voices and all of you have helped me to understand the prison in ways I would never have imagined at the beginning of this journey – thank you. Inspiration and interest also come from colleagues of the Independent Monitoring Board, good people at National Prison Radio, Inside Time, KickStartTV, Leaf and Life Channel.

I am indebted to Professor Tim O'Sullivan for his time, humour, pragmatism and patience over the many years I have known him, as well as Professor Brian Williams (1952–2007) for his nurturing support in the beginning of my research. Of significance I must record here how Professor Lorraine Culley, Professor Derek Layder, Dr Nicky Hudson, Professor Dave Ward, Annie Britton, Professor Rob Canton and Dr Charlotte Knight have untiringly encouraged me.

Finally, Philip, for making our home a haven, a safe and fun place to be. This project saw the birth of our beautiful daughters, Olive and Lois, to whom this book is dedicated.

1
Research Foundations

This book is about the role of in-cell television in a male adult closed prison. Its focus is to capture the experience of television use by prisoners within the prison context.

1.1 Introduction and rationale

1.1.1 Research origins

The impetus for this book arose from work on the consumption of mass communications in a closed male young offenders' institution which I completed in 2001 followed by a focused study on television (Knight 2012). British studies, Jewkes's (2002a) and my earlier research in 2001 came at a time when in-cell televisions were just being introduced to prison cells in England and Wales. The introduction of television in prisoners' cells, following New Labour's announcement by the Home Secretary Jack Straw in 1998, revealed some interesting effects on the prison environment. The British research could not systematically document these effects, as in-cell television at this time was only available to 'privileged' prisoners. In-cell television is now firmly fixed into the prison environment. This introduction took 12 years to complete from its official launch to the last prison receiving television in cells in 2010. Installation was not straightforward and many cells had to be modernised to receive electricity. There were, however, approximately 1000 prisoners who benefited from in-cell television from 1991 and this disparity in availability of in-cell television called for an official review (Ministry of Justice [MoJ] personal correspondence 2011). The research that was carried out provided a snapshot of its early introduction and its effects were limited to those prisoners who complied with current behaviour management strategies. The *Incentive and Earned*

Privilege (IEP) system, introduced in 1996 (PSI 11/2011), following a review of disturbances at HMP Strangeways by Lord Justice Woolf in 1990, sought to manage prisoner behaviour much more robustly. Policymakers were tasked with ensuring that prisoners complied with the prison regime. Incentives were needed in order to motivate prisoners and in-cell television became a key incentive to enable prison staff to encourage compliance. Along with other incentives such as access to goods and services, visits from friends and family, time out of cell and access to work and education, the IEP system sought to organise prisoners based on their compliance and behaviour. Within limits, the more prisoners complied with the prison regime the more access they were allowed to goods and services. Non-compliance could lead to privileges being withdrawn and prisoners placed on a 'basic' regime. The introduction of in-cell television and other privileges received highly contested focus in public discourse, as an index to broader concerns about the penal system going 'soft on' criminals and losing its direction. In defence of this, in-cell television became framed in political rhetoric. In-cell television was therefore positioned as an earnable privilege for 'deserving' prisoners; for example, those who proved to be drug free (Hansard Vol. 314, 1998). The Prison Service employed television to directly manage behaviour, a method which is directly mirrored in many households with children (Silverstone 1999a).

Tracing the introduction of mass communications into British prisons is difficult, as scarce public historical or policy documents report their introduction. Staff and prisoners anecdotally related[1] that early access to mass media was originally through newspapers and magazines. It was common practice for staff to read out news in chapel every week. By 1954 prisoners could directly access radio and newspapers, under supervision. Radio was broadcast onto prison landings, shortly followed by prisoners' opportunity to buy their own transistor sets. Films were sometimes shown in communal areas like the chapels or gyms on a weekly basis. Communal television sets were introduced to 'association' areas where prisoners spent leisure time out of their cells in some prisons from the 1970s, but this was never formally standardised. Prisons, therefore, are media-poor environments.

Only one prison contributed to a formal evaluation of in-cell television (McClymont 1993), which outlined concerns about the decline in prisoners attending associations and other activities; a theme also echoed by Jewkes (2002a). It was also noted that in-cell television had an influence on the atmosphere in the pilot prison, where it was observed that prisoners appeared calmer (Jewkes 2002a). Despite claims to 'monitor closely' (Hansard Vol. 314 1998) its introduction to prisons, no official evaluation has been carried out by the Ministry of Justice (Home Office[2]). This study therefore marks the only independent evaluation of in-cell television since its official introduction.

1.1.2 Research foundations

The sociological perspective underpinning this book departs significantly from the recent trend in prison research based on measuring 'what works' agendas and assessments of prisons as 'performing' enterprises (Raine and Wilson 1997; Liebling 2004). The dominance of performance-related research has eclipsed the sociology of imprisonment (Simon 2000; Wacquant 2002; Liebling 2004). These changes have resulted in the prison culture and its prisoners and staff becoming increasingly lost, even invisible, in managerialist discourse (Liebling 2004:203). Access to prisons to conduct sociological research is difficult, as prisons' resources are locked into key performance targets, as well as managing high numbers of prisoners with limited resources. Furthermore, pressures to reduce reoffending and a move to foreground victims' rights are also evident (Williams 2002). Many offenders come to prison with a range of complex physiological and psychological needs (Prison Reform Trust 2009; Scott and Codd 2010). In addition, a significant proportion of prisoners return regularly back to prison (Padfield and Maruna 2006). The cost of incarceration, set at £45,000 per year per prisoner, highlights the cost of using prison as a punitive instrument; for some, this is too much for the tax payer to bear (Prison Reform Trust 2010). Prisons are therefore under extreme pressure to perform and the sociological dimensions of prison life are not a priority. The sociological paradigm brings the human experience to the fore and is a mirror image of the policy and strategies that are routinely implemented (Simon 2000:288). As Jewkes (2002a:x) observes, audience research in prison is limited, yet provides a curious site for audience investigation. Gersch (2003:53) highlights the 'uses and gratifications' which can generate peculiar effects in the prison environment:

> The notion of 'escape' gains special meaning in the prison context, where the media are one of only a few links for inmates to the outside world.

Researchers of prisoner audiences have been uncomfortable with the frameworks and typologies of audience behaviour derived largely from research on audiences in domestic settings. One example is Jewkes's modification of the 'uses and gratifications' model defined by McQuail et al. (1972) to account for how the structural features of the prison can impact on prisoner agency and their responses to their incarceration. Her work moved away from the deterministic typology of uses and gratifications model to highlight how prisoners' *motivations* can capture the role that media has in their lives. Through conversation she was able to document the ways in which the male prisoners interpreted and made sense of their experience and also of themselves. The *meanings* they reported provided a view of their subjectivity and how it is negotiated within the prison setting. In a similar way, Vandebosch (2000) highlighted that prisoners had 'media related needs' and increased degrees of dependency on media use. A common finding across most of the prison audience, including my earlier research, is that prisoners actively draw upon media resources in powerful and active ways during incarceration. All of the studies challenge the view that prisoners are passive both to the system and to the messages they consume through mass media. As much broader research on audiences has shown, media consumption is an active phenomenon in which audiences negotiate power, meanings and identity (Silverstone 1999a). Media can also transform time and space and provide an insight into how public and private life is negotiated and resisted by audiences (Moores 1995a). Prisoner audience research has found that these features take on heightened meanings for people in prison.

My earlier work (Knight 2005c) raised some important questions about the role of media consumption in relation to its time-passing qualities. Media use helps to fill time with meaningful activity. Broadcast media can help to minimise boredom, and at this stage I interpreted this in relation to the inescapable 'empty' time that prisoners routinely endure especially behind their cell doors. Upon review of prisoner audience studies, boredom and the experience of the prison cell remain underexplored. These studies had not sufficiently mapped time and space in relation to media use or the kinds of 'excursions' (Moores 2006) prisoners were making. In light of overcrowding, prison cells that were once intended for single occupancy are now mostly accommodating two or more prisoners (PSI 2750); these dynamics impact significantly on the management of time and space by prisoners. Other than Gersch's (2003) insight into communal viewing and the hierarchies of access and selection based on race in US prisons, little is known about the dynamics of sharing cells. Therefore, the everyday living arrangements between cell co-occupants remains an enigma and more generally are a relatively unexplored feature of prison life. Cell-sharing received much attention when Zahid Mubarek was murdered by his racist cell-mate, Robert Stewart, at HMYOI Feltham in 2000. This brought about a policy review to risk-assess cell-sharing. Now that all cells in England and Wales have the capacity to have in-cell television as standard, this dynamic deserves attention.

These prisoner audience studies have consistently fallen short of interrogating the feelings engendered by media reception. Jewkes (2002a) demonstrates how the 'pains' of incarceration are managed (or not) through media use with *implicit* reference to emotion. Vandebosch (2000) also discusses the therapeutic qualities of media use but does not report sufficiently on the nature of media's effects on well-being. Garland's (1991) thesis on the use of punishment highlights that emotionality is central to the ways in which punishment, like imprisonment, is both managed and experienced by its stakeholders (see also Crawley 2004). To this effect, according to Garland, emotionality is actively controlled by penal agencies or the 'rationalisation' of punishment (1991:177). As Hochschild (1983) found, organisations or settings demand composure of emotion. These 'feeling rules' are also valid in the prison setting (Crawley 2004). Crawley found that in this context certain feelings are tolerated and accepted and others are not. The 'inmate code' is also thought to be a powerful force on the ways in which prisoners interact and do their time in prison; 'prisonisation' or prison socialisation (Clemmer 1958). The regulation of emotion is therefore part of socialisation. In a landscape where some, if not most, emotions are purposefully masked, the salience of media, especially broadcast media, has been identified as psychologically nourishing (Zillman 1988). It is claimed that television has 'care-giving' qualities and is a particular site for achieving 'ontological security' (Silverstone 1999a). This begins to indicate that media use stretches beyond pure functional and environmental features (Lull 1990, 1988). Silverstone's work has paved the way for a fuller exploration of the kinds of emotive relationships audiences have with television, and prisoner audience research should not be excluded from this. The sociology of imprisonment continually points to the pains and harms of the incarcerating experience and yet these have not been fully developed to account for specific forms of emotionality and how they become, or the extent to which they are registered as, painful. The deprivation models developed by Sykes (1999) and Goffman (1991) are significant, but their models of deprivation do not cater for the emotional dimensions of institutional life. Goffman's (1991) discussion of a 'civic death' on entering an institution is powerful, yet lacks the emotional vocabulary to deal with how incarceration is felt by inmates. Even alternative models such as prisonisation and importation models may also be accused of the same omissions (Clemmer 1958; Irwin and Cressey 1962).

These aspects of prison life, with television firmly rooted within it, present ever pressing challenges. The government's response to the green paper *Breaking the Cycle* (MoJ 2011) sets out a series of aims whereby time in prison should be better spent or 'purposeful'. Historically this has been an aim; with the mission statement to get prisoners to 'lead a good and useful life' (Prison Rule 1), this is now becoming intensified. Achieving purposeful activity has been an instrumental and guiding target for prisons for some time (PS7100, PS4350), yet the current claims to engage all prisoners in work and training are now for the first time going to be linked to the 'payment by results' policy. Here prisons will compete to deliver provision and support for prisoners in order to achieve the aims and objectives set out in the government response. Prisoners' use of time is therefore a renewed issue and scrutiny of their time is about to enter the debate much more fiercely than in the past. Secretary of State for Justice Kenneth Clarke added to this response:

> too many prisoners are able to pass their time in prison in a state of enforced idleness, with little or no constructive activity. Prisons must become places of hard work and training, where prisoners are expected to work a 40 hour week, with money from their earnings deducted to support victims' groups.
>
> (MoJ 2011:1)

This perspective highlights how the Prison Service is criticised for allowing prisoners to 'sleep through their sentences' (London Evening Standard 2011). How in-cell television is framed within these discussions remains uncertain, but it is likely that television viewing by prisoners will be attributed, as it has been historically, as a passive and non-productive activity. Yet rhetoric about making prison 'hard' and where prisoners will be expected to make reparation or 'payback' and take up 'treatment' may not necessarily position the current incentives system too favourably. Jewkes (2002a:x) explains that this 'sits awkwardly alongside the prison service's self-proclaimed aim to engage prisoners in purposeful activity' (ibid.:x). The anxieties about watching television, especially within the prison environment, hark back to concerns about the 'effects' model. Here viewers, particularly the disenfranchised and vulnerable, are susceptible to the unrelenting enticement and powerful messages that mass communication delivers. Jewkes argues that this perspective 'misses the important point that media resources fulfil a wide range of motivations and gratifications and desires, many of which are felt acutely among the confined' (ibid.:xi). As Jewkes and others (Vandebosch 2000; Gersch 2003) have demonstrated, media use by prisoners is an important route to power and control; it is one of the few activities and aspects of their lives where they can make choices for themselves. The purposeful negation of autonomy and choice that prisons actively construct may contradict the current government's aim to get prisoners active in meaningful ways.

Rose, in his discussion on governance, shows that the state's project to cleanse society of pathological groups requires a 'neo-hygienic strategy' (1999:188). Inculcating the individual in this project 'it is necessary and desirable to educate us in the techniques for governing ourselves' (ibid.:221). Therefore the extent to which prisoners are expected and encouraged to self-govern can also be traced within the prison setting (Pryor 2001; Bosworth 2007). If the government plans for 'payback' are going to be ratified, 'vocabularies of the therapeutic... [need to be] deployed in every practice addressed to human problems' (Rose 1999:218). The prison regime, now with in-cell television, currently provides prisoners with an additional site to 'look inwards' (Rose 1999:227). The extent to which forms of self-regulation are mobilised with communication outlets like television remain an unexplored dimension in prisoner audience research.

1.2   Research on prisoners and audiences

This book is based on a qualitative study, which uses an ethnographic research strategy to explore the role of in-cell television in prison. The foundations of this study are informed by Layder's (2005) theory of 'domains' and his 'adaptive' approach. Together these theories have provided a conceptual and practical guide to the research process. An ethnographic strategy was selected to operationalise the research, by employing television-use diaries as well as semi-structured interviews with prisoners and staff. The research was conducted in a single prison (local adult male closed). Decisions to employ this methodology are informed by qualitative traditions of research carried out with prisoners and media audiences. This short section provides an overview of some of those influences and how they have shaped the design of this study. This takes into account the role of the ethnographic approach, methods for capturing data, accessing and reaching the prisoner audience and the ethical implications of undertaking this type of research.

1.2.1 Ethnography

Moores (1996) as well as others (Silverstone et al. 1991; Gray 1992; Jewkes 2002a; Bird 2003) have adopted ethnographic strategies in their work on audiences of mass communications. Although methods of data collection and immersion in the field may differ from 'traditional' ethnographic strategies, audience reception studies can also share the same intentions (Moores 1993a:4). These include Moores's (ibid.) own work on satellite television and Jewkes's (2002a) study of male prisoners' media use. The critical ethnographic approach[3] adopted by Moores (1993a) 'is committed to critically analysing culture as well as describing it' (ibid.:4). Moores asserts critical ethnography can

> ...take extremely seriously the interpretations of the media constructed by consumers in their everyday routines. At the same time, it [ethnography] is not afraid to interrogate and situate their spoken accounts...
>
> (Moores 1993a:5)

However, Moores asserts that accessing television audiences is difficult for researchers, because the 'private sphere of the household' is physically separated from the public sphere (Moores 1993a:4). Lull (1990) and Hobson (1982) also report such difficulties, explaining that viewers' consumption of television is also a private activity. Similar challenges are also relevant to prison researchers, as they are often constricted by the nature of the regime and the willingness of social agents to disclose personal and private information. Consequently, there is 'insufficient knowledge about the ordinary world of the prison' (Crewe 2005:349). Interrogating private activities, like watching television and imprisonment, cannot duplicate the traditional ethnography where the ethnographer is immersed within the field of study for extended periods, thus moving beyond the anthropological roots of this tradition (Hammersley and Atkinson 2010). Moores (2006:3) asserts that media use in everyday life is taken for granted and ethnographic strategies can allow researchers to access social reality in systematic ways (ibid.:14). Moores (1993) makes the point that ethnographic strategies allow researchers to interrogate everyday life with television, even though they have spent no more than a couple of hours in a household. In prison environments visiting researchers are also constrained by time.

An ethnographic strategy can help to illuminate meanings, motives, action and feelings of social actors,

...attending to the meanings produced by social subjects and to daily activities they perform, qualitative researchers have frequently sought to explain those significances and practices by locating them in relation to broader frameworks of interpretation and to structures of power and inequality.

(Moores 1993:5)

The value of an ethnographic strategy lays in its capacity to provide a mixture of techniques by offering an account of social reality in its natural setting (Hammersley and Atkinson 2010:3). In the context of the prison this means that a critical description of the impact of television on prisoners, prison staff and prison culture can be reproduced. Audience research asserts that private modes of media consumption should fully take into account the context of this activity (Silverstone et al. 1991). Adopting Layder's sociological model provides an important platform to qualify the relationships between the domains in everyday life. Television consumption, as research has shown (see Chapter 4), is not an isolated activity and encompasses a range of diverse and complex activities and interpretations. In essence an ethnographic approach can allow the researcher to locate the phenomena of inquiry across an intricate web of networks, action and subjectivity by also paying attention to broader social structures and discourses.

As Alasuutari (1999) identified the 'ethnographic turn' celebrates 'natural settings' research within predominantly domestic contexts (see Morley 1980; Moores 1989, 1995; Lull 1990; Ang 1991; Gray 1992; Silverstone 1999a; Wood 2009). This important body of work highlighted the social, political and economic complexities of family life, revealing much about features of class and gender in relation to audience relationships with mass communications. Significantly, this body of work helped to identify much about the felt experiences of domestic life and the spatial and temporal dimensions of everyday life. There has been a smaller raft of studies that shifted their focus to audience receptions outside the domestic sphere. McCarthy's (2003) study of television in public places captures the influence of context on television reception: that audiences' use of television is modified depending on the context in which it is received. Hajjar's (1998) study of media use within a nursing home also supports this perspective. These shifts in context have enriched debates about theoretical models of audience activity. In particular, the body of prison audience research has extended understanding about the ways in which audiences make sense of their relationships with mass communications. Jewkes's (2002) revision of the 'uses and gratifications' model proposed by McQuail et al. (1972) identified that prisoner audiences explained their reception behaviour in terms of *meanings and motivations*.

1.2.2 Ethnography in prisons

The value of the prison ethnography is best summarised by Jewkes (2013) where she argues that this approach can counter the tide of prison statistics, account for social interaction and relationships, allows the researcher a voice and counters the dominance of psychological assessments and auditing. Yet reaching the private and inner sphere of the prison is increasingly hard to achieve. With limited resources and policy agendas driving a 'what works' evaluative research culture and a focus on the growing size of the prison population, the prison ethnography is in danger of disappearing from view (Simon 2000). As Wacquant (2002) has famously articulated, this 'eclipse' shifts the felt, everyday experiences of prison life off centre and thus skews understandings of our prisons. Liebling (1999b) further talks about 'the absence of pain' in quantitative research and she stresses the importance of emotions in research and the field of criminology. Ethnographic accounts of the prison go some way to reaching the emotive dimensions of prison life, but much of this dialogue has routinely drawn on Sykes' typology: the pains of imprisonment. Qualitative prison research relies heavily on this model of pain. However, more recently, Crewe (2011) has suggested that contemporary penal experiences mean that 'new' pains are emerging. Crewe's analysis (2006) is located within the ethnographic tradition and his access and closeness to the field and those that inhabit these spaces means that he is able to develop and continue important discussions about the ways in which incarceration is felt by prisoners and staff.

As Simon suggests, the creeping invisibility of prison social order means that 'the prison regime is now hostile to the production of inmate discourse' (2000:290), thus the voices of the prison experience are muffled and de-centred by the ebb of prison sociology. With these aspects in mind prison ethnography has a complex role to play in the penal landscape (Jewkes 2013). Sensitivity around the ways in which prison ethnographies are reproduced by researchers requires careful handling. Robust methods and modes of inquiry, along with credible modes of analysis, as well as the inclusion of researchers' narratives, means ethnography can, with integrity, continue to enliven the penal landscape and put people at its centre. This monograph seeks to mirror these values.

1.2.3 Capturing data

1.2.3.1 Structured television-use diaries

Television's role in the use of time and routine has waned in recent audience research and 'critical reception' seems to have dominated the audience research (Moores 1996:7). Academic audience research has largely progressed along a qualitative paradigm, and mapping and measuring time (in quantities) in relation to television consumption is largely constrained to the television industry. The quantitative techniques of audience measurement have received criticism, based on the assumption that this will not necessarily provide a clear and precise image of audience behaviour (Moores 1996:5; see also Ang 1991). Silverstone et al.'s ethnography of householders' use of technology adopted time-use diaries, along with other methods such as interviews, in order to access and record *private* consumption of household members which provide 'an objectification of a week's activities, and one that can be cross-examined' in interviews (1991:214 – see also Zimmerman and Wieder 1977:484). They argue that time-use diaries provided the 'first indication... of the space-time geography of the home' (ibid.). Gershuny and Sullivan (1998) also assert that time-use diaries can offer researchers a valuable gateway into understanding the sociological features of everyday life.

Prison audience research has not benefited from the same analysis of television that has taken place in traditional 'domestic' settings such as that collected by the Broadcast Audience Research Board. Whilst the use of diaries can provide illustrative detail they cannot be analysed independently, rather they are illustrative to the setting's routine, which can be built upon through descriptions made by prisoners based on their own viewing repertoires and experience of the prison. The design of the diary format adheres to what Corti (1993:137) describes as 'structured', where the respondent makes entries and annotations to the format provided by the researcher. Each day of the diary sheet contains 24 separate hourly slots to record the television programme watched according to the time of day. The other fragments allowed the respondent to note where the programme is watched and whether this was in the company of their cellmate.

Using this particular method harnesses important theoretical propositions in relation to 'social domain' (Layder 2005), in that agency and structure cannot be fully interrogated unless all domains are fully captured (Layder 2004:49). The diaries provide access into the *social setting* in which television is consumed. It is possible to identify points at which television flows into prisoners' lives and 'the kind of 'journeys' that are made' with television (Moores 1993:366). Furthermore, diaries can account for the kinds of *contextual resources* that diarists are accessing through television, such as types of television programmes selected.

1.2.4 Semi-structured interviews

Building on the data from the diaries to produce rich, interpretive accounts of consumption, interviews provided an opportunity to understand the context of viewing (Moores 1996:6–7). Rather than observe them, the most reasonable method to understand the activity of television consumption was to directly ask prisoner respondents about their experiences. These principles also applied to staff, since they are directly engaged in prison life. The role of the prison staff was also important and a wave of interviews was also introduced to capture their views of prisoners' television consumption and access.

Interviews are co-constructed and the balance of power between the interviewer and interviewee is not equal or neutral. As a tool for data collection interviews are based on a complex mix of values, beliefs, agendas and power of researcher and researched. Bird (2003:14) identifies in her ethnography that interviews are 'power charged verbal encounters' and that participants have different goals. Hammersley and Atkinson (2010:102) advise that

> All accounts must be interpreted in terms of the context in which they are produced. The aim is not to gather 'pure' data that are free from potential bias. There is no such thing. Rather the goal must be to discover the best manner of interpreting whatever data we have, and to collect further data that enable us to develop and check our inferences.

Commentators have stated that the prison and its people are routinely 'silenced' (Liebling 1999b; Wacquant 2002). O'Connor (2003) asserts that interviews are incredibly powerful forms of interaction, especially for prisoners. They provide what she calls 'new conversations' and are an 'act of autobiography', whereby the interviewees can take control to counter the lack of autonomy they routinely suffer, and thus have the capacity to be restorative (see also Liebling 2002). In accounting for the diversity of people's experiences, Holstien and Gubrium's (1995:117) concept of the 'active interview' acknowledges the shifting and evolving dynamics during these encounters. Short biographies were prepared to describe the prisoner sample and also a list of prison staff and their roles can be found in Appendices 1 and 2.

1.2.5 The research site

The research site visited[1] and described in this book is a local,[4] adult male category B closed prison with an occupancy of under 1000 prisoners, a relatively small occupancy compared to other local prisons. HMP X's (HMP X from herein) purpose, apart from securing prisoners and protecting the public, is to serve the courts in the surrounding area. As a result, many of its prisoners spend time on remand, awaiting sentence. Other prisoners are convicted and often spend most of their sentence serving their stipulated time. Longer-term prisoners, including lifers and those on indeterminate sentences also find themselves at this prison, awaiting places at other prisons. Most adult male prisoners will experience a 'local' prison at some stage of their incarceration. The movement of prisoners through this establishment is phenomenal (over 200 per calendar month) compared to other prisons like training and dispersal prisons. HMP X offers limited activity or curricula for prisoners staying there. Opportunities for work are mainly restricted to the maintenance of the prison itself such as cleaning, orderly work, laundry, kitchen work and peer mentoring. Education is provided both in a designated department and on the prison landings. Many of the prisoners come from the surrounding area and visits therefore are used and accessible to most (but not all) family and friends in a visits centre. This prison also has a healthcare facility (hospital) and some prisoners are able to spend time recuperating in this facility. This prison also has a Vulnerable Prisoner Unit, a First Night Centre, a segregation facility, a large kitchen with one serving counter, chapel and multi-faith room, exercise yards, sports pitch, gym, library and specialist centre for prisoners withdrawing from drugs and alcohol. For staff, offices are located on each landing and it has administrative offices, meeting and training rooms, gatehouse and a staff room.

1.3 Ethical conduct

Liebling et al.'s (1999) 'appreciative' approach seeks to resolve the tensions that can arise in prison fieldwork, and can highlight 'both ethical and emotional strengths' across the research setting (Liebling et al. 1999:443). Following Liebling's and others' leads (Jewkes 2002a; Crawley 2004; King and Liebling 2008) sensitivity was paid to *all* aspects of the research from its inception (knowing the field of inquiry, what others have done and said): designing the methods and research instruments (including how best to speak to people), my behaviour and 'performance' in prison, understanding the dynamics, protocols, prison rules, treatment and handling of data and presentation of the findings. The nature of television reception studies means they seek information on a 'private' activity and 'involves making public things that were said or done in private' (Hammersley and Atkinson 2007:212). As a result 'making the private public may have undesirable long-term consequences' (ibid.). Finding resolutions between gathering responses from participants and maintaining their privacy can be achieved by ensuring that, as Hammersley and Atkinson suggest, people have 'a right to control information relating to them, and that they must give their permission for particular uses of it by researchers' (ibid.:213).

1.4   Theoretical underpinnings of the research

Shaping the structure of this research was the employment of Layder's (2006) 'social domain theory'. It was useful in offering a diagram of social reality which provides a constructive synthesis of structure and agency. Furthermore it also provides an extension of these dimensions as what he calls 'domains' of structure and agency; *contextual resources, social settings, situated activity* and *psychobiography*. His theory therefore enables researchers to interrogate and understand aspects of social life including emotion that researchers have not been able to approach via other theoretical models. Moreover, his theory has also been influential in shaping this research strategy, scoping and interpreting the fields of study and also providing an 'adaptive' analysis.

The fields of emotion and governance in this study have been enabled by the use of Layder's theory of domains, which have permitted a review of relationships or 'linkages' between these concepts. Rather than condense social life based on either structure or agency, it has been possible to expand upon the 'linkages' between the four domains Layder defines. Hence, this study captures how television use in prison is *felt*, as well as appreciating and acknowledging the broader structural elements of prison life *with* television. The affective qualities of prison life have been routinely documented in sociological commentaries and typically the 'pains' or 'harms', which are in essence shorthand for the emotionality of prison life. Seeking to measure the affective outcomes of watching television in prison would not necessarily capture the impact of the social settings and contextual resources on the feelings and experiences of the temporal and spatial qualities of cultural life with in-cell television in prison. Layder's theory of social reality and contemporary audience ethnography (Moores 1993a) is adopted in this study to capture these features, using a range of methods and strategies. In Layder's view, to ignore these qualities would result in the presentation of an 'emptied-out vision of the social world' (2004:9).

This provides an overview of Layder's theory and defends its appropriateness. Other major theories have also contributed to this thesis and have helped to orientate this study, especially Rose's (1999) theory of governance set out in *Governing the Soul: The Shaping of the Private Self*. These are supplemented at different points in the research along with Garland's (1991) thesis on the 'rationalisation' of punishment, and Silverstone's thesis on ontological security, television's contribution to the moral economy of a setting and the care giving qualities of television. Moores's (1989, 1995a) extensive research on radio and satellite television has been important in defining this study as ethnographic and more recently his ideas on migration and place were applicable in extrapolating the spatial and temporal effects of viewing television in prison cells (Moores 2006). His work has been influential in assisting a conceptualisation of space, place and social relations. Lull's (1990) typology of the social uses of television and Jewkes's (2002a) 'meanings and motivations' of media use have provided important frameworks for interrogating the uses and gratifications of television viewing at the design of research tools and analysis phases of the research. Jewkes (2002a), Liebling (1999a), Liebling et al. (2001) and Bosworth et al. (2005) have also provided essential guidance on conducting research in prison settings and have directed the execution of the research in the field as well as the subsequent handling of the data. Layder's (2004) own work on emotion has also provided additional theoretical resources.

1.4.1 Theory of social domains: Unpacking social reality

Social domain theory developed by Layder offers the researcher a model to understand 'social reality as multiple interrelated domains' (2006:272) as well as practical research strategies to adapt both the design of their research and a route to connect their work to social theory. This enables 'ontological variety' as well as 'disciplined epistemological inclusiveness... to incorporate and reconcile the equally valid insights of objectivism and subjectivism' (ibid.:293). General theory approaches, like grounded theory are considered 'inward-looking', which means emergent data is forced through a particular lens. Layder welcomes an adaptive, flexible and synthesising approach, where researchers can draw upon a range of theories at different stages. This approach enables the researcher to escape theoretical dead ends or forced pre-conceptions. He argues that they 'artificially compact the nature and scope of social reality... [and] complexity is lost' (ibid.:273). Overall Layder finds other models of social reality too reductive, as they flatten structure and agency. Layder recommends that researchers need to rethink the structure–agency dualism because 'social behaviour arises in the interplay between the creative inputs of individuals and the pre-existing social resources' (ibid.:15). He argues that dualism brings about 'singularities' whereas social life, when investigated and explored, can only acknowledge 'single' dimensions of social life (ibid.:9).

In resolving this, his model of social reality outlines four distinctive 'domains' (see Figure 1.1). He identifies 'personal' aspects of social life as 'psycho-biography' and 'situated activity'. These are the components which are directly felt and experienced by individuals. Moving away from the centre of this model are 'social settings' and 'contextual resources', which are impersonal and remote from the individual yet influence the personal experiences of social agents and vice versa. Layder emphasises that social processes move continually and dynamically; as a result, time and space and domains are 'stretched out' (ibid.:273). Forms of power can also be traced across these domains, for example across social relations and action. Layder asserts that 'power must be

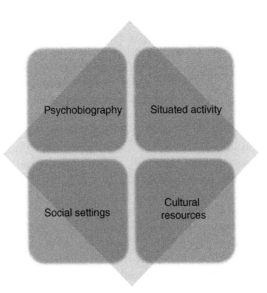

Figure 1.1   A model outlining Layder's theory of social domains (2004)

construed as an amalgam of influences – individual, interpersonal, positional, discursive-practical, social-structural... and symbolic' (2004:17). Social life is therefore a complex mixture of these forms of power, which social agents are influenced by.

1.4.2 Psychobiography

This domain maps a social agent's experience of social reality over time and can account for the ways in which they are socialised or can account for the effects of their 'critical experiences' throughout their life (Layder 2006:274). For Layder the psychobiography 'embraces the unique subjective configuration of emotional-cognitive capacities acquired... during the course of their personal and social development' (2004:10). Expanding upon this he argues that 'we are emotionally unique beings, not simply rationally self-reflexive agents choosing the most appropriate way of maximising our satisfaction' (2006:275). Emotions, he argues, can therefore be 'disruptive' to social relations and action and can thus powerfully impact on the ways in which the remote aspects of social life, such as settings and contextual resources, are perceived and organised. It is the emotionality of individuals for Layder that makes the 'fit between the individual and society... imprecise, imperfect' (ibid.:275). Emotions are not always visible to the observer and yet they can provide an insight into how individuals respond to a particular experience. Emotions are not always under control either, and at different times individuals have different levels of commitment to a social situation and the broader social enterprise which they inhabit. At the heart of this is a person's 'ontological security'[5] or a person's 'inner psychological security' system.

Layder argues that ontological security cannot be fully attributed to trust in the environment in which a social being is placed or situated. Instead, Layder suggests,

> Ontological security is an ongoing, emergent accomplishment and not a mechanical outcome of everyday routines... It is more accurate to think of it in terms of a partial, fleeting achievement, hewn from the 'chaos' of social interaction... [it] is directly implicated in the same quest for control.

> (2004:42–43)

This security, for Layder, is never achieved and is always 'unfinished' (ibid.:42). He argues that it is possible to experience anxiety and security and disappointment and trust simultaneously throughout social relations. Therefore, our feelings are more often than not contradictory. He describes this as one feature of 'inter-personal' control (ibid.:13) or 'personal control' (ibid.:24). This type of control signals what Layder refers to as 'need claims' (ibid.:27). He argues that the self has an 'executive centre' which allows emotions to 'intrude into the flow of awareness', for example to deal with threats to the self (ibid.:25). Layder asserts that to accomplish personal control, 'protective devices' are employed to minimise or abolish threats to an individual's well-being. Once the need claims are worked out an individual can then attempt to act upon them and deal with the emotions as if they were in a queue (ibid.:27). Layder recognises that social agents therefore have the capacity to transform or have 'psychological resilience' (2006:276); yet the competence and ability to cope with everyday life is not the same for everyone and failures of interpersonal and personal control are also commonplace (2004:89). He also refers to the capacity that social agents have to alter and adapt to their circumstances. This is evident for example in prison settings, where some prisoners are much more able to cope with incarceration than others (Cohen and Taylor 1972; Liebling 1999a). The techniques and adjustments made by some prisoners, for example those sentenced to life in prison, are varied and are not fixed, as they can evolve and change over time (Sapsford 1978; Jones and Schmid 2000). The psychobiography is therefore striving for personal control across social relations; fuelling this, according to Layder, is anxiety (2004:43). The need to have an alert and functioning inner 'basic security' system is fundamental to how an individual engages in social relations. Imprisonment puts pressure on one's executive centre to find solutions to restore basic security.

1.4.3   Situated activity

This domain is the 'main gateway' between the psychobiography of a social agent and the domains of settings and contextual resources (Layder 2004:48). Situated activities are usually short, as they mark the arrivals and departures as encounters in social life (ibid.:44). Hence, they are a 'gathering point' for power which becomes drawn into the activity between and amongst social agents (ibid.:50). The transactions between individuals in this domain of social reality are where 'meaning is created' and brought to life (see also Blumler [1969], Goffman [1990] and Garfinkel [1967] Layder 2006:277). These theorists generally agree that it is the process of interaction in situated activity that can demonstrate the roots of meaning as a form of action, and reject the notion that private and personal constructions of meaning do not influence the ways in which humans interact within this domain. Layder refutes this line of thought and asserts that 'subjective attitudes and feelings' or the 'inner' world (ibid.:278) play a vital part in the way meaning is constructed and made sense of in situated activity. Equally 'external' features like gender, ethnicity and class are also influential in the ways in which situated activity is encountered. Therefore, meaning needs to be appreciated and interrogated as 'an amalgam of subjective, external and situated influences' (ibid.:278).

Encounters are not emotionless and some can unsettle and thwart basic security. For some 'avoidance' of situated activity or withdrawal from social encounters can resolve these tensions. Several sociological studies of prisoners show that some prisoners withdraw from prison culture in an attempt to avoid psychological and physical harm (Irwin and Cressey 1962; Cohen and Taylor 1972; Sapsford 1978; Jewkes 2002a). Yet this is not altogether feasible or completely beneficial. Layder describes situated activity as having a 'compelling enticement' (2006:279). An opportunity to gain reward through inclusion, approval and identification can readily be achieved by direct interaction with others. Moreover, situated activity provides opportunity to achieve 'validation and support' of their emotional needs (2004:25). Layder argues that humans can employ control in encounters in three distinct ways: self-control; mutual/personal emotional satisfaction; and managing life situation. By self-control, Layder refers to the levels of composure during interaction: the area in which 'feeling rules' are learnt by social agents (Hochschild 1983). By mutual emotional satisfaction, he refers to the degrees to which humans can understand and be sensitive to the needs of others, which is often a 'mixture of altruism... manipulation and self-interest' (2006:280). Finally, a situated activity provides a network which can often mirror their own circumstances and usually involves the kinds of people inculcated into their life situation, for example the family or workplace. It is also here where one's and others' life situations are assessed by the self and the degrees to which these can be 'ratified' (Goffman 1990). This domain therefore acts as a filter between the psychobiographical and the impersonal or structural domains.

1.4.4 Social settings

Settings are the domain in which situated activity directly occurs and they are 'local aggregations of reproduced social relations, positions and practices' (Layder 2006:280). Layder describes formal and structured settings like schools or prisons, as highly structured in terms of routine and hierarchies, a feature of what Goffman (1991:15) defines as 'total institutions'. Informal settings are less structured than friendship groups or family networks. In formal settings, emphasis is placed upon the people within these settings, based on their role and status. As a result, interaction and modes of action are defined by these expected positions; for example, a prisoner will wear a different set of clothes from a prison officer, distinguishable by a 'uniform'. Within informal settings these roles are less distinct and observable and coercion to adopt certain roles is not principally organised or formally orchestrated either through reward or punishment. However, convention and ritual which influence the ways in which groups or networks organise and interact with each other are also powerful in informal settings. These influences are drawn from a wide range of resources and are not necessarily reproduced directly within the setting. Not only does social convention influence informal settings, but personal interpretation has more freedom and opportunity to influence this kind of setting. For Layder, settings are the closest point to situated activity and can thus influence the ways in which activity is organised and experienced (2004:47).

1.4.5   Contextual resources

This domain is the 'most encompassing' featured in Layder's theory (2006:281). He defines two features of this domain: distributional and historical accumulation of cultural resources. By distributional, he refers to the material and cultural resources available and accessible to groups based on gender, age, class, ethnicity and status. Instead, these are *influencing* but not determining. A social agent's ability to access goods and services in a given context is influenced by these factors and can thus shape the ways in which situated activity and the inner self is experienced, endured and managed. Contextual resources are also influenced through the range of cultural resources that have been accumulated over time, such as knowledge, artefacts and representations in the media and popular culture. Layder argues that these are the 'ultimate source of societal values' which allow for dominant and sub-cultural values to manifest themselves, akin to Bourdieu's (1977) theory of habitus. These can directly shape how social settings can be organised and how individuals engage with them. These are the resources that we draw on, to inform us about ourselves and others. They provide a material foundation in which cultural and 'ideological elements rest' (ibid.:282). Like settings, contextual resources are not, according to Layder, entirely subjective; they are enlivened and mobilised by social action through activity. One example is that the aims of imprisonment have historically become relatively independent; it is not until imprisonment is turned into action that its aims are brought to life. This process finally determines the prison as a setting. The ways in which situated activity is organised to punish prisoners for their crimes are, for example, secured by the imposition of deprivation on liberty and autonomy (Goffman 1991; Sykes 1999). Resources therefore provide the fuel or the power to organise the social life of the prison in these ways. Layder (2006:283) argues that each different 'domain embodies a different form of power' and as a result power is both subjective and objective. Media, including television, are an important source of contextual resources, and the ways in which social agents access and subsequently interpret and employ these are an important feature of audience behaviour. The degrees to which audiences can access these resources can influence other domains.

1.4.6 Adaptive theory

Layder's theory of social domains also provides an important foundation for this research into television in prison. Following this 'adaptive theory' (2005) this research has been designed and executed to incorporate flexibility and draw upon deductive and inductive procedures within the research strategy. Like Layder, I wish to exploit the 'influence' that both deduction and induction can have on each other by finding 'linkages' in order to ensure 'that rational forms of proof, demonstration and validity have a continuing role to play in empirical research and in the theorizing that results from, or feeds into empirical (primary data gathering) research' (ibid.:139).

By unpacking social reality in the shape of his domain theory, different aspects can be interrogated, and thus subjective and objective perspectives can be drawn in. Layder notes that other theorists have rejected objectivism in their work and he is fearful that this does not allow researchers to acknowledge features of social reality which are distinctive and independent (ibid.:141). His view is that of moderate objectivism, thus influencing the ways in which social reality is organised. As a result the researcher begins the empirical exercise realising that social reality is 'complex and dense ... formed from the multifarious interconnections between agency and structure' (ibid.:142). Layder's goal is 'to produce an enhanced or more accurate rendering of the nature of social reality under scrutiny ... [and] the adequacy of knowledge is reflected in the formulation and presentation of ever-more powerful explanations of social phenomena' (ibid.:142). In these ways, adaptive theory therefore encourages researchers to consider the links and relationships between structure and agency, and insists that consideration cannot be given exclusively to either the structural *or* subjective features of social reality. Instead, the research can 'disembed' these components and analyse them. Layder suggests that the researcher abandons the tendency to privilege only one aspect (or at least one at a time) of social reality. He advocates using the most appropriate theory in different stages of the research process, for instance in the analysis and design. Layder recognises that the onset of research is not neutral of theory. He highlights that theory can provide a 'scaffold' which can also accommodate new and different theories to deal with the incoming information (ibid.:150). As a result some theories may be provisional. He explains that theories can act as 'templates against which data can be evaluated' (ibid.:152). In some cases the original model may also be challenged by the incoming data or by the analysis phases; in these instances, features of the model may have to be abandoned to allow the next stages to proceed. These theories, however, have played an important role in orientating the development and elaboration of final concepts.

1.5 Overview of the book

The organisation of this book is influenced by Layder's (2006) social domain theory.

Chapter 2 is a conceptual discussion, outlining the major discourses on the use and application of imprisonment. This chapter also reflects on the major policy changes (in England and Wales) that have been influential in shaping the ways in which contemporary prisons have begun to make way for the introduction of in-cell television. Close attention is paid to the ways in which *control* and *care* are delivered in prison and how *emotion* is managed within this setting. This chapter ends by introducing previous research on media access and use in prison. The social, cultural and political landscape of the prison is well documented and in order to delineate the relationships prisoners have with television it is important first to appreciate the ways in which prison is organised, conceptualised and legitimised.

Chapter 3 discusses literature based on prisoners' experience of incarceration. Here key theories based principally on empirical research are discussed to interrogate the ways in which the experience of prison is felt by prisoners. A discussion of the techniques prisoners employ to adapt to and cope with prison life is included. This chapter focuses on the ways in which *care* is experienced and the extent to which prisoners are permitted to access and engage in a range of *communicative* opportunities.

Chapter 4 departs from the prison focus and reviews sociological and psychological audience reception research. In doing this, a review of the impact that particularly broadcast media has on everyday life, typically in domestic settings, is presented. This discussion goes on to outline the composition of the television audience and how media scholars have discussed this phenomenon. This leads to an important review of the uses and gratification models utilised by audience reception researchers. A brief section is included to discuss important psychological research relating to the ways in which television is employed as a mechanism for audiences to manage their daily and emotive lives. The chapter ends by reviewing the small body of prisoner audience research in line with the themes identified in this chapter.

Chapter 5 charts access to and availability of television, focussing primarily on the accounts that describe the introduction of in-cell television into the prison landscape. This acknowledges the rationale of its introduction, the perceptions of its introduction and the ways in which access to television is sustained. This chapter also includes the findings from 14-day television-use diaries completed by nine male prisoners to map television consumption. This discussion provides important contextual detail in relation to the *setting* and provides background to account for *situated* and mediated activity (Layder 2004). This also identifies how access to and use of television in this setting is negotiated across the mechanisms of control in the prison. This chapter sets the scene of the prison with in-cell television, and allows the voices of prisoners and staff to be fully amplified in the subsequent chapters. Without this contextual information the inter-relationships between setting, knowledge and resources, situated (and mediated) encounters and the psychobiographies of prisoners cannot be realised (Layder 2004).

Chapter 6 discusses the ways in which prisoners' use of television serves broadly as a series of 'uses and gratifications' in order to actively manage their own emotions whilst in prison. This chapter exclusively centres on the voices of prisoners and charts the kinds of emotive responses both described and expressed during the interviews. The ways television is employed (or not) by prisoners for therapeutic means, signals an important contribution to prisoner audience studies. The ways prisoners 'look after themselves', using television, stresses the emotive experiences of the men in prison (Layder 2004). This takes the audience ethnography away from the traditional forms of interpretations based on power, that is, gender, age and class and instead foregrounds the emotional experience of prison and use of television. The sociological interpretations of prison life repeatedly acknowledge the 'harms' and depriving effects of incarceration, and much time has been spent on relating these to the relational and structural features of the prison.

Chapter 7 articulates how in-cell television as both medium and object is inculcated into the enterprise of 'self-regulation' (Rose 1999). This chapter includes data from prisoner and staff interviews. It reviews and considers how emotions in prison are ordered, managed and scrutinised by both staff and the prisoner themselves. It also assesses what Garland (1991:177) refers to as the 'rationalisation' of punishment. Contrary to Prison Service agendas, television in prison has a significant and overwhelming therapeutic function. It outlines how prisoner respondents in this sample are highly selective in their viewing repertoires. The desires to access educative material through mediated encounters and also to make attempts to remain engaged with public life are, for some, paramount. In-cell television coincides with care and control discourses and these aspects are not easily ratified in the prison environment. The placing of television serves as an important object of control across all domains in the social reality of the modern prison and most saliently, control through mechanisms of surveillance can assist in the project of self-governance; television it seems is placed most appropriately in the cell to support this enterprise. The chapter ends by reviewing the digital landscape of prison settings.

Chapter 8 presents an integrative concluding discussion. It begins by reviewing domain theory recommending that mediated activity is incorporated into this model based on the findings. This chapter goes on to document the major conclusions of the study in showing how in-cell television is at 'work' in the prison context and the impact of in-cell television extending social relations.

2
Perspectives on Prison

This chapter documents the different perspectives on prison, and examines how historical, cultural and sociological factors have shaped the modern prison. The material presented here charts how penal practice is mobilised, with attention to the themes of care and control in line with Garland's (1991:174) 'sensibilities' of punishment. It is no accident that the introduction of in-cell television coincides with major discourses of imprisonment, and the effects of television and other mass media are also reviewed here. Rose's theory of governance is helpful in extrapolating the effects of control and regulation, and signal prison as a 'psy shaped space' (Rose 1999:266).

2.1 Core discourses about prison: What prisons do

Discourses have been placed on the prison; their meanings are culturally bound and these are dependent on different audiences (Wilson 2002). It is sensible to accept that these should be combined in order to interrogate the legitimacy of imprisonment. For example, principles of care are not often cited as a core theme of incarceration, rather terms like 'punishment' and 'treatment' are usually assimilated with the purpose of prison. Yet the concept of self-regulation (Rose 1999) has become increasingly apparent in liberal society, and this too can be applied to the prison (Bosworth 2007). Rose suggests that the human soul has become embroiled in the aims and objectives of the social enterprise. Prisons, therefore, collude with prisoners to take care of themselves by the 'therapeutic expertise in which this work was enmeshed' (1999:275). Therefore, key discourses on prison concur with Rose's observations such as the prison being 'a hub of a programme movement for mental hygiene' (ibid.:131) and this is enabled by surveillance. In addition, the wave of preoccupations with *pathology* and *abnormality* in the 'psy' sciences, was taken up by the state in attempts to minimise harm and attend to reform. This grand project of surveillance has come to dominate the ways in which social agents are controlled (by themselves and also others) (Layder 2004).

2.1.1 Legitimacy

The Prison Service in England and Wales currently states that 'the purpose of the training and treatment of convicted prisoners shall be to *encourage and assist them to lead a good and useful life*' (HM Prison Rules 1991 my emphasis). Sparks (1994:14) captures this in terms of 'legitimacy' and he refers to the 'endlessly recurrent arguments about which philosophical principles animate or justify the imposition of criminal sanctions'. These principles underpin how the state and society have legitimised prison: as acceptable and palatable. Sparks notes with Bottoms (1995) that 'to seek legitimation from prisoners' is regularly overlooked and often hidden from popular consumption. Denying prisoners a voice is clearly an ingredient in this legitimisation, as Sim (1994:265) remarks 'the accountability of prisons within a liberal democracy' is perplexing. Wilson (2002) also adds that the complexity of such discourses can also be attributed to the fact that the audiences of prisons are three-fold 'the public (including politicians and commentators); penal staff and the prisoners themselves' (2002:366). Hence, discourses are endlessly discovered and re-discovered and anxieties about imprisonment result in aspects of care being stifled by the ' "legitimacy" agenda' (Liebling 2002:141).

Sparks et al. (1996) explored the legitimacy concept in their study of two English prisons. Underpinning this exploration was their interrogation of social order; the types of social order and how power is distributed. They found that much of the legitimacy debates were positioned from the perspective that what prisons do to prisoners is 'non-legitimate', in that it is non-consensual and coercive (1996:302). They found that by observing social relations across the two prisons that both state and prisons were sensitive to the legitimacy principle and thus responded to this in different ways. Coercion was not identified as a governing principle. Instead the social life of the prison demonstrated how social agents tried to get relationships 'right' (ibid.:313). They argue that the problem of order in prisons requires certain practices by social agents to prevent conflict yet this order is not always secured. In avoiding conflict the adoption of what they call 'crime prevention' strategies are employed to maintain order. By fostering techniques to achieve by compliance by prisoners, control and order can be achieved if physical safety and psychic security are established (ibid.:327). In their view, achieving these to ground the legitimacy of what prisons do to prisoners requires delicate and sensitive handling by both prisoners and staff.

Emphasis on prison reform is also culturally and historically diverse. Synthesis can occur thematically and it is generally agreed that 'traditional goals of the prison have been built around the institution's power to combine punishment, deterrence, prevention, incapacitation and rehabilitation' (Sim 1994:113). Prisons have not always been an apparatus of the state and the system for dealing with criminals and deviants was managed or administered locally and not nationally (Jewkes and Johnston 2006:2).

Changes began to take place during the mid-19th century where 'increasingly, prisoners became cut off from wider society' (ibid.:2). Foucault's (1991) *Discipline and Punish: The Birth of the Prison*, first published in 1977, records that the process of punishment was intentionally removed from public view. The execution of criminals moved from the public gallows to the private enclaves of the prison.[1] Postwar Britain was shaken by the events of the Holocaust in Europe and torture of the body entered the public's imagination as unethical, distasteful and uncivilised (Garland 1991:224). Thus, punishment became what Garland (1991:174) described as rationalised, and the emotionality of punishment became increasingly hidden from view, in part to control and assist with the civilising process that Elias (2010) describes. Emotions such as distress, shame and pleasure come under control, and this process of rationalisation tempers emotive responses (Layder 2004:17)

Rationalised techniques can be conceptualised across major principles; *separation, contamination, deprivation and surveillance and more recently managerialism and responsibilisation*. Figure 2.1 highlights how these dogmas are interrelated and are dependent on each other, and highlights that this is what a modern penal practitioner needs to *do* to transform social agents into prisoners. These are important in order to understand how prisoners are able to engage in social relations in prison.

2.1.2 Separation

The principle of *separation* first emerged as a result of the transference of local governance of prisons to the state in 1877 (Wilson 2002). In England, Pentonville was the first prison purpose built by the state with the 'separate system' in mind. Pentonville's routine and regime entailed prisoners being contained in isolated conditions and all of their

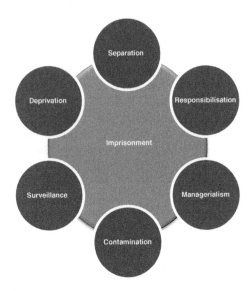

Figure 2.1   Concepts of imprisonment

time being spent away from others. This was peppered with visits to chapel for religious instruction and exercise, where masks and outward facing booths were used to avoid further interaction. This 'formal' setting (Layder 2006:280) was highly regulated and structured through narrow outlets such as religious instruction. Forsythe's (2004:759) historical account of early modern prisons outlines these methods 'were deliberately designed to restrict rigidly communication between prisoners'. The 'prohibition of communication' (ibid.) is often an overlooked reality of prison life. Separation was problematic and difficult to manage, and so verbal utterances were strictly prohibited between prisoners and staff, known as the 'silent' system.

Prisons were in the business of limiting social relations. Foucault's (1991:248) model of imprisonment includes the 'political-moral schema' whereby prisoners are coerced into isolation and subjected to a hierarchy of power and control, limiting autonomy and control over minor aspects of their everyday life, and the prisoner is forced to look inwards. The moral economy of the prison relies on this technique by reducing the interactive and communicative rights of prisoners as forfeiture for their criminal behaviour. It was also believed that preventing and minimising interaction in this environment should reduce the contaminating effects of other people's character and behaviour. The communicative rights of prisoners can also be evidenced in research into media use. Although the 'separate system' disappeared, research and policy highlights traces of this technique, and shows that communicative and interactive opportunities are still limited and conditional, such as screened telephone calls, censoring of mail and lock-up. Pratt (1999:282) notes that changes can be traced through changes in the design and architecture of new prisons, and the onset of welfarism brought about 'a shift away from less eligibility' thinking. Balancing penal aims with public attitudes to punishment was a difficult concept to manage; he notes that 'it became necessary to counterbalance this more enlightened form of punishment with assurances that a level of suffering would still be inflicted' (ibid.:282). Some consider prisoners to be undeserving and thus are expected to forfeit a whole range of rights including communicative and also care.[2]

2.1.3   Contamination

Separating and disconnecting criminals from public life and then from each other is also synonymous with the concept of *contamination* (Sykes 1999:15). Contamination is readily assimilated with the 'techno-medical model' (Foucault 1991:248) where infection can be spread and cause illness. The removal of undesirable elements, that is, the criminal from mainstream society can reduce contamination or the spread of criminality (the disease) and can be quarantined in the prison. The management of further contamination is sought through using separation techniques and minimising cross contamination.[3] Prisoners are therefore subject to scrutiny and examination with a view to curing, treating and standardising them. Criminality is treated like sickness and constraining the disease of disorder requires technical observation and surveillance (Section 2.1.5).

De Viggiani notes that 'penal institutions are generally sick places' (2007:115) and that illness and insanity are commonplace in modern prisons. He highlights that 'some individuals begin their prison sentences with pre-existing health problems that may even precipitate their criminal behaviour ... if they have an existing drug problem or personality disorder' (ibid.:119). Sickness is two-fold in prisons. First it can be 'imported' into the prison and prisoners bring with them a range of health and social characteristics (see also Irwin and Cressey 1962). Second, imprisonment actually harms prisoners, such as the incidence of insanity (see Forsythe 2004) and is therefore 'indigenous' to the prison. This process is also described by Cohen (2007) as 'iatrogenic', borrowed from Illich's (1985) theory of iatrogenesis where things are made worse by the processes of intervention. The 'deprivation' model of imprisonment, whereby prisoners are deprived of a series of needs or nourishment are experienced as 'pains' (Clemmer 1958; Sykes 1958). The process of denying liberty, goods and services, heterosexual relationships, security and autonomy means that a prisoner's 'inner strength—begins to waver and grow dim' (Sykes 1958:79). Goffman (1991:26) describes how institutions like prisons achieve control by stripping individuals of personal artefacts and employ a series of deprivations as a mechanism for managing prisoner behaviour. Goffman refers to this as 'trimming' or 'programming' in order 'to be shaped and coded into an object that can be fed into the administrative machinery of the establishment, to be worked on smoothly by routine operations' (ibid.:26). He also refers to 'interpersonal contamination' (ibid.:35), whereby proximity to other people means the body and mind is always in danger of being contaminated,

> ...the inmate undergoes mortification of the self by contaminative exposure of a physical kind, but this must be amplified: when the agency of contamination is another human being, the inmate is in addition contaminated by forced interpersonal contact and, in consequence, a forced social relationship.
>
> (ibid.:35)

The metaphor of death, as Goffman suggests, to describe incarceration captures the sensation that prisoners endure and their disappearance from the 'living' world means that separation is total (Jewkes 2010:26). Withdrawal or introversion is therefore not uncommon (Sapsford 1978:138). A retreat into the deep interior (Martel 2006) means that situated activity in prison can be lessened with little or no interaction from prisoners and this minimises disruption. Moreover, the regulation of social relations (situated and mediated) allows the prison to minimise contamination. Restraining and limiting these social relations minimises what is perceived to be harmful and above all enables prison officials to control not only prisoners' bodies but also their minds.

The 'cleansing' of new prisoners is characteristic of reducing contamination upon entry to the institution (Goffman 1991:35). Pratt (1999:285) suggests 'cleanliness was normalised by the 1895 Prison Rule 33 that the prisoner "shall be required to keep himself clean and decent in his person". Encouraging self-respect and self-care began to emerge, with improvements to clothing and laundry facilities. It was not until 1996[4] that 'slopping out' was abolished and in-cell lavatories were fully installed in British prisons and so the 'civilized prison had also become the sanitized prison' (ibid.:287). These policy and practice developments coincide with wider structural changes emerging in wider society, as observed by Rose the 'neo-hygienic strategy' (1999:188) sought to clean up society in an attempt to prevent and reduce pathology and abnormality. Furthermore 'techniques of reformation and remoralization' (ibid.:227) were adjoined to this strategy and 'linked to doctrines of social hygiene and mental hygiene' (ibid.:228) whereby individuals were coached into 'techniques of the self', and 'each individual was to become an active agent in the maintenance of a healthy and efficient polity, exercising a reflexive scrutiny over personal, domestic, and familial conduct' (ibid.:228). These civilising techniques acted as a catalyst for the project of self-regulation (Elias 2010).

Pratt (2000) writes that 'appropriate and various tactics of reform, educative and industrial training and rehabilitation would work on "souls" of prisoners to bring about their normalization' (2000:129). Early modern prisons adopted the view that the mind was in need of disinfecting, and mechanisms like religious teaching were believed to cure deviant behaviour – or moral reform. The prison chaplain played an important role in delivering institutional aims and assisted in treating the mind through religious education. Prisoners were encouraged to look inwards at themselves to achieve reform as Rose suggests 'not underestimate the use of coercive powers to enforce morality' (1999:227) and 'rites of the self-examination bring the soul's moral disorder and danger to bitter consciousness, achieving detachment from sinful inclination' (1999:223). Thus, prisons were cautious and restricted 'intervention'. The contaminating effects of outside influences contravened the aims of punishment. Before 1954, prisoners were updated weekly in chapel, when newspapers were read out to the prisoners. This was abolished and newspapers and radios were for the first time permitted inside prison in England and Wales (Prison Commission 1954). The concept of contamination was therefore coming under review.

2.1.4 Deprivation

Depriving prisoners of certain liberties is synonymous with imprisonment (Goffman 1991; Sykes 1999) and there is careful attention paid by institutions to restricting and controlling what kinds of access prisoners can have to artefacts, interaction and also treatment,

> ...the imprisoned criminal literally suffered civil death...still stripped of many of his civil rights....
>
> (Sykes 1999:65–66)

Of Sykes's list of 'pains', the loss of autonomy is brought about by the serial depletion and denial of making choices for oneself. Instead 'he is subjected to a vast body of rules and commands which are designed to control his behavior in minute detail' (ibid.:67).

Tension between prison officials and staff and prisoners are commonplace. Sykes (1999:70) describes that 'custodians' refusal to give reasons for many aspects of their regime can be seen in part as an attempt to avoid such an intolerable situation'. He makes reference to these techniques as a way of reinstating childhood, the prisoner is conditioned to the role of a child insomuch that they are dependent on the institution in order to meet their basic needs (ibid.:70) and subservient to their carers (see also Bosworth 2007). Goffman (1991:26) notes that 'staff often feel that a recruit's readiness to be appropriately deferential in his initial face-to-face encounters with them is a sign that he will take the role of the routinely pliant inmate'. He also observed the 'initiation' of new inmates (ibid.:27) and this process relates to learning one's place in the system. Goffman expands upon the techniques staff employ to remind and restate control, such as controlling possessions (types and volume), moving prisoners to different cells or even establishments, carrying out security searches, perpetuating myth and folklore of prison, maintaining anxiety, medical and security examinations and denying privacy through regular observation, censorship and surveillance.

2.1.5 Surveillance

Surveillance is also a mechanism for asserting control and compliance and also for ensuring levels of deprivations are maintained. Foucault's (1991) description of the 'carceral network' explains that surveillance is a feature of moral reform, and this can be extended to other institutions like schools and hospitals. The need to watch over people is a significant feature of governmentality, as Rose (1999:135) states, 'they established a regime of visibility in which the observed was disturbed within a single common plane of sight ... regulation of detail'. Surveillance has been continually legitimated and safeguarded in all aspects of the life of a prison, in so much that surveillance becomes normalised and habitual. Privacy is not readily granted and most forms of social action occur publicly. Goffman (1991:17) argues that this 'rational plan' is where 'all aspects of life are conducted in the same place and under the same single authority'. Prison institutions work hard to limit free spaces where inmates can 'engage in a range of tabooed activities with some security.... Free places are backstage to the usual performance of staff-inmate relationships' (1991:205). Bentham's 'Panopticon' circa 1785 was designed to guard against free spaces and optimise surveillance.[5] This model was adopted by Foucault as a metaphor for the prison. Following this, Rose suggests everyday life is colonised by a 'delicate matter of the harnessing of micro-fields of power to enable extension of control over space and time – or what I have termed government at a distance' (1999:xxii). Rose supports Foucault's perspective that changes in the punitive world, primarily the prison, are instrumental in shifts of wider governance and social control. Rose recognises that the shift from punishment of the body to the soul has meant that 'the aspirations of government to be articulated in terms of the knowledgeable management of the depths of the human soul' (ibid.:7). The administration of control and care relies therefore on degrees of self-regulation,

> Through self-inspection, self-problematization, self-monitoring and confession, we evaluate ourselves according to the criteria provided by others. Through self-reformation, therapy, techniques of body alteration, and the calculated reshaping of speech and emotion, we adjust ourselves by means of the techniques propounded by the experts of the soul. The government of the soul depends upon our recognition of ourselves as ideally and potentially certain sorts of person, the unease generated by a normative judgement of what we are and could become, and the incitement offered to overcome this discrepancy by following the advice of experts in the management of the self.
>
> (ibid.:11)

Potentially being distracted by oneself or applying focus on the self can help to achieve good order and discipline in prison. Instead of displaying resistance to prison staff, prisoners are encouraged and subsequently rewarded to engage in 'techniques of the self' through mechanisms like worship, education, work, good health and respecting others. The 'individualizing gaze' (Rose 1999:135) leads the person to themselves and thus allowing prisons to achieve largely controlled and 'settled' environments. The success of a prison achieving reformation of its prisoners in these ways is questionable, especially given high rates of re-offending. Prison reforms have made prisons more 'publicly accountable; prisoners have been given a number of legally enforced rights' (Pratt 1999:291) and privatisation of service delivery across the contemporary prison sector is commonplace. Hence, discourse of incarceration is reignited in public debate, with calls for accountability and desire to 'recreate the distance between prison inmates and the rest of society' (ibid.:292). Care of prisoners is locked into these paradoxes, as Pratt warns,

> Exhortations to 'take care of ourselves' are likely to break many of the chains of interdependencies that something like a century of welfare thought had firmly put in place: sympathy for and responsibility towards others is eroded by feelings of suspicion and intolerance, particularly of those who are thought to endanger us.
>
> (ibid.:293)

2.1.6   Managerialism and accountability

The management of offenders both in prison and the community is harnessing new technologies (Pratt 2000:132). In addition, shifting emphasis in penalty can be evidenced in the move away from care to the *management* of risk, 'monitoring offenders by means of electronic surveillance begins to take place of care through individualized counselling; and computer based actuarial calculation of risk supersedes clinical diagnosis' (ibid.:132). Pratt argues that these changes haven't lessened the harms of punishment, they have been increased, 'while their intervention with offenders has been premised on aspects of "care" ... what we may now be witnessing are more overt forms of surveillance and control' (ibid.:135) and according to Garland (1991:186) 'now forms an essential part of the power-knowledge network of penal power'; care then is *control*. Through the deployment of experts, punishment has become a technical occupation (Cohen 2007:164). Achieving success in penal practice is a difficult exercise for penal experts and the practice of tightening up surveillance and control has led to a 'narrower projection of what the punishment of offenders can achieve com[ing] into existence' (Pratt 2000:136). Within the contemporary prison 'new managerialism' and 'therapeutic gloss' have appeared (ibid.:138). Assessment and supervision of offenders is linked and so 'risk rather than crime comes to play a crucial role' (ibid.). Overall punishment is becoming 'rationalised' and emotions are silenced.

Bottoms (1990) demonstrates that the Prison Rule 1 aim, 'a good and useful life', is limited and unrealistic to achieve (1990:39). His suggestions to review the aims of imprisonment include secure custody, order, respect, care, hope, encouragement, regimes (ibid.:45). The May Committee (1979) debated the concept of humane containment and terms like respect and care were associated with this principle. However, it was felt that this idea was 'an ontologically incomplete concept' (ibid.:48). As Pratt (2000) warned, the emphasis on security and risk are fore grounded in the objectives outlined in the Prison Service's statement of purpose. Management of the prison is core to these objectives, with emphasis on treatment of prisoners in humane and decent ways following on. However, care and respect are absent from such statements. Contemporary policy is measurable and accountable and achieving outcomes like care, respect and humanity can complicate 'performance'. However, the adoption of Liebling's (2004) *Measuring the Quality of Prison Life* (MQPL) model has sought to address these kinds of gaps; a technique seeking to capture the 'softer' aspects of prison life.

Measurements of success of punishment and rehabilitation are important indicators for uncovering the contemporary position on the purpose and role of prisons today. Pratt argues that recently there are additional themes to penalty, these include *exclusion, shame* and *incapacitation* (2000:143). Recidivism and reconviction rates are routinely cited as a measure of success and are often the barometer employed by government and public alike (Martinson 1974; Pratt 2000:142). This is complicated by self-harm, suicide and racism which have more recently risen up the agenda and *accountability* has begun to enter prison discourses. Foucault (2009) suggests that 'the prison has been a factory for producing criminals; this production is not a mark of its failure but of its success' (2009:13). It is the 'economy of illegalisms' (ibid.:13) that transcend all aspects of culture and practice that have normalised the practice and outcomes of the prison, in which control and surveillance have taken hold. He concludes that 'there can be no reform of the prison without the search for a new society' (ibid.:24). Simon (2000:292 see also Dilulio 1987) reports, there has been a de-centring of the prison experience in favour of the purposes of prison in preference to assess 'less certainty of failure' or performance. This 'closing off of social science knowledge to the prison' (Simon 2000:292) means that the ethical and moral features of the prison are silenced in favour of managerialist assessments of prison performance, driven largely by economic and political scrutiny.

Liebling (2004) refers to the Woolf Report (1991) as a trigger to the ways in which prisons are now managed. This report instigated an overhaul of management and the use of performance indicators and some changes to the ways in which prisoners were to be treated. The value of these changes is not straightforward and in daily practice complex policy is 'refashioned in shorthand' (Liebling 2004:204) with 'slippery words like "care" and "relationships" [that] came to inhabit prison landings' (ibid.:2004). An increase in time out of cells, for example, saw increased violence, escapes and drug use (Prison Service 1994 in

Liebling 2004:204). High-profile incidents saw the 'rediscovery of the prisoner' (2004:205) which coincided with political rhetoric and public sentiments on crime. Others, like Carlen still assert that 'prison is for punishment' (2002:115) and concepts of care are obscured.

2.1.7 Responsibilisation

Carlen suggests that 'responsibilization strategies which displace from state to prisoner' (ibid.:116) are now ensuing, and the prison emerges as a beneficial service for prisoners Carlen's discussion echoes Rose's (1999) theory of 'self-regulation' that prisons have become 'an opulent shareholder in the modernistic fashioning, retailing and consumption of new therapies and "psy" sciences' (2002:116). Carlen makes the point that prisons have become successful in the reinvention of its ideologies and this is how prisons continue their 'carceral function' (Foucault 1991). Now self-governance is central to the prison experience (Hannah-Moffat 2001; Bosworth 2007). Bosworth (2007:67) also highlights that this encouragement for 'prisoners to govern themselves' is fuelled by managerialism. Getting prisoners to self-inspect and look inwards, through the language of responsibility, evocatively presents 'inmates as citizens or consumers with all the freedoms such associations imply' (ibid.:81).

One such reinvention occurred in 2002 with the *Safer Custody Programme* that sought to place 'care' at the centre of its ethos and thus the 'decency agenda' emerged (Liebling 2004). Prior to this, earlier initiatives by the service to manage increasing numbers of suicides were not sufficiently operationalised and numbers continued to rise.[6] Liebling (2002:140) explains that there were barriers to effective intervention, and this care by staff was stifled by pressures of population, security and resources. In addition, the era of market testing hung over the service, which fuelled the urgency to 'perform'. Liebling notes the 'moral economy' of the prison can struggle, with reductions in trust in institutions (2004:205). Consequently, performance measurement research marginalised the *feelings* of prison life (ibid.:206). Liebling notes the disappearance of such explorations 'ceased with the demise of the rehabilitative ideal and the arrival of managerialist concepts of service delivery' (ibid.:206) and leaving services with the dilemma to punish and rehabilitate.

Liebling's important work on 'what matters in prison' (ibid.:207) seeks to understand a range of complex social and moral factors such as respect, trust, fairness, safety, decency, order, support, humanity and well-being (ibid.:207). Measuring and accounting for these kinds of factors can uncover a prison's 'dominant cultural pattern' (ibid.:210) or 'how morality works' (ibid.:213). Yet the emotive aspects of prison life still remain marginalised in such interrogations.

The current decency reforms do not mean prison life for prisoners and staff is 'easy' or achieving its statement of purpose robustly. As Liebling warns 'reform in many ways strengthens the capacity for the prison to punish' (2002:147). Many areas of prison life have experienced 'reform' but the use of prison by the wider judiciary has piled enormous pressure on the Prison Service. The insertion of 'care' agendas like safer custody and also decency are exacerbating these demands. Safer custody is difficult to achieve when numbers of prisoners have increased dramatically in the last decade and prisons have become 'overcrowded'. Reforms and re-reforms are an inevitable part of governmentality and thus reform remains 'unfinished' and incomplete (Carlen 2002:119).

More recently, racism in prisons has been 'discovered' following the murder of Zahid Mubarek in 2000. The inquiry (House of Commons 2006) listed HMYOI Feltham's failings to 'care' for the victim and challenge racist behaviour amongst prisoners and staff. Consequently, race equality statements and race equality officers have appeared, with outlets for prisoners and staff to record grievances as racially motivated (PSO 2800, 2006). Health has also been subject to scrutiny recently with the delivery of healthcare changing from in-house to the charge of the local Clinical Commissioning Group. Also education for prisoners is contracted out to around 28 different providers delivering education and training (Knight and Hine 2009). The extension of mental health and drug and alcohol misuse services has brought about important cultural changes to the overall delivery of service within prisons, with dedicated units to deal with detoxing prisoners. Prison sites are no longer isolated monopolies, charged by one organisation. The concept of 'total institutions' with a 'single rational plan' (Goffman 1991) has disappeared and now a range of agencies deliver service and support to prisoners' needs, often with competing aims and agendas. With this, additional anxieties about the role and purpose of the prison are evolving and locating the delivery of 'care' must acknowledge these current developments. The penal apparatus is an emotive one and managerialism and responsibilisation which professes rational outcomes across the business of the prison silences the emotive experiences of the prison (Garland 1991).

2.2 Dichotomies on prison and imprisonment

Governance (self-regulation) in prisons has emerged and is gaining momentum. It is necessary to look closer at the features of the prison and its effects in order to examine prison culture. Two themes have been selected in order to highlight how social relations in prison is routinely problematised (Rose 2000; Miller and Rose 2008):

1. *public and private*
2. *harm and healing*

Dichotomies are a constant concurrent feature of the discourses about imprisonment. In addition, aspects of governmentality and control as discussed by Rose (2000) result in tensions about imprisonment being expressed as an array of different claims about the value of the prison apparatus, Rose cites Simon's (1993) concept of a 'post-disciplinary society' and Castel's (1991) idea that risk has replaced dangerousness (2000:321). Moreover, the business of control 'practices manifest, at most, a hesitant, incomplete, fragmentary, contradictory and contested metamorphosis' (ibid.:322) and so practitioners and policymakers are also confused. Potential solutions are in abundance and responsibility for control and security is devolved most often to local settings; in this case the prison, the prison staff and also prisoners. The expectations of control agencies like prisons are also far reaching, sometimes contradictory and potentially unrealistic (Rose 2000:322).

2.2.1 Public and private

Martel's (2006) account of women's experience of segregation in Canadian prisons highlights the dichotomy between public and private spheres within the prison. She explains that consideration for space cannot be divorced from time as 'prison practices are...heavily scripted spatio-temporally speaking' (2006:595) and the 'carceral schedule' becomes vital for prisoners (ibid.:597). Finding safe and meaningful space inside prison is difficult to achieve and thus prisoners can be deprived of 'psychological space' (ibid.:600). Many aspects of prison life are performed publicly, yet the prison is often invisible and can go unnoticed by the wider public. The idea of public and private has to be understood from two perspectives: a) the existence of prison *in* society: the exterior; and b) *inside* the prison: the interior.

Most prisons belong to the social enterprise, they are owned and controlled by the state (achieved by the Prison Act 1877 in the UK) and funded through the public purse; their aims are public.[7] Yet prisons are not open to all as the average citizen cannot freely access the prison space. Physical access to prisons is strictly controlled, regulated and limited to a small sample of people; prisoners, staff, official visitors and family and friends of prisoners under certain strict conditions. The identity of the prison is produced and reproduced by the public. Aspects of prison life are debated and documented in political and cultural spheres.[8] Prison inspections are not new and expert visitors to prisons have produced a huge volume of official reports throughout history (Stockdale 1983). As Jewkes and Johnston (2006) report, 'political and media institutions invariably lend themselves to a single analysis; on matters of crime they function together, with dominant media representations... then communicated to audiences in such a way as to satisfy public appetites for retribution' (2006:290). The degrees to which the general public can remain informed on issues relating to *their* prisons is limited.

Transactions that occur within the *interior* of the prison are routinely accounted for, documented, measured and subsequently scrutinised by experts in the promise of transparency and performance measures and thus are public. Outputs from this kind of positivist information are routinely made available to wider prison audiences.[9] These serve as a mechanism for transparency, accountability and also legitimacy of prisons themselves, but they also continue to re-assert the tensions and anxieties about prison. In relation to legitimacy, many of these documents list endlessly the failings of prisons.

There are few private spaces; privacy is kept to a minimum and is graded according to the social agent's role and function with the prison setting. Surveillance is potentially constant and all forms of social life and situated activity occur publicly. Discretion is applied in certain situations where privacy can also be upheld, such as medical treatment, legal visits, administration, meetings and record keeping, but in the main privacy is denied and being in the prison means that it is a visible and open experience for all social agents. Prisoners' bodies and minds are subject to public scrutiny by their keepers and this increases prisoners' desire for privacy (Foucault 1991; Goffman 1991; Sykes 1999).

Martel (2006:601) explains that the cell is both public and private, 'yet they take on an intensely heightened private and individualized character', by the use of personal artefacts and opportunities to access 'small-scale temporal operators' such as eating meals or watching television (ibid.:596). Privacy is only ever partial in prison. The prevalence of overcrowding now means that most people serve a sentence in co-occupancy with other people. Moreover, security mechanisms like the window hatch on the door do permit staff and prisoners passing by to take a look inside. The crammed nature of imprisonment results in most people being able to hear if a noise is made and therefore the notion of surveillance is not just confined to visibility, it is also auditory.

Contact with the outside world is strictly controlled and monitored, for instance contact with family either in person or through telephones or letters. Surveillance is paramount with routine scrutiny and censorship of letters and telephone calls, the regulation of visits from family and friends including high level recording of visitors via personal information and more recently biometric information, as well as the role of CCTV in visit areas, exercise yards and corridors in the prison: these all make prisoners routinely visible. Surveillance is paramount for staff to achieve high levels of control.

2.2.2 Harm and healing

The Prison Service in England and Wales has taken on board the need to reduce harm. The extent to which this extends to minimising personal pain (psychological and physiological) as documented most famously by Sykes (1999), Cohen and Taylor (1972) and Zamble and Porporino (1988) could probably be contested. In the era of managerialism, harm reduction is not restricted to the delivery of care in its truest sense, where the major discourses of imprisonment, separation, contamination, deprivation and surveillance are upheld: instead, ensuring prisoners are cared for in a way that does not lay blame at the door of the prison. Global and local literature circulated to prisoners in England and Wales regularly joins up responsibility with care, in that it is the prisoner's job to seek care.

Mechanisms to minimise self-harm and also suicide, through *Assessment, Care in Custody & Teamwork* (ACCT) policy (PSO 2700, 2007) require prison staff to monitor prisoners in such a way that it provides a profile of what actions the staff are performing in order to observe the prisoner. However, the multi-disciplinary approaches adopted here, which include prison, healthcare and mental health teams should result in vulnerable prisoners receiving appropriate care and in particular 'treatment' for their behaviour, low mood and despondency.

For Bosworth (2009), healing is left for the self to attend to. Healing can be closely assimilated in reform and rehabilitation but more specifically this is emphasised as 'self-improvement' (ibid.:179). As a site of potential 'self-improvement' prisons do offer opportunities for prisoners such as the provision of education, training and employment, access to healthcare, opportunities for worship and faith, improved fitness and access to a range of cognitive behavioural programmes. Yet less is known about the informal mechanisms adopted in prison to aid transformation. The degrees to which these types of opportunities increase healing and reduce harm remains widely debated.

The experience of prison denies choice, yet choice is crucial for change and 'self-improvement'; the opportunities in prison are in reality limited and sparse. Most saliently the role that education has 'on' the prisoner experience is often caught up in concerns about recidivism and their post-prison experience, rather than transformation. However Hughes (2004) and also Ruess (1999) remark on the relevance of learning in prison as a mechanism for softening the harms of incarceration. However, much of the commentary and research often frames learning in prison as a problem, largely extended by the features of the prison itself, such as resources, the quality of teaching, overcrowding and relevance (Knight and Hine 2009). Most famously Martinson's (1974) evaluation stated that the range of interventions offered to offenders (including prisoners) means that 'nothing works'. Despite such criticism, prison services continue to frame educative and therapeutic opportunities in prison as a route to healing. Yet the degrees to which prisons are equipped and resourced to address these barriers are problematic, as prisons often struggle to engage prisoners in sustained or meaningful 'purposeful activity' (PS04350, PS7100).

2.3   Managing behaviour and delivering care: Making room for in-cell television

Evidence presented in this section captures the dominant available literature and policy[10] with respect to managing behaviour, care and communicative opportunities in contemporary prisons in England and Wales. Bosworth's (2009) analysis of prison policy and prisoner hand-books in England and Wales and the USA employs the governance framework by observing that the deployment of responsibility and care is left regularly with the prisoner. In an era of rights and responsibility, the prison services on both sides of the Atlantic inculcate this doctrine in their business. The appearance of the 'Decency Agenda' does 'indicate a desire to raise the standard of care' but at best can be interpreted as 'welfare rhetoric' (ibid.:182). With these changes, the official introduction of in-cell television from 1998 in England and Wales requires scrutiny alongside these debates.

2.3.1   Care and control: Prison policy

The PSO 2700 launched in 2007 seeks to prevent suicide and self-harm in prisons in England and Wales. Prior to this single document a range of service instructions in relation to this area were administered, and for the first time this policy encompasses an exhaustive account of close management of this kind. Suicide and self-harm are highly sensitive issues, where scrutiny by staff is often inevitable. Liebling's (1991, 1999a) research on suicide and self-harm has helped to raise awareness of best practice with respect to prevention in prison. The *Safer Custody* agenda captures some of Liebling's extensive recommendations, but sadly not all. These include important attention paid to the induction of new prisoners into prison life and an induction programme that assesses and understands prisoner vulnerabilities (PSO0550), the launch of the personal officer scheme to enhance relationships between prison staff and prisoners (PSO 2700), ensuring a multi-agency response to vulnerability, purposeful activity (PS4350, PS7100) and communicative opportunities. In addition, the cell-sharing risk assessment (CSRA PSO 2750) framed as part of the violence reduction strategy, carefully reviews all prisoners' ability to share cells. These kinds of mechanisms are intended to make the prisoner governable by reasserting responsibility for their care.

2.3.2   Communicative opportunities for prisoners

In 1996, the National Framework for the Incentives and Earned Privilege system (PSO 4000 and revised in 2011 PSI 11/2011) was introduced to all prisons in England and Wales, an initiative launched in response to several high-profile prison disturbances in 1990. Access to goods and services is aligned to the prisoner's behavioural performance. This system states that the scheme must function on at least three tiers: basic, entry/standard and enhanced;[11] as a result this 'scheme places all prisoners under constant monitoring' or surveillance (Bosworth 2009:176). On induction to prison, prisoners are placed on the entry regime which is reviewed within one month of coming to jail. PSO 0550 for Prisoner Induction outlines a range of provisions for new entrants to prison life. With respect to their 'communication needs' (PSO0550: 2.3), the prison is directed to establish these, including literacy, disabilities and contact with family and friends, as the Prison Rules state 'special attention shall be paid to the maintenance of such relationships' (Prison Rules 1991:II:4). The order also stipulates that new prisoners are provided with writing materials, postage and also telephone credit to ensure contact with family is made quickly.

The IEP system aims to encourage responsible behaviour, effort and achievement, commitment to sentence planning and to bring about a disciplined, controllable and safer environment for prisoners and staff.

If a prisoner acts irresponsibly, privileges can be removed. The PSI 11/ 2011 outlines the key earnable privileges as:

- Extra and improved visits
- Eligibility to earn higher rates of pay
- Access to in-cell TV
- Opportunity to wear own clothes
- Access to private cash
- Time out of cell for association

(HMPS 2011:6)

The privilege level determines the volume and frequency of the opportunities listed above. With this in mind it is anticipated that prisoners will be motivated to progress up the privilege system.

Depending on factors like security and logistics, Governors may introduce other privileges; these are known as local IEP. An example of this is access to quilts rather than standard bedding, an additional gym session, access to films on DVDs. This local IEP system does vary from prison to prison and discretion of the prison's Governor is permitted. PSI 11/2011 outlines that in-cell television is made available to 'standard' and 'enhanced' prisoners and that it is 'forfeitable', just like other privileges. Prisoners also have to pay for their in-cell television at £1 per week for each set and these funds support entire provision including the purchase of television sets. Typically two people share a cell and this cost is shared. PSI 11/2011 stipulates that the availability of television in-cell

> …can be a strong incentive to good behaviour and regime participation, and can aid order and control by occupying prisoners' time and reducing boredom and tension. It also helps to maintain contact with the outside world.

(HMPS 2011:8)

From the Prison Service's perspective the role of in-cell television has important influence on controlling behaviour, conduct and mood of prisoners. The Service also recognises the value of remaining connected to wider society via mediated outlets,

> Governors have discretion to prohibit the showing of any material they consider unsuitable, taking account of the age of the prisoner and any other local factors. Governors also have the authority to

remove sets in individual cases if in-cell TV appears to be damaging a prisoner's treatment or increasing the risk to the public on release.

(ibid.:15)

The option of censorship is therefore available and this could suggest that the content of television programming is not suitable in some circumstances (see Chapter 7). The Service recognises that television is a possible route of contamination or harm, which in turn could upset the smooth running of the prison. However, the order also recognises the therapeutic role that television can have for disabled prisoners 'judged to need the mental stimulus of TV' and also those at 'risk from self-harm/suicide may be considered for in-cell TV irrespective of privilege level' (ibid.:15).

The IEP policy outlines that prison establishments are required to make this system fair, consistent and accessible to all prisoners. Forfeiture of television is also applicable, meaning staff have the power to remove in-cell television based on IEP status (basic), as a result of an adjudication, breaching the contract, for security reasons and where it is considered 'detrimental to a prisoner's behaviour or treatment' (ibid.:16). In accordance with the Prison Act (1952) the Prison Rules also clearly articulate the power to intercept communicative opportunities (section 35A) and all forms of communication are permanently recorded. This relates specifically to interpersonal communication between prisoners and other people, especially through telephone and letters. The rules do not mention that this is applicable to mass communications, but in theory the prison has the authority to do this if deemed necessary.

Liebling et al. (1999) evaluated the IEP system and identified that most prisoners felt it was fair but there were discrepancies in the policy. The evaluation found significant variations in the IEP system, particularly in the definition of 'good' and 'bad' behaviour across different prisons. Prisoners noticed these differences when they were transferred to other prisons, and as a consequence exacerbated perceptions of unfairness amongst prisoners surveyed. The evaluation recommended that the effectiveness of the IEP system could be improved by implementing a 'personal officer' framework. This also needed to be supported by training staff in objective decision making, using prescribed procedures, welcoming contributions from other staff and providing feedback to prisoners. It was however noted that the IEP has improved staff–prisoner communications and given quieter prisoners more opportunities to be noticed and rewarded.

The introduction of in-cell television was not informed by research; rather it was framed as an incentive to rationalise prisoner behaviour. There was pressure to standardise behaviour management and the kinds of access to goods and services prisoners had across the prison estate. Prisons were acting independently of global policy and hence the IEP system brought about some standardisation.

2.3.3 Media use in prison: Research

This final section introduces prison audience research and reflects on what these studies have found in relation to the dominant discourses as reported in this chapter.

Prison audience research confirms that prisoners' access and use of the media eases *deprivation* endured in prison. As Lindlof (1987a:180) reported, use of media is 'deemed vital to the inmates' wellbeing'. The effects and influence of media use on easing the direct pains of imprisonment have been noted by Lindlof (1986, 1987) and also Vandebosch (2000:529) as 'therapeutic'. Some researchers have found that dependency on media in prison becomes more focused (Lindlof 1986:353; see also Vandebosch 2000; Jewkes 2002a, 2002b; Gersch 2003, 2004). Researchers also found that media use is actively employed to counter different types of deprivation. Knight (2000, 2005a), Lindlof (1986, 1987) and Vandebosch (2000) agree that media use is a psychological distraction from the regime and its people. Jewkes (2002a) also explains that media use provides material to stay psychologically intact and provides a place to withdraw. Vandebosch (2000:539) explains that the pains of imprisonment are accentuated by lack of activity and respondents ranked interactive and communicative activity very highly in prison. Knight (2005b) reported boredom as a significant experience of incarceration exacerbated by minimal activity and a monotonous regime (see also Harrison et al. 2004). In achieving autonomy and privacy Jewkes (2002b:218) found that in-cell television began to privatise 'leisure time' and the effects of television assisted 'ontological security' (ibid.:222). Gersch (2003) however found that television viewing in US prison dormitories or day rooms meant that her respondents were less motivated to watch television. Instead they turned to other media which permitted increased privacy, such as reading or listening to music. Bonini and Perrotta (2007) also found that the conditions of cell-sharing in Italian prisons meant that radio was much more attractive to assist in achieving privacy by using personal headsets.

The need to secure some privacy means that in some instances the points of access and structural organisation of daily life in prison can modify how prisoners are motivated to access certain types of media. However, much of the research also highlights that the deprivation model is not the only motivating feature of the consuming behaviour of prisoners, as Vandebosch (2000:531) explains prisoners bring their 'media baggage' with them. Overall research suggests that media use in prison is both a direct response to the conditions they endure as well as importing of their own values and tastes.

The effects of *separation* from the outside world can also be eased by media use. All of the research confirms that it provides a direct route to transport themselves outside the prison walls and thus connect and become close to the outside world. Bonini and Perrotta (2007:1991), however, note that this concept of 'escape' is not always significant. Instead modifying space and time can enable resistance and survival of the prison as a mechanism to adapt to and cope with incarceration and minimise the disconnection from everyday life and prevent 'cultural jet lag' (see also Gersch 2003, 2007). Moreover, Jewkes (2002b) and Lindlof (1987b) agree that separation from the outside world is not the only mode of separation that occurs. Prisoners deliberately and actively construct their own forms of separation from their immediate setting and media use is instrumental in creating 'distance' from the monotonous regime and the pains of incarceration. Thus through media use prisoners can actively disengage from situated activity by transferring to mediated activity. As Jewkes (2002b:212) describes, this allows prisoners to 'tune-out' of prison life. Vandebosch (2000:531) also reported that prisoners' heavy use of television creates 'presence' in the prison cell thus enabling audiences to feel close to the outside world, as well as distance from other prisoners (see also Knight 2005b:28; Bonini and Perrotta 2007:184; Gersch 2007:9). Being able to separate from the direct setting is not always straightforward and the constraints of the environment often mean that control over this is difficult to achieve. Sharing space, particularly the cell with others, means that choice and opportunities to modify time and space according to one's own needs is routinely stifled (Lindlof 1987; Gersch 2003).

Instead of top-down *surveillance*, as described by Foucault (1991), prison audiences are also active in modes of surveillance themselves. In countering separation, remaining connected by watching and listening to broadcast media or reading a daily newspaper enables prisoners to engage in public life (Bonini and Perrotta 2007:185). Thus media has a 'panoptical' (ibid.:187) quality to extend social relations beyond the confines of the prison cell. By attuning to their prison circumstances renewed forms of citizenship become apparent through focused viewing of news, for example (Jewkes 2002b:214). All of the researchers observed that watching crime documentaries or films were increasingly attractive to many prisoners. Yet as Lindlof (1986:188) found the representations of crime, especially on television, failed to offer or even confirm the reality of the experience. Gersch (2004:14) noted that some genres provided an inward gaze, to observe themselves and thus attempt to establish control of themselves in an environment where control over most aspects of their life is intentionally denied.

In countering deprivation and separation, prison audience research has also identified that these techniques help to avoid or minimise *contamination*. Jewkes (2002a, 2002b) found that prisoners work hard to counter the contaminating effects or harms of incarceration. Media have enhancing benefits for prisoners; for example, she found that the respondents routinely selected material, particularly on television and radio, that was educational and informative, such as documentaries and current affairs (2002b:216). However, media use was not always considered beneficial and selection was also framed in some instances as contaminating. The time and space that broadcast media can permit means that prison audiences are 'folding into oneself' (Bonini and Perrotta 2007:189). The introspection or thinking time is complex and often contradictory for the lone prisoner. Vandebosch (2000:533), Knight (2005b:28) and Gersch (2007:10) highlight that the desire to minimise the contaminating effects of imprisonment means that prison audiences become increasingly more attached or dependent on media use. As Knight (2001) described, the communicative poverty that prisoners experience exacerbate the desire to have social relations (situated and mediated). Acts of self-separation using media are also directly related to the need to minimise harm. Harrison et al. (2004:13) and Knight (2001) also found that respondents directly attribute media use and access as a safety mechanism; minimising direct harms like self-harm, bullying, violence and even suicide. Yet research on suicide does not associate television as a preventative measure.

Some of the studies reported on the impact and relationship between prisoners' use of media and managing control by staff. Jewkes (2002a, 2002b) and Knight (2001, 2005a, 2005c) identify that the provision of in-cell television and access to funds to purchase other media like radio and print media is based principally on the IEP system. Lindlof's research in the USA also confirmed that provision operated using the same principles. Lindlof (1987:183) noted that this system of behaviour management enabled the institution to 'displace some of its activities' by prisoners' use of television in their cells. Jewkes (2002a, 2002b), along with Knight (2005c) also noted that respondents had witnessed that prisons had become quieter and less disruptive. Harrison et al. (2004:15) along with Jewkes highlighted that there was an erosion of interaction between staff and prisoners and staff were becoming fearful that in-cell television was the direct cause of this. Television and other media are framed as conditional based on prisoner performance in line with *managerialist* discourses. Jewkes (2002b:222) suggests this is 'reproducing disadvantage and deprivation', as the status of prisoners based on the degrees of opportunities they are afforded is counterproductive. Knight (2005a:29) also observed that organising prisoners based on their privilege status is a continuation of the forms of control and power that manifest and exist across the prison and providing in-cell television under these terms continues to legitimise imprisonment. For Jewkes this actually normalises control and power, and prisoners become tacitly compliant. In this setting, the lure and attractive features of television are powerful. With increasing emphasis on managerialism and responsibilisation, the placing of television into prison cells requires renewed interrogation.

2.3.4 Summary

The overarching aims of imprisonment continue to legitimise the use of prison. This review of research, policy and commentary highlights that prisons control and regulate all aspects of the prisoner experience and exerting these kinds of control continue to deprive, separate, observe, and manage prisoners. Yet recent research has begun to document the prevailing shifts in governmentality, away from direct observation of the state to the individual (Rose 1999). The prisoner is forced to have a relationship with their own self. Through the process of introspection reformation is believed to occur. Punishment has moved beyond the body and is now considered to target the mind or 'soul'. The aims of imprisonment have become normalised, which in turn reasserts its legitimate place in the social enterprise. More recently control is framed, perhaps misleadingly, as care. Foucault (2009) raised important questions about the continuing use and appropriateness of prison in the social enterprise. It is evident that the aims of imprisonment are often fudged and competing, and now it is not necessarily clear what the social enterprise wants prisoners to be. As a result the ethical and moral perspectives become obscured. Shifting agendas make it difficult to ascertain what aspects of prisoners' lives need to be managed to achieve the ideal prisoner. The privilege system (IEP), as outlined here, normalises and perpetuates the aims of imprisonment, especially deprivation and separation. The introduction of in-cell television is also framed along these same lines. Its introduction was not informed by research, but instead deemed a reasonable, palatable and cheap incentive to maintain order and discipline in an era when resources are becoming increasingly restrained. Jewkes's (2002a) influential research found that prisoners' access to mass media helped to minimise deprivation and separation. Prisoners were disappearing from view, to be with television rather than 'in' the prison. As this chapter has outlined the broad and far reaching aims of imprisonment relating to resources and settings (Layder 2006), the next chapter will focus on research and theory relating to the prisoner experience, focusing specifically on the domains of psychobiographies and situated activity.

3
Prisoner Perspectives

This chapter outlines the prisoner experience which locates the *psychobiography* and dimensions of action in *situated activity* (Layder 2006:274). This chapter begins by describing the 'pains' of incarceration, paying particular attention to two key theoretical models; *deprivation* and *importation*. A fuller discussion of the subsequent harms of incarceration is explored, focusing on the techniques prisoners adopt to protect their *well-being* and sustain their *status and identities*. The final part examines more closely the coping strategies prisoners employ with respect to *social isolation, deterioration, time management* and *emotion*.

3.1 Pains and deprivations

Sykes (1999) and Goffman (1991), along with others (Clemmer 1958; Cohen and Taylor 1972), have collectively defined a 'deprivation' model of imprisonment, whereby the social context (the prison) actively and knowingly deprives prisoners of access to most aspects of social life. Here, the norms and values of the setting in which they are placed determine how the individual will behave and thus adjust (or misadjust). These responses are 'indigenous' to the prison setting which sustain cultural codes and convention. Goffman's (1991:16) reference to the 'total institution' asserts that the domains of social reality are contained within the institution. Here a 'process of assimilation into the inmate community' (Adams 1992:278) occurs whereby prisoners begin to 'adopt the normative proscriptions of the prison culture' (ibid.:278) known as 'prisonisation' (Clemmer 1958).

3.1.1 Indigenous/deprivation model

Sykes's (1999) description of pains in his book *The Society of Captives* is a useful benchmark for understanding the kinds of losses prisoners can encounter. In summary, these include deprivations based on *liberty, goods and services, heterosexual relationships, autonomy* and *security*. These kinds of deprivations are particularly understood as felt experiences; they are psychological and social. For Sykes 'loss of liberty is a double one – first, by confinement to the institution and second, by confinement within the institution' (1999:65) and that participation in public life is forfeited 'stripped of his civil rights such as the right to vote' (ibid.:66) a 'civil death'. Sykes also observed that imprisonment limits prisoners' 'standard of living' based on material ownership and opportunities for consumption of goods and services. Sykes acknowledges that 'basic needs are met' (ibid.:67), yet 'material impoverishment' (ibid.:66) is sustained. Hence, poverty is imposed on the inmate and this has deep psychological implications, resulting in 'personal inadequacy' (ibid.:68). Prisoners are unable to make choices and the prison tactically thus denies prisoners autonomy. Sykes employs the analogy of a child, suggesting prisoners are infantilised, characterised by qualities like 'weak, helpless, dependent' (ibid.:71). The active storing of human beings in close proximity amplifies the risk of contamination by exposure to pathological individuals or violence. This threatens one's sense of security which in turn 'arouses acute anxiety' (ibid.:78) because the prison is unpredictable.

Goffman's (1991:16) theory of the 'total institution' from his book *Asylums*, pays close attention to the ways in which prison inculcates the inmate into a way of life within closed settings. In achieving this Goffman argues that 'the barrier that total institutions place between the inmate and the wider world marks the first curtailment of self' and that institutions like prisons 'strip' individuals of their previous roles in order to transform the individual into an inmate (1991:24). This is achieved by routine techniques like the issue of standard clothing, loss of civic rights, volumetric control of personal artefacts and limiting contact from the outside. Together these bring about withdrawal from 'his home world' (ibid.:25). This process results in what Goffman calls 'the mortification of the self' (ibid.:26) whereby deep anxieties surface.

Goffman's work (1990) on social interaction offers the concept of a 'mask' as an adaptive response to social situations. The 'front-stage' selves are presented in public situations and opportunities to revert to the 'back stage' and allow the mask to drop are limited in environments where privacy and intimacy are systematically denied. Hence anxiety and deterioration can manifest.

Cohen and Taylor's (1972) work in *Psychological Survival* details observations of HMP Durham's high security wing, housing predominantly long-term prisoners. Central to their interpretations is the nature of time experienced by the prisoners in their study. They observed that time is experienced differently because 'time may become an open landscape' (1972:87) and for prisoners 'it has to be served rather than used' (ibid.:89). Prison routines and regimes focus clearly on the prescribed activities of prisoners such as work, education, worship and visits. Conversely prisoners are usually locked in cells much of the prison day without structured activity. These routines are total and fixed to ensure the institution operates to accommodate staff, workloads and security. A common response is that time is sought to be used and consumed and terms like 'killing time' or 'doing time' describe the process to diminish the abundance of time. In responding to this prisoners seek to own time; 'do your time and not let your time do you' (ibid.:90). Cohen and Taylor observed that prisoners 'live for the present' (ibid.:91). Biographical accounts from prisoners document the techniques employed to prevent pains associated with time (Serge 1978), and often report how the past and the future are often imaginatively suspended (Zamble and Porporino 2013). Imprisonment interrupts temporal relationships by disrupting one's life-course as trajectories of time are considered broken (Jewkes 2005b; Wahidin 2004; Roth 1963). Techniques to divide, differentiate, mark, speed up and slow down time contribute to the 'survival' of the pains of imprisonment (see Section 3.3).

3.1.2   Importation model

Irwin and Cressey (1962) observed that prisons were not successful at achieving their institutional remits and aims; to reform and rehabilitate (Maruna and Roy 2007). Despite correctional methods they wondered why the indigenous models of imprisonment were failing to produce compliant, social and moral citizens. Jacobs found that 'much of what has been termed inmate culture is actually imported from outside prison' (Jacobs 1974:395).

Schwartz (1971) describes this failure as 'cultural drift' suggesting that prisonisation is not merely a mechanical matter of socialising individuals in a particular direction. Deviation or even prisoner resistance away from the institutional aims and ethos result in prisoners responding in a range of ways to the prison setting.

The pre-prison experience was found to have an impact on adjustment to prison. The ways in which prisoners 'do their time' are linked to the prisoners' outside life. Irwin and Cressey's (1962) study of inmate culture offers a typology of prisoner subcultural membership; 'deviant/thief', 'time doer' and 'gleaner'. For the 'deviant' mode, these prisoners continue to subvert and reject the dominant ideologies of control and order. They may find themselves involved in the underworld of the prison and thus continue their criminal career. These prisoners are likely recidivists who are often at odds with prison rules and regulations and involved with disciplinary procedures. The deviant groups do not consider imprisonment painful and their coping strategies are displayed in their regular resistance to the norms and values of the establishment that holds them, thus they find an 'adaptive niche' in the prison subculture (DeLisi et al. 2004:370). The 'time doer' often adapts to prison life by withdrawing from deviant members in an attempt to avoid infractions. This prisoner seeks out opportunities to minimise his or her pains of imprisonment by occupying their time with work and activities in order to diminish time. Imprisonment for these prisoners is an interruption to their life-course and returning to the outside world is their main focus. This prisoner does not necessarily seek to change his or her pre-prison behaviour and identity, rather incarceration 'freezes' or interrupts his or her life, as a result this prisoner is preoccupied by marking, using, filling time to preserve his or her own sense of self. The 'gleaner' however takes on board many of the institutional aims and objectives in order to use his or her time productively and thus gain from the opportunities the establishment can offer. This prisoner, like the 'time doer', actively seeks out opportunities to fill his or her time, but seeks to change. This prisoner is compliant, often described as a model prisoner, and seeks out others who share the same values. Education or work is an opportunity to construct a post-prison self that is ethical and moral.

Following this typology of prisoners, Crewe's study captured in his book *The Prisoner Society* (2009) examines how social relations operate within the prison. His typology of the prisoner, like Irwin and Cressey's model, examines how social interaction interplays with a prisoner's adaptation to prison life. His analysis presents a thorough account of the ways in which prisoners interact with each other, staff and the prison system. Moreover he manages to capture the varying attitudes and practices in relation to friendship, solidarity, trust and identity. Crewe makes distinguishing links between the prison structure in terms of levels of power and control (e.g. IEP system) and the ways in which prisoners respond to this. Like Irwin and Cressey, Crewe is able to note the varying and complex ways different groups of prisoners orientate themselves towards what he calls 'soft power' (2009:109). In particular, distinguishing characteristics identified in his analysis are aligned to prisoners' relationships with drugs, their ethnicity and their local community.

Criticisms of the key models of imprisonment suggest that the experience of prison includes pre-prison and prison variables (Dhami et al. 2007:1085). Some studies have acknowledged both models (Crewe 2009; Jewkes 2002a; Vandebosch 2000; Thomas 1977; Toch 1977). As Dhami et al. suggest, 'both approaches are viewed as compatible because life before prison can help to shape how inmates experience and respond to deprivations' (ibid.:1088). Therefore it is not now uncommon to accept that 'integrated' approaches to understanding the experience of prison offer appreciation for deprivation and the pre-prison experience. This integrative approach thus accepts the influence of the 'domains' of social reality which includes a range of 'resources' that social agents can draw upon and access (Layder 2006:281).

3.2   Harms of imprisonment

Prison service policy both in Britain and North America have responded to the harms that 'disconnection' from wider society can have. Late-modernity has seen the 'normalisation' of certain activities and methods of communication. Unsurprisingly the introduction of radio and television was in part a response to 'civilising' the prison as well as a mechanism for minimising harm (PSO 2700).

Preventative measures to minimise the separation of prisoners from their families and friends include communicative opportunities for prisoners. Many studies cite this loss as the most painful and also harmful (Liebling and Krarup 1993; Toch and Adams 1986). Prisons are 'communication'-poor environments (Knight 2000) and this kind of poverty also impacts on psychological and sociological factors, such as well-being and status/identity. Prison audience research has found that media use is instrumental in softening the harms of imprisonment and access to media in prison is tacitly acknowledged by the Prison Service as a mechanism for prisoners to develop strategies to enhance well-being and mitigate assaults on identity and status (see PSI 11/2011- IEP).

3.2.1   Protecting well-being

Limiting opportunities for interaction with the outside (and inside prison) can threaten security and cause distress (Lindquist 2000). From Layder's perspective the lack of control within a given setting means that the self can become disconnected from the wider social system and impinge on one's self-identity (2004:59). Finding ways to redeem control are fundamental to the healthy functioning of an individual's psychobiography (ibid.:92). Layder identifies that a driving factor is the avoidance of helplessness and he argues social agents work hard to control this (ibid.:30). Finding ways in a constrained setting to remain 'well' are at the heart of much of the evidence that reports on the techniques prisoners employ to deal with the harms of incarceration and maintain their ontological security. Wooldredge (1999:235), for example, found that well-being in prison is enhanced by 'program participation, more frequent visitation, and no experience with victimization'. Greer (2002:117) also found that women prisoners developed techniques to manage their emotions, which include emotional diversions, spiritual pursuits, blocking exercises, self-reflection and humour in order to proactively manage their emotional responses to incarceration.

Jacobs (1962:401) found that gang membership serves as a network to offer 'psychological support'. Identification or connection to a social group in prison is therefore beneficial to adaptation, but also a functioning route back to the outside. However, earlier studies, based in the USA, have been criticised for over-simplifying this kind of solidarity amongst prisoners, for example, 'the drugs culture that exists in all prisons has created a "dog eat dog" environment in which individuals are unwise and unwilling to put their trust in fellow inmates' (Jewkes and Johnston 2009:49–50). Crewe found that solidarity was not as pronounced as Jacobs describes, instead he found that 'emotional empathy and sympathy for the plight of others were more common' (2009:334).

Withdrawal from situated prison life is not uncommon and long-term prisoners often distance themselves from short-termers or remand prisoners (Sparks et al. 1996; Sapsford 1978). They often seek out other long-termers in order to share similar timeframes (Cohen and Taylor 1972). It is not uncommon for many long-term prisoners to actively minimise direct contact with family and friends in order to isolate themselves from the outside. Other forms of withdrawal come in response to harms such as the fear of or actual violence, bullying, exposure to sex offenders or strained relationships with family outside prison (Liebling and Krarup 1993). The active and routine control of communication with the outside world, through use of telephone, visits and letters, is sometimes too painful for prisoners to maintain. Prison policy in England and Wales is therefore responsive to some of these needs and 'maintaining family contact', and is a core feature of decency and safer custody agendas. However, these practices still do not replace a sustained and ongoing form of interaction and can add additional strain on relationships. Prison staff note that relationship problems are a key signal to distress in prison, knowledge of a 'bad phone call' may alert staff for closer surveillance of a prisoner to ensure his or her well-being is preserved (Liebling and Krarup 1993).

3.2.2   Sustaining status and identity

Incarceration is an assault on prisoners' identity. As Jewkes found the 'meanings and motivations' (ibid.:116) prisoners demonstrated through their selection of specific media content reveals how the fears and anxieties present in prison life can be managed through media use. Some of her observations suggest the effects of access to mass communications 'normalises' the prison environment. In preserving and constructing masculinities, media may serve as a mechanism to sustain what Bourdieu (1977) describes as 'habitus' or a series of references points about one's culture. Media texts offer prisoners a range of resources to draw upon that enable them to actively sustain masculine (as well as class, ethnic, age, sexual) identities (Jewkes 2002a:54).

Criminal hierarchies are evident in prison culture based on criminal and also prisoner identities. For example, the 'inmate code' (Irwin and Cressey 1962) is a powerful cultural resource that sustains such dominant cultural practices. Jewkes argues that this 'is clearly as bound up with aggression and violence as it is on the outside' (2002a:56) and that these kinds of responses assist in prison adaptation and survival.

Jewkes makes it clear that media use, and the rejection of it, are significant in managing harm. Broadcast news often allows prisons to remain connected to the outside world, which some prisoners however acknowledge 'they could play no part in' (ibid.:121) and therefore these prisoners actively distance themselves as citizens from matters that non-prisoner audiences take for granted.

Vandebosch (2000) also identifies, similar to Lindlof (1987), how selection of mediated material is assimilated to criminal identities. She suggests that 'the degree of (subjective) criminal involvement manifests a particularly strong predictive power:...also display a deviant pattern of media use' (ibid.:541) selecting genres such as 'action, police and gangster movies, prison fiction, erotic...heavy metal, punk and hardrock...legal news, disasters and accidents'. She also found that television is consumed at a higher rate, brought about by long periods of lock-up and high levels of noise. Vandebosch frames these findings in relation to the respondents' 'media related needs' which can 'prevent, solve or at least lessen some typical prison problems' (ibid.:534).

Jewkes and Vandebosch (also Knight 2005) agree that prisoners' communicative needs are amplified and result in what Vandebosch describes as 'media dependency' and suggest that prisoners have a 'strong television dependency' reflected in their increased intensity of use and the personal value they place on it (ibid.:541). Lindlof states 'that the configurations, frequency, and gratifications of media use depend on their adaptability to the incentives self-selected by inmates for a sustainable institutional career' (1986:352). Therefore, criminal and institutional identities can also shape cultural tastes and these selections help to maintain a self that the prisoner deems beneficial.

Other challenges include cell-sharing and the synergy between inmates 'may hinge partly on the extent to which successful methods for mutual goal attainment in negotiating content and temporal issues of media use are achieved' (ibid.:353). Vandebosch (2001) confirms that prisoners who demonstrate a 'higher degree of subjective criminal involvement watch television more because they are bored, want to pass time, have nothing else to do, or want to relax' (ibid.:560) and seek out more 'action police and gangster movies, and series, prison movies...and erotic television programs' (ibid.:561). In addition 'the preference for informative radio programs decreases as the criminality score rises...stronger preferences for harder and socially disvalued music genres such as heavy metal, punk, and hard rock' (ibid.:562). Types of news are also carefully selected by those with increased criminality identification, especially judicial news and also disasters and accidents (ibid.:564).

3.3   Coping and surviving prison

It is the 'styles of coping, and the social life that emerges in the process of coping' (Liebling 1999a:286) that deserves attention. Layder suggests that there are healthy and unhealthy forms of control a person can adopt, and that this affects the kind of relationship one has with oneself (2004:26). Lazarus and Folkman (1984:141) explain that there are two different forms of coping: *problem-focused coping* (sometimes called approach coping), which seeks to control or transform the stressful situation, and *emotion-focused coping* (sometimes called avoidance coping), which seeks to avoid stressful events or situations. It is suggested that emotion-focused coping is more productive in settings where the individual has little or no control, for example, the prison (Rokach 1997; Gullone et al. 2000; Mohino et al. 2004). Greer (2002:122) found that incarceration requires women prisoners to modify their 'emotional management techniques' in order to rationalise and cope with their experience. Four major concepts are discussed in this final section to highlight how prisoners cope with social isolation, deterioration, time and space, and their emotions.

3.3.1   Social isolation

Responding to enforced social isolation is not uniform for all prisoners. Feelings of social isolation are said to be amplified in the 'the early period of confinement [which] subjects prisoners to a great deal of stress and a feeling of disorientation' (Liebling 1999a:286), increases the risk of suicide and self-harm and 'isolation from relationships or a breakdown in communication' (1999a:297) could inflame suicidal feelings. In addition, those prisoners who attempted suicide were reported to have 'fewer visits, wrote fewer letters... they had slightly less contact from the probation service... they kept in touch with the outside slightly less and found it marginally harder to keep in touch with the world outside, preferring to forget it' (ibid.:314). Social isolation is said to be amplified for vulnerable groups and they are 'more likely to spend time in their cells doing nothing; fewer would (could) read or write, or do anything else' (ibid.:315). Hence, Liebling asserts that it is important for services to know and understand how prisoners occupy their time (especially inside their cells), identify their levels of boredom, and offer purposeful activity or 'methods of occupation and distraction' (ibid.:315–316); 'inactivity is a central variable' (ibid.:316).

The desire to 'communicate' is for Vandebosch and confirmed by Knight (2000, 2005a) a symptom of the deprivation and pains imposed in prison settings: the kinds of communication poverty experienced, heighten the need and desire to communicate. Harrison et al. (2004) found that prisoners 'used television as a part of their coping mechanisms... and the ability to withdraw from other activities was a benefit' (ibid.:13).

The enforced separation or loss of freedom means that 'these "pains" are aggravated by the deprivation of material goods and services... that media resources – and in particular, television... are a rare pleasure that take on a level of importance which few of us in the outside world can fully appreciate' (Jewkes 2002a:91). Despite the pleasures media can offer, they can also accentuate the feelings of separation (ibid.:91). Some of her respondents avoided media consumption for these reasons. Others reported the importance of remaining 'in touch' with the outside world because of their distance from it. She also noted that some prisoners try to re-create the feeling of home, to which television is central (ibid.:93). They also used broadcast schedules to establish domestic routines, bringing them closer to social practices of the outside and narrowing the sense of separation (ibid.:95). In an environment where sociability is limited and sometimes risky, television especially provides the 'company' of others, that is, personalities and characters.

Forsythe (2004) found that during the early modern era prison regimes were 'designed to restrict rigidly communication between prisoners' (2004:759) and which the 'enforced loneliness rendered the prisoner docile and tractable prone to remorse and amenable to advice, instruction and admonition' (ibid.:760). The 'separate' and 'silent' systems (see Chapter 2) were intended to encourage introspection in order to seek repentance and reformation. These systems were subject to criticism, particularly noting the harms that these techniques of control could cause, such as insanity and mental deterioration (ibid.:761). Prisoners became restless, suffering from insomnia, verbal outbursts and violence (ibid.:762). Prisoners employed 'ingenious methods' (ibid.:763) to overcome social isolation and enhance communicative opportunities, such as Morse code on water pipes, talking without moving lips, facial expressions and hand gestures (ibid.:763). In the absence of family, prisoners endure a longing for 'contact', and these became intensified at different times such as Christmas (ibid.:765; Jewkes 2002a:105). Prison biographies and observations in research also account for prisoners keeping 'pets', usually birds or rodents, that they tame and care for (ibid.:767; McConville 1995:478; Jewkes 2002a). The appeal of social interaction and intimacy is compelling for prisoners and developing techniques to counter social isolation and loneliness are powerful (Layder 2004:26).

3.3.2 Deterioration

Qualitative accounts of prisoners regularly feature the fear of deterioration, decay and decline. The socialisation into prison culture influences the prisoner in a number of ways and for some this imposition on their psychological and physiological well-being is difficult to manage especially given that a range of resources and opportunities are not accessible (Greer 2002). Jewkes suggests 'prisoners are concerned about being cut off from the outside world ... that on release they will be as aliens in an unknown world' (2002a:21) and therefore maintaining contact, knowledge and skills means that their transition back into the community will be easier. The fear of losing touch is not just social, it is also psychological. Johnson and Toch (1982) remark on the implications of imprisonment on the self, deteriorating on a cognitive level and not being able to think and process effectively or sustain mental agility, losing independency and becoming passive. Cohen and Taylor also remark on these elements, noting that any sense of autonomy and subjectivity in action and thought might be lost and thus become 'a dead thing' (1972:109). Zamble and Porporino (2013) use the analogy of a 'deep freeze' to explain how prisoners prevent deterioration, yet their study does not conclude that prisoners actually psychologically deteriorate; instead they work hard to prevent this.

Deterioration is linked to time, and it is especially significant during periods of disruption to one's life course. Like illness, imprisonment interferes with and dislocates the common order and flow of one's life, inducing a sense of disorientation and threat to one's 'ontological security' (Layder 2004:42). For some, illness and imprisonment is short and temporary for others it is long and permanent. These kinds of disruption are for some 'embodied' (Becker 1997:12). As with illness when bodies begin to fail or age, we can feel vulnerable and seek to find explanations within our cultural domain, to validate the disruption. For some prisoners, the fear of physical deterioration is often expressed in the need to stay fit and healthy and some aspire to youthfulness, attractiveness and agility. It is no surprise that gyms, especially in male prisons, are sites which are heavily populated and used by prisoners. Prisoners are forced into idleness, as work or activity is rationed, and finding outlets to avoid deterioration have a heightened significance (Gramsci 1971).

The quest for mental stimulation (and even sedation) is also a priority for many prisoners. For mental stimuli some prisoners demonstrate a thirst to 'learn' new skills, and perform tasks that require mental agility and physical dexterity. Mastering prison crafts like matchstick modelling has become part of the 'archetypal' prison tradition and folklore (Jewkes 2002a:101). Other less legitimate activities like brewing 'hooch', gambling, drug dealing and tattooing are also significant. By overcoming boredom and endless periods of unstructured time through activity and pursuits it 'restores a sense of self-worth' (ibid.:101). Boredom is a significant emotion in prison. A bored person needs to find meaning in his or her situation and is thus compelled to overcome the effects. Barbalet (1999:631) suggests that bored people will search out meaning and this often includes risk taking or even conflict. The prevalence of bullying, violence, drug-taking and racketeering in prison are potential releases from the boredom prisoners encounter.

Diversionary and blocking techniques are considered by some prisoners as a proactive mechanism to sustain personal control (Greer 2002); in particular, some types of television programmes are considered more appealing than others, with some preferring quiz shows (Jewkes 2002a:92). Jewkes links this to Cohen and Taylor's study suggesting that television viewing could create 'possible mental and physical deterioration, and feared being reduced to a vegetative state, almost literally a "couch potato" (ibid.:92). She stresses that it is 'more to do with how prisoners *feel* about the possibility of their mental and physical health eroding' rather than it actually deteriorating (ibid.:98). Cohen and Taylor (1972:105) remark that prisoners can develop 'obsessive concern with signs of deterioration' as there 'were examples of people who had turned into cabbages'.

Conversely, mental stimulation is not always desired, and some prisoners find ways to escape arousal and seek opportunities to sedate themselves. Cope's (2003) study into young offenders' use of cannabis in prison highlights some of the advantages of sedation through drug use and other means. Her respondents found that cannabis helped prisoners to sleep and 'a way to control, repress and suspend time' (Cope 2003:168). Other advantages included opportunities to alter realities whilst high; a form of mental escapism (ibid.:168) from the harsh environment in which they are placed. In addition the routine and patterns of use in prison also provide inmates with a schedule 'to demarcate' time by having an 'activity' to focus on. Cope also found that respondents preferred certain drugs over others, suggesting that cannabis and heroin are 'prison drugs' (ibid.:169). The sedative qualities of these kinds of drugs provide prisoners with a technique to overcome some of the painful experiences such as isolation, especially during the night whilst locked up in their cells. Liebling (1999a) suggests that drug and alcohol misuse (before and during prison) are indications that they struggle to cope and that this is a risk factor for suicide and self-harm. However, Cope finds that drug-use in prison was believed to be protective against such harms in prison, a 'form of self-medication' or 'numbing' (2003:170) and thus asserting 'their status as a prison coper' (ibid.:170), and resist prison socialisation or 'prison mentality' (ibid.:172). Paradoxically, drug-use and supply in prison is fraught with difficulty and drugs are common in modern prisons (Crewe 2006:348).

There is much debate about the addictive and soporific qualities of television (Alasuutari 1999) and respondents in Jewkes's study are also aligned to some of these debates (2002a:102). Some of her respondents were fearful of the addictive nature of television and how it may quite easily interfere, distract and disrupt their progress in prison (ibid.:103), yet others welcomed these kinds of outcomes (ibid.:129). She also noted how prison staff were perceptive of the 'plug-in-drug' principle and that 'the increasing reliance by prison authorities and staff on using television to occupy and pacify an otherwise potentially volatile population represents an important change in philosophy and purpose of imprisonment' (ibid.:174- see also Crawley 2004:125).

3.3.3 Time management

It is generally agreed that time feels qualitatively *different* in prison (Sykes 1958; Cohen and Taylor 1972; Wahidin 2004) and this is often experienced as disorientating. Coping with deterioration and social isolation is also impacted by time. Time becomes focused as prisoner experiences are

- Equated to a period of time i.e. their sentence length
- Strictly regulated and organised i.e. routine
- Unstructured i.e. periods of empty time

Cohen and Taylor note that the qualitative difference of time in prison for long termers is that it is central to punishment, it 'served rather than used' (1972:89). The 'landscape of time, past and the future, and the actual significance of the present moment insistently occupy the mind' (ibid.:91). Imprisonment deliberately disrupts one's timeframe. Long-term prisoners have two options, by 'surrendering himself to this meaningless world as a life project or obsessionally thinking about the future – a near certain way of doing hard time' (ibid.:92). They also observed that given the totality of the regime and routine, that each day and hour is rarely different, prisoners need to find ways to 'mark' time, to slice up hours, days, weeks and years spent inside, which they note are not provided for by the institution or the staff. As a result prisoners take on this responsibility, 'to create stages themselves. They build their own subjective clock in order to protect themselves from the terror of the "misty abyss" ' (ibid.:95). For example, achieving mental or physical progression through learning skills, studying or exercise (ibid.:95) and thus 'marking out improvements over time' (ibid.:96) whereby the 'external clock may be partially abandoned in favour of such subjective markers as changes in mood or feeling' (ibid.:96). They suggest there is a 'lack of a chronology of events' (ibid.:96). Instead they argue prisoners create or seek out events and interruptions or observe the passing of other prisoners through the system. They suggest that some prisoners have surrendered the fight to decline and instead turn their energy towards 'learning how to deteriorate' (ibid.:105).

3.3.4 Managing emotions

Socialisation assists social agents to manage emotion in different settings (Crawley 2004:46). As a result, many forms of social interaction require 'emotional labour' (Hochschild 1983) in settings which 'suppress or re-present' our 'own private emotions to make them appropriate or consistent with a situation' (Crawley 2004:47). Also 'different zones offer different degrees of emotional freedom' (ibid.:48), and experiencing environments which limit emotional freedom could mean that people 'become estranged from their own feelings' (ibid.:48). Crawley asserts that 'emotions are controlled by those in power defining what is meant by emotionality, and then imposing a pathology on expression of emotions' (ibid.:48) brought about by structural pressures. This is particularly relevant in prison settings. Crawley's work on the lives of prison officers outlines the 'emotional labour' involved in this work. Following this model, Greer (2002:119) also observed that female prisoners were expected to retain emotional composure; 'individuals become cognizant of definite feeling rules (emotion norms and display rules (expression norms)) through their encounters with others'. Thus emotion is controlled to account for the situated activity in line with a setting's contextual resources (Layder 2004:18). The cultural code of prison is harsh, in that emotion of prisoners and staff is heavily regulated and the freedom and opportunities to display certain types of emotion are limited (Crewe 2009:334). Critics of Goffman's concept of 'mask' state that the performative nature of interaction overlooks feelings and how emotions are managed (Scheff 1988). As Crawley states prisons are 'emotional places' (2004:130) and this is 'a topic that has largely escaped academic attention' (ibid.:130).

Crawley argues emotion is central to the everyday work and practice in prisons 'through the day-to-day performance and management of emotion that the prison itself is accomplished' (ibid.:130–131). Thus to ignore emotion erases the social reality of everyday life (Layder 2004:24). For Crawley, 'the management of prisoners' emotions is attempted at both the level of the institution and at the level of the individual officer' (ibid.:132). Garland (1991) observed that the 'privatization of disturbing events' to include punishment contribute to what Elias (2010) defines as the civilising process. Garland argues that penal practice has become 'sanitised' and 'rationalised' and so emotions are thought best to be concealed from public view or contained to specific activities (1991:235). For example criminal justice interventions such as cognitive behavioural therapy encourage offenders to 'address' their emotions and behaviours associated with offending. It is well documented that HMP Grendon's therapeutic regime is not easy for prisoners to endure (Wilson and McCabe 2002; Smart 2001). In this therapeutic context emotions are essentially expected to be displayed and channelled within a therapeutic framework. Consequently, Grendon is a setting in which emotional freedoms are increased and prisoners are encouraged to 'inter-act in a more reflexive and considered way' (Jefferson 2003:132). Yet this remains the exception. As in Crewe's study of a Category C prison, mechanisms to control and regulate social relations and emotion are 'designed to enhance legitimacy' (2009:113). The process of rationalisa-tion is therefore adding further pains to the experience of incarceration by amplifying feelings of 'frustration and fatalism' (ibid.:113).

Crawley suggests that prison officers are key to managing 'the emotions that prison generates within *them*' (2004:132), the ways in which officers achieve this are by managing and presenting their own emotions in certain ways. These for Crawley are synonymous with 'machismo' (ibid.:132) displaying courage, authority, fearless instead of 'non-masculine' emotions like stress, fear and anxiety (ibid.:133), she argues that male officers are careful not to communicate too many 'female' emotions such as care and compassion, conversely female offi-cers rely on these to avoid conflict (ibid.:133). Hence there is a landscape or 'emotional map' (Hochschild 1983) that officers and prisoners learn. Expressing emotions in a prison environment is a risky business, for prisoners showing anger can result in disciplinary action and time in segregation, or if a prisoner is distressed, upset or depressed this can stigmatise the prisoner and make him or her vulnerable to other pris-oners (Crawley 2004:139). Like officers, prisoners find 'emotional zones' within the confines of the prison space and these zones are understood to serve an emotional purpose (Crewe et al. 2013). For example, prison gyms are zones to display aggression through the outlet of exercise, prison chapels often witness emotional outbursts like sadness, grief or loss, and visiting areas permit affection. Less is known about the prison cell as an 'emotional zone', as Martel (2006:600) found, feelings of lone-liness are experienced most frequently during locked up periods, we also know that prisoners enjoy and find pleasure in leisure time, accessing media and accomplishing crafts and writing letters home, all of which take place in the prison cell.

Emotions are relevant in coping, yet the surfacing of emotion in prison settings is routinely framed in much of the literature as not pro-ductive. Emotions are considered harmful and destructive, and interfere in the grander project of punishment. Layder (2004:13) highlights that control is widely debated, yet scarce attention is given to personal con-trol. It seems maladjusted and poor copers receive the most attention in prisoner literature; good and ambivalent copers are often ignored, and little attention has been given to 'healthy' forms of personal control. Coping and the emotions that are involved manifest on a continuum and prisoners find themselves adept at coping and also disabled at different stages (Mohino et al. 2004; Rokach 1997). It is established that television and other media provide audiences with opportunities to experience, witness and feel a range of emotions and moods (see Chapter 4). Much less is known outside the psychological paradigm however, about how audiences *explicitly* manage or govern and regulate their emotionality with media in everyday life. This omission applies also to the small raft of prison audience research. In accounting for the range of emotions prisoners experience, a more explicit description of this is needed in relation to media use in everyday prison life. As Zamble and Porporino (2013) highlight, prisoners' personal control is likely to involve a range of emotions that require continuing management. With the injection of media and specifically in-cell television into the prison landscape, opportunities to work through the range of threats (or not) towards ontological security are now ever more extended and diverse:

> ... some men sink into depression and hopelessness, while others feel comfortable, contented, or even happy. From our results we can say that most fall somewhere in between, coping day by day and minute by minute, and surviving intact and more or less unchanged ....
>
> (ibid.:15)

3.3.5 Summary

Overall, prisoners experience varying degrees of deprivation and employ different protective devices to counter the pains of imprisonment. The limits of interactive encounters in prison amplify the harms of incarceration. Therefore media interaction has a significant role to play as a protective device and is thus valued highly by prisoners. Evidence presented here begins to suggest it assists in problem-focused coping and most significantly in emotion-focused coping (Lazarus and Folkman 1984) to deal with social isolation and deterioration, as well as managing time and emotion. This chapter has highlighted the linkages and interplay between the social domains of prison life. A prisoner's psychobiographical status is acutely challenged by the setting in which he or she is placed, and the constraints within prison complicate access to cultural resources. Situated activity is often displaced by mediated activity in the prison setting as a mechanism for coping. Prison audience research has begun to highlight the role of media use in terms of coping and harm minimisation. Yet this review indicates that the field of emotion in the sociology of imprisonment remains underdeveloped, as Elias states

> Every investigation that considers only the consciousness of men, their 'reason' or 'ideas', while disregarding the structure of drives, the direction and form of human affects and passions, can from the outset be of only limited value.
>
> (2010:486)

Thus including emotion can provide a more embodied examination of social action and social reality, and this needs further interrogation within prison audience research. There is a danger that the prisoner experience is becoming 'over-rationalised' (Frazier and Meisenhelder 1985) and thus it is timely to introduce the vocabulary of emotion in prisoner audience research. This will enrich and bring prison thinkers and policymakers closer to *what matters* in everyday life. In order to understand more closely the prisoner audience, the next chapter examines the *audience* in more detail, by examining theory and research of television audiences. Building on the themes developed in this chapter, the next chapter considers the role of the audience and how they respond to everyday life, culturally, socially and emotionally with television.

4
Audiences of Television

This chapter departs from the previous two chapters and introduces theory and research on the audiences of television. Drawing from sociological studies of mass communication consumption, it also examines significant research on psychological responses to television use. This chapter is wholly focused on what audiences *do* with television rather than what television does to audiences. By considering the kinds of relationships audiences have with television, research evidence can highlight the kinds of journeys audiences are making with television with some understanding of what factors motivate these transactions (Moores 2006). This chapter will outline the impact that television has on the experience of everyday life (Silverstone 1999a), who these audiences are and what research has suggested about the nature and composition of audiences. It will also review how audiences employ television to enable a range of strategies to manage their daily and emotive lives. This chapter ends by reflecting on this literature with respect to the prison setting and reports what research has identified with respect to media use by prisoners: it draws from an extensive literature, yet selects key studies and insights to consider the dimensions of viewing television in non-domestic settings.[1]

4.1 Television and everyday life

The extensive work of Silverstone and Moores has been significant in providing research based evidence to account for how television enters 'lived cultures' (Moores 1993a). In summary, their work has been influential in accounting for how the introduction of mass communications, particularly in the home, has had a significant impact on the ways in which social relations have developed across a number of areas in everyday life. By observing the kinds of journeys social agents make with television, it is possible to observe the linkages between social domains, which can reveal the sociological effects of everyday life itself. Silverstone and Moores agree that the context in which television is received and consumed cannot be ignored and thus aspects of their work have important significance in understanding the dynamics and interplay between all social domains.

Silverstone's account in *Television and Everyday Life* (1999a) is a synthesis of empirical studies of television using sociological and psychological traditions. Silverstone asserts that he is 'trying to provide an account of what I have to call the *experience* of television: the experience of television in all its dailiness, in all its factuality' (1999a:2 italics in original text). He articulates that human experiences in modern everyday life are neither straightforward and the

> ...palpable integration of television into our daily lives [has] emotional significance, both as disturber and comforter; its cognitive significance as an informer and misinformer; its spatial and temporal significance, ingrained as it is into routines of daily life; its visibility, not just as an object, the box in the corner, but in a multitude of texts...its impact both remembered and forgotten; its political significance as a core institution of the modern state; this integration is both complete and fundamental...
>
> (ibid.:3)

These dilemmas transcend all aspects of daily life and Silverstone begins his discussion by proposing that individuals, institutions and society at large are problematised by order. The transformation of the modern world brought about by 'technology-led changes' (ibid.:2), as a product of industrialisation, have had social, economic and political consequences. These consequences to social reality include sets of anxieties, and thus television is for Silverstone (see also Moores 2004) a vehicle for securing order and managing anxiety which manifest in everyday life.

Silverstone does not offer an explicit description of these anxieties, but uses Giddens' account of 'ontological security' (2009:92) as a response to how individuals manage their sense of self and social relations. Like Giddens, he acknowledges that ontological security is learnt. In order for this to be mobilised, humans are required to actively engage with people, places, events and institutions. In essence the actual experience of these interactions permits the development of trust and as a result they realise, albeit unconsciously, tensions, threats and hazards.

Giddens argues that 'what is mastered is an extremely sophisticated methodology of practical consciousness, which is a continuing protective device...against the anxieties' (2009:99). He notes that the sites in which ontological security is developed have been modified since technological and economic developments. Giddens' concept of 'time-space distanciation' (ibid.:21) is a feature of this, and human experiences have begun to move away from situated or face-to-face encounters to mediated modes of interaction through electronic media such as television and radio. Layder's view of ontological security adds that this is never completed (2004:42).

Mediated relations are risky and according to Giddens are 'not for the most part psychologically satisfying' (1989:279). Silverstone's work extends Giddens' ideas by synthesising this with the psychological approach: object relations theory, which helps to unpack the space that television occupies in culture including the personal. Television provides space for social action and experience; it is also a place for the development of security, trust and comfort and thus attachment,

> ... television will become a transitional object in those circumstances where it is already constantly available or where it is consciously (or semi-consciously) used by the mother-figure as a baby sitter: as her or his own replacement while she cooks.... The continuities of sound and image, of voices or music, can be easily appropriated as a comfort and a security, simply because they are there.
>
> (Silverstone 1999a:15)

Television is thus a care-giver, and this is reinforced by the fact that 'television survives all efforts at its destruction...it is eternal' (ibid.:15). The care giving qualities are enhanced because 'television is a cyclical phenomenon. Its programmes are scheduled with consuming regularity. Soap operas, weather reports and news broadcasts provide a framework for the hours, days and weeks of the year' (ibid.:15). Trust and comfort is for Silverstone sustained through the familiar and the predictable' and television can reliably provide these features (ibid.:19).

Moores's (2004, 2006) more recent work contributes important theory to that of Silverstone, in particular the concept of 'experiencing' television and other media with specific focus to the 'feelings' of living in a mediated world. Moores's foregrounding of emotion here is considerable, yet still remains underdeveloped in the shape of empirical study. Moores considers the 'relationships, meanings and experience' with special attention paid to the 'circumstances of technologically mediated communication' (2004:69). Thompson's (2011) typology of interaction is pivotal to Moores's discussion, and he argues that mediated interaction is not sufficient to explain the unique nature of experiencing media like television. To distinguish these differences the term 'mediated quasi-interaction' (Thompson 2005:33) can be adopted. Thompson's interactional theory claims that non-face-to-face interaction, mediated or quasi-mediated means that interaction has 'different spatial and temporal characteristics' (ibid.:32). He explains that these forms of interaction become 'stretched across space... stretched out or compressed in time' (ibid.:33). For Thompson, mediated interaction relates to contact between people at a distance, for example through letters or telephone, which require technology to facilitate the dialogue. Unlike direct interaction, mediated interaction means that the scope of cues such as body language becomes restricted. For mediated quasi-interaction he refers to media such as broadcast and print and thus one significant difference is that the dialogue is potentially open and without boundaries; the media's messages have the capacity to reach large and unknown receivers. The opportunities for receivers to respond are also restricted and thus do 'not have the degree of reciprocity and inter-personal specificity' (ibid.:33) and thus relationships manifest as what he calls 'non-reciprocal intimacy at a distance' (ibid.:34). The term mediated interaction however is readily adopted to account for all non-face-to-face forms of interaction, in short the absence of direct co-presence and symbolic resources that individuals exchange dialogically. Layder's (2004) account of situated activity emphasises co-presence within this domain, alternatively co-presence at a distance can be viewed as a version of activity that is mediated in which exchange of dialogue is extended or stretched beyond a direct or intimate encounter; thus mediated activity. Layder does not explore the concept of mediated interaction in his discussions of social relations.

Moores extends the concept of 'mediation' as forms of action; *intimacy, grief, pathologisation, sociability,* and *doubling.* These facets for Moores are characteristics of mediated quasi-interaction. For 'intimacy at a distance' he relates to Horton and Wohl's (1956) 'para-social interaction', whereby audiences connect and relate to television personalities. Moores reiterates that encounters with television characters are not sporadic but routinised and 'serialised' and audiences build up relationships over time (2004:75). Audiences have comfort in knowing when they will appear, because they are habitually available. Meyrowitz claims that 'media friends' are best explained when personas unexpectedly die and that the many 'people may experience a sense of loss... new genre of human grief... the media provide the most ritualized channels of mourning' (1985:120). Grief of this kind can stir emotions of loss, despite the fact that most audiences haven't met the dead persona, yet these emotions for some are real, felt and genuine.

Moores however does identify that the 'bond of intimacy' can also be problematic, particularly for some social groups. Pathologisation outlines how vulnerable groups of people identifying with characters and even events can become obsessive (Horton and Wohl 1956). Moores is cautious about this type of application to social groups and this in itself is a mechanism for labelling deviancy. Pathological audiences are located and described only within certain social groups such as children and women and these typologies are morally and culturally constrained. Compulsive mediated relationships for these groups present a 'problem' for social order; they challenge the social norm. Sociability is a defining characteristic of much of Moores's earlier work, also explored by Scannell (1996). Sociability as described by Scannell has specific outcomes for individuals, because 'they seek nothing more than the pleasure of each other's company' (1996:22). For audiences elements of pleasure in media consumption can propel their choice; people are not forced to consume mass media. However the construction of certain media texts like news and chat shows offer a mode of address which makes them inherently sociable; meaningful, accessible, familiar and conversational; thus audiences are drawn in. Central to this is what Scannell describes as the ways in which mediated interactions construct a 'mood of interaction' (ibid.:147), or as Moores describes a 'mood of sociability' (2004:86) and that the construction of moods is not homogenous, particularly for the receiver. Readings of particular texts are framed by a vast range of diverse sociological and psychological biographies of individuals such as gender (see Morley 1997). Moores extends the concept of sociability further in the recognition that media talk is conversational by use of everyday language.

Moores explains that 'when place gets doubled in practices of electronic media use, it is necessary for us to recognise how social relationships can be pluralised too' (2004:99). He describes that this has allowed for 'simultaneous mixing of interactions, in that they allow for a consideration of how physical and mediated proximities intersect, having various relational consequences' (ibid.:102). Moores's earlier work expands on the problem of mediated interaction reflected in a number of studies he conducted. The 'mediated interaction order' (2000:135) encompasses both the dynamics and consequences of mediated interaction, such as the 'arrangements of time and space' (ibid.:136), 'cultural experiences of modernity' (ibid.:136). Overall Moores claims that television, as well as other media, allows individuals to get close to interactions, situations, times and places. Moreover, television provides a kind of social glue which can regularly provide comfort and distraction from the problem of order. Hobson (1982) noted that television content, like soap operas, provides opportunities for audiences to share experiences. Talking through problems and events can provide an opportunity for individuals to work through their own problems and recheck their moral and emotional positions and practice (see Wood 2009; Gorton 2009). The transformations of social relations as a result of the use of and access to mass communications can also be evidenced in a small body of literature which charts the 'domestication' of technologies (Berker et al. 2005).

4.1.1 Inserting television into everyday life

Silverstone (1999a) and Moores (2004) present rich descriptions of the construct of 'domestic' by offering historical and cultural accounts of communications in the domestic sphere. In addition, the work of Spigel (1992) and O'Sullivan (1991) provide important historical accounts of the introduction of television into the home during the post-war periods 1940–1950. The domestic sphere, like television, has its own history and the collision of television with domestic life has resulted in renewed understandings of everyday life. The term domestic encompasses different categories as it

> ... subsumes home, family and household, and one which is an expression of the relationship between public and private spheres .... The domestic is being seen as increasingly isolated and removed from the mainstream of modern society, and only reachable through technical and heavily mediated forms of communication.
>
> (Silverstone 1994:50–51)

Moores's (1988:31) research on radio describes how this brought about a movement from public life towards the 'interior'. With radio, homes became much more welcoming places; it provided some families with opportunities to come together. Equally Spigel (1992) noted the same outcomes with television's introduction to North American homes. She also reported that interior spaces were deemed by some to improve living conditions (1992:113). This research also remarks on the ways in which householders accommodated the object into their living spaces and the extent to which they made room for the radio or television.

In the early years of their introduction, radio and television were perceived as luxurious items and thus treated by householders in largely formal ways. Radio and television consumption were framed as events; typically with families gathering together to tune in (Moores 1988:28; O'Sullivan 1991:163). Both O'Sullivan and Spigel report that within a relatively short period of time the uptake of television rapidly increased during the 1950s, gaining momentum during the post-war periods. Television soon became 'naturalised' into the spatial and temporal features of everyday life (O'Sullivan 1991:178).

O'Sullivan observed that television impacted on the ways in which space was used within the home and how leisure time was used (ibid.:167). However, the encroachment of broadcast media's entry into the private sphere raised anxieties. As Spigel observed broadcast media was represented as a 'unifying and divisive force in the home' (1992:9). Despite the attractiveness of radio and television, television particularly was perceived as an intrusion into private family life (Moores 1988:26). O'Sullivan noted that respondents reported feelings of guilt and that television got in the way of other domestic or leisure activities (1991:168). Spigel found that television was often represented across a range of cultural artefacts as a metaphor for disease and that television was considered by some to be contaminating the social body (1992:113).

Spigel (1992) and also Moores (1993) identified how the domestic space became zoned, whereby, instead of the unification of householders consuming the same broadcast at the same time, householders were beginning to withdraw into separate private spheres within the home itself (ibid.:65). For Spigel, television was framed as the new 'patriarch', adjusting the dynamics of power within households (1992:60). O'Sullivan noted that conflict about the scheduling of television viewing in the household created tensions that had not been experienced before. In particular, householders with children feared that their children may become corrupted by broadcast messages (Spigel 1992:50). Hence families began to negotiate how family members, particularly children, accessed and received television. However, for women, broadcasts provided important companionship and connection to the world beyond (temporally and spatially) the domestic sphere (Moores 1988:33; O'Sullivan 1991:177). Broadcasters set about targeting their audiences and thus modes of address allowed audiences to be directly identified. As Moores found, broadcasters set about encouraging and instructing mothers to adhere to idealised roles of motherhood and to take direct responsibility for their children and family. For Spigel television became an 'instrument of social sanitation', a mechanism to bring social agents under control (1992:111). Moreover broadcasters provided children with their own programmes broadcast at a time to coincide with times of the day when their carers were particularly busy, such as the lead up to meal times. The care-giving qualities of television tacitly smoothed television's entrance to the family home and despite anxieties television and radio became accommodated into everyday life (Silverstone 1999a).

A significant theme identified most extensively by Moores is the impact that broadcast media has on human geography. Television audiences can be 'simultaneously staying home and imaginatively going places' (1993b:365). Drawing on Giddens's notion of time-space distanciation, consuming mediated interaction has a 'disembedding mechanism' (ibid.:372) and thus audiences are able to extend their 'reach' and access places and times beyond their immediate private experience. As a result new communities emerge. With the introduction of satellite television in the 1980s, some audiences were able to take refreshing and alternative sets of mediated excursions. Hence audiences' identification with cultural life began to transcend local and even national boundaries (ibid.:368). Indeed Spigel and also O'Sullivan report the emotive facets of the kinds of relationships audiences have with their television sets and programmes and the extent to which this is intertwined in the daily practices of everyday life. The dynamics of family and private life, through inquiry into media use, can uncover an often silenced facet to everyday life. This body of work provides important criteria for evaluating the effect of in-cell television's introduction to prisons.

4.2   The television audience

4.2.1   Who are television audiences?

The nature and composition of audiences is complex and routinely described by theorists as problematic (Ang 1991; Silverstone 1999a; Bird 2003; Gorton 2009). In contemporary society everybody is part of an audience, knowingly and unwittingly. Audiences are also difficult to observe as they are plural and diverse in nature – consisting of sub-groups (Moores 1993:2 see also Silverstone 1999a:151).

This departs from traditional or 'mediation' models of the audience, where an audience is the receiver of messages and is thus subject to the effects of the medium. Silverstone (1999a:134) explains that this model relies on the effects of technology, ideology, culture and text on the audience and some proponents of this model suggest the receiver is inherently passive. Although this model has significance, most audience research located within the sociological paradigm has favoured the 'reception' model (ibid.:143). This model characterises the active nature of the individual which accounts for how viewing experiences are inherently social and also takes into account the levels of engagement (see Radway 1984).

Alasuutari (1999) captures the development of the fields of inquiry in audience research and defines three overlapping generations of this work as *interpretive communities, reflection on the everyday* and the *ethnographic turn*. These phases are thematically arranged rather than sequenced based on a chronology of research. The first, 'interpretive communities' is the body of work which draws upon post-structuralism or discourse theory. Within this phase Alasuutari includes the influential work of Hall (1980) who defined the model of audience interpretation as encoding/decoding. Hall's theory contributed significantly to an understanding that audiences are active and the ways in which audiences or viewers relate to texts is associated with the ways in which they make sense of the texts they consume or 'decode'. Here audiences actively position themselves and this directly influences the effect of the message received. Morley's study of audience interpretation, *Nationwide Audience* (1980), was directly influenced by Hall's model, in which he found relationships between socioeconomic status and the decoding positions of different audiences.

The second generation includes a direct progression from Morley's first study to his *Family Television* (1986). This phase focuses on the reflection of the everyday in which this body of research draws heavily on feminist and also fandom theories. The work of Brunsdon (1981, 1986), Ang (1991, 1993), Gray (1987), Radway (1984) and Hobson (1982) all contributed significant theory to account for the ways in which women in particular negotiate their daily lives where media also features. The third phase, the ethnographic turn, locates research as essentially ethnographic; employing ethnographic research strategies to locate and map the role of mass communications in everyday life in their natural settings. Lull (1990), Moores (1988, 1996), Silverstone (1999a) and Morley (1986) sought to capture the nature of privatised consumption within domestic settings.

All of these bodies of work have provided empirical and theoretical insights to account for the composition of audiences and the conditions under which individuals negotiate their daily lives with and alongside mass communications. Much of the research presents the audience as acutely gendered, insomuch as their maleness or femaleness is intertwined within the conditions of media consumption. In locating the role of social identities upon reception, emphasis on context has become increasingly valid to researchers. In order to appreciate for example the role of pleasure in media consumption, Ang (1993:9) emphasises the need to locate and position viewers' subject positions within broader social contexts in order to understand their interpretations. Silverstone (1999a:154) stresses the importance of social context and relations in sites of reception in order to fully appreciate the ways in which television viewing is active. Morley (1988: 38) asserts that research needs to account for the 'domestic complications'.

Overwhelmingly the nature of ethnographic work in this area, which is also subject to criticism, has often dangerously slipped into what Morley (1997) describes as 'essentialism'. Reflecting on his own work, Morley (1997) offers a critique of his *Nationwide* project and *Family Television*. Morley recognises how his interpretation of family domestic life with television presents family life and also viewing activity as acutely gendered.

Morley's study of family viewing of television saw the disappearance of text from audience reception work (Silverstone 1999a:150). Morley's focus was to account for the 'natural' viewing context and to document the activity of viewing television rather than audience responses directly to television texts. Alongside Lull's (1988, 1990) work on family viewing, Morley explored the significance of power and gender within social relations in domestic settings. Interviewing families (including children) he suggested how men and women use television differently, at this stage he accounted for overlaps and blurring of some of these differences, primarily based on gender. For example he found that men are attentive to television and women watched distractedly. Men, he found, liked to plan their viewing whereas women were less likely to do this. He also found that women prefer fiction and men prefer to select factual based programmes. He also asserted that men and women negotiate time and space within the domestic landscape differently; for example men returned home from work to a site of leisure, whereas the women framed the household as a site of work: thus active television consumption was often described as a guilty pleasure for women (1997:153). These differences were identified directly by Morley at this point as a direct influence of broader social structures based on power such as patriarchy.

Morley (1997:159) refers to Ang and Hermes's (1991) account on the problem of gender essentialism (ibid.:160) and acknowledges 'a reductionist form of analysis which takes "women" as a simple, natural collectivity with a constant identity', as a result gender dominates the discussion. Assuming a gendered consumption of media results in emphasis on relations of power being foregrounded at the cost of not fully examining features like everyday routines, for example in relation to use of time and space. Ang and Hermes (1991:6) highlight that these facets are also considerable to relations of power. Morley states that his sample fails to include other variations of 'family' or household units (1991:163). As Lull (1989) discovered in his investigation of family viewing in India, he observed how television was positioned, which directly impacted on the seating arrangements of viewers. Moreover, Medrich (1979) and Kubey (1986) found variations amongst disadvantaged (economically and educationally) households' viewing behaviours.

Morley also responds to his work reflecting on the psychological needs of audiences. He briefly acknowledges that his interpretation of gendered consumption relates to the different ways social agents are expected to respond to texts and their act of viewing. Morley fails to extend this discussion beyond the scope of psychoanalytical perspectives adopted by screen theorists. His interpretations begin to suggest the kinds of control and constraints different social agents have with emotionality. Hence the ways in which viewers talk about television adhere to the emotive conventions of social life or 'feeling rules' (Hochschild 1983). Despite his praise for Lemish's (1982) research on television consumption in public places, his self-critique unsuccessfully takes inspiration from the possibilities that viewing of television is not always located within the home. McCarthy's (2003) analysis of television in public spaces offers insight into the modes of spectatorship. She observes that television in public spaces like shops and bars has a significant impact on how television is consumed and interpreted (see also Lemish 1982). In addition, the small body of research on prison audiences has begun to open up important discussions about the nature of audiences and the conditions in which consumption occurs (Lindlof 1986; Vandebosch 2000; Knight 2001; Jewkes 2002; Gersch 2003; Bonini and Perrotta 2007; Hajjar 1998 – on nursing homes).

Silverstone et al.'s (1991:132) discussion 'on the audience' is also valuable and highlights the tensions of inquiry in an attempt to guide reception theory towards the 'multiplicity or to measure the extent of its contradictions'. Central to Silverstone's thesis is his discussion of 'active' audiences. He is cautious to wholly accept that all audiences are 'active' and the nature of television viewing itself further complicates this term. As Livingstone (1990:193) suggests 'an active viewer need not be alert, attentive and original'. Silverstone's point is that the activity of television viewing can occur in different modes. From a theoretical perspective, he usefully draws upon the relationship between activity, action and agency (1991:152). He highlights that audiences have 'psychologically and sociologically defined differences' (ibid.). Silverstone refers to Radway's (1984) work on women's consumption of romantic fiction and he highlights consuming action 'does not necessarily lead to greater liberation' (ibid.). Silverstone suggests that audience research often overstates the active qualities of viewing and to a degree he argues this can represent audiences as 'free and unfettered' (ibid.:155).

Silverstone, Moores and Morley all agree that to understand the audience, ethnographic research strategies are necessary to highlight the 'dynamics' of everyday life, and to account for how social agents 'move in and out of "the audience"' (Morley 1997:197). Moores (2006:1) has more recently recommended that audiences are conceptualised by their 'habitual movements' in everyday life (including media use). This also acknowledges that this can occur outside the traditional domestic sphere (McCarthy 2003).

4.2.2   How television is used in everyday life

This section highlights some of the ways in which television audiences make sense of their use of television and motivations for its use. As Silverstone (1999a) has highlighted, such use is not always meaningful or even obvious, and the presence of television in daily life permits a number of sociological and psychological functions. The enticement of television is not always an attractive proposition either. This section will introduce two influential typologies which provide an important framework for reviewing the function of television in everyday life.

The first model known commonly as 'uses and gratifications' originates from the work of Katz and Lazarsfeld (1955) later refined by McQuail et al. (1972) and has been influential on audience reception theory. This model locates four 'uses and gratifications' of mass communications as:

1. **Diversion**: a form of escape or emotional release from daily pressures
2. **Personal relationships**: companionship via television personalities and characters, and sociability through discussion about television with other people
3. **Personal identity**: the ability to compare one's life with the characters and situations within programmes, and hence explore personal problems and perspectives

4. **Surveillance:** a supply of information about 'what's going on' in the world

According to this model audiences are motivated to use and access media for a range of 'rational and emotional needs' (Silverstone 1999a:143). The uses and gratifications model intimates that selection and consumption of television is acutely conscious and assumes that audiences are complicit in their selection of material. This model combines psychological and sociological qualities. Some critiques suggest it is not sufficiently sociological as it fails to review the context of consumption (Morley 1997:54).

Silverstone notes this model is 'based on the idea of sociability: that the individual was embedded in a network of neighbourhood, community and group relations' (ibid.:144). It provides a range of opportunities for individuals to be social, to interact and engage. Like situated activity, viewing and listening incorporates modes of interaction and exchange, yet it is well documented that mediation and its product, reception, is not the same as face-to-face situated interaction (Thompson 2005, 2011). Personal value in mediated interaction should not go unnoticed and the uses and gratifications model stresses the sociological and psychological resourcefulness of media use.

Lull's (1990) study is a sociological extension of the uses and gratifications model. His ethnographic study located in North American used participant observation and in-depth interviews with family members. His analysis defined a model to describe the 'social uses' of television within family homes:

Structural:
1. *Environmental instrument*: background noise, companionship and entertainment
2. *Regulative*: to punctuate time, create talk patterns and plan activities

Relational:
3. *Communication facilitation*: experience illustration, common ground, conversational entrance, anxiety reduction and agenda for talk
4. *Affiliation/avoidance*: verbal contact, family solidarity, family relaxant, conflict reduction
5. *Social learning*: decision making, behaviour modelling, problem solving, value transmission, information dissemination, substitute schooling

6. *Competence/dominance*: role reinforcement, substitute role portrayal, intellectual validation, authority exercise, gate-keeping and argument facilitation

(1990:35)

The 'structural' uses of television explain that individuals employ television as an 'environmental resource' (ibid.:35) and as a companion to the home's routines, offering a background noise. The structural features include television as a 'behavioral regulator' (ibid.:36), that is, punctuating time. He found that people manage their lives around the television schedule, for instance eating, bedtime and chores. It was also observed that conversation may be shaped by these routines and he noted that people adapt their leisure time around television.

For the 'relational' uses, Lull describes how family audiences arrange their social situations around television. The behaviours or responses in relation to this were divided by Lull into four uses or functions. The first is 'communication facilitation' or a mechanism to create or enter conversation such as permitting children to access adult conversations. Lull noted atmospheres can be adjusted with television. Another function is concerned with 'affiliation/avoidance' which is 'a resource for the construction of desired opportunities for interpersonal contact or avoidance' (ibid.:38). Television viewing facilitates family solidarity and shared emotive experiences. As for avoidance, television viewing is considered as a distraction from tension and conflict. Television allows space for fantasy and pleasure that can bear on interaction with others, such as promoting intimacy between couples.

Lull identifies 'social learning' function where media can deliver a range of information. Lull also argues that 'television provides an abundance of role models which audience members find socially useful' (ibid.:41). Parents can use television as a tool to educate their children, especially programmes that align to values that marry to their own. Moreover for adults, television can be a place to help build opinions and accomplish interactions such as control of children's viewing. In addition, access to television is dependent on behaviour too and often recruited as a tool for reward and withdrawn as punishment. Decisions about who gets to watch which programmes are a matter of dominance, aligned to gender and age. He also added that 'some viewers capitalize on the one-way nature of television by verbally assaulting the characters, newscasters, or commercials' in attempts to exert dominance over content (ibid.:42). Equally 'family members often use television as a validator of contested information, thereby demonstrating intellectual competence' (ibid.:43).

Lull's work is important for recognising the social functions of television, especially within the 'family sphere'. The extent to which either of these models is appropriate for non-domestic settings remains limited. The work of McCarthy (2003) on television in public places and also Hajjar (1998) on television in nursing homes captures some the features of non-domestic use of television. These outline some of the qualities of the uses and gratifications tradition, yet do not offer a typology. More assertively, Jewkes' (2002a:10) study on men in prison directly modifies the uses and gratification model to account for 'motivations sought' and 'meanings desired' (ibid.:63).

Her critique of this model includes how the gratification model emphasises agency over structure or context and thus ignores the conditions of reception. Jewkes found that modification was necessary in her study of prisoners in order to also explore 'internal gratifications' much more explicitly (ibid.:116). She was able to overcome difficulty in locating 'identity' through their narratives by tracing their self-reflexive accounts of media use in prison. Other criticisms of the gratification approach include the premise that power and interest in media use and access is equal (Elliott 1974:251). Morley accuses this model of being too open and grounded in function rather than meaning (1997:52). Gersch (2003:54) found that such typologies were not necessarily reflective or responsive to the prison audience due to the conditions and challenges the context brings to prisoners. Ang (1991) is also critical and is cautious to accept that all audiences cannot be as active as these typologies would assert. As Jewkes and Gersch already identify, this is particularly salient for prisoner audiences. Yet as Jewkes acknowledges, these models are useful 'orienting device[s]' (2002b:206). Hajjar (1998) highlights the fact that the effect of control and regulation in institutional settings (nursing homes) remains underdeveloped in such typologies since many of her sample had little control over what programmes were selected, as this was in the hands of their carers (ibid.:18).

Vandebosch's (2000) interpretation of the uses and gratifications model focuses on the potential for media use to be 'therapeutic', especially for prisoner audiences using media to combat the pains of incarceration. As Blumler (1979:22) recognises, too much of the gratification research is framed in terms of 'environmental deprivation' and little has been developed to describe the nourishing qualities of media use with respect to personal control or the emotive dimensions of everyday life, as these models are principally functionalist (Layder 2004). The next section explores television viewing from a psychological perspective. The inclusion of this material is necessary to illustrate how audiences use television to manage their life situations and emotionality. Little sociological work in audience studies has explored the emotive dimensions.

4.3   Television and mood management: Television as antidote

Lull's (1990) concept of 'social uses' of television provides a useful framework for identifying what audiences do with television, yet such models fail to include how audiences' affective responses to everyday life are implicated in this process. This research has mostly taken place in North America and employs both media theory and psychological theory (social psychology and cognitive behaviour) by making use of psychological assessments in the shape of questionnaires using scaled responses (psychometric tests) and by employing quantitative analysis. Hence, little attention is paid to the social and physical conditions in which television is used. This body of research can highlight important relationships and configurations of how individuals respond to material from television. Moreover sociological studies have rarely provided a full account of audiences' emotive responses to everyday life. An explicit description of the affective dimensions of social reality remains underexplored within the sociological paradigm (Gorton 2009).

Mood management is a term which can be explained as something that

> ...applies to the selection of any type or genre of communication...as well as to selections within these types of genres ....Needless to say it deals with all conceivable moods rather than with a single, specific affective state, such as dissonance...individuals strive to rid themselves of bad moods, or at least seek to diminish the intensity of such mood.
>
> (Zillman 1988:328)

He argues that Festinger's (1957) selective-exposure theory 'posits that exposure to counter-attitudinal messages produces dissonance, an experience that is noxious and that individuals are striving to terminate' (1988:327), similar to what Layder (2004) defines as 'need claims'. The importance of pleasure in media use is widely documented in sociological audience research (Radway 1984; Ang 1993). The physical, economic and social constraints of daily life mean that television is a medium that can overcome some of these barriers and moving between different or mediated experiences is practical for many audiences.

Zillman offers a typology for mood management theory. First 'mood-impacting characteristics' (ibid.:331), which can be understood as 'excitatory potential' relating to the intensity of moods as a result of received messages. He describes how certain stimuli can resolve certain moods, for instance exciting messages might help alleviate boredom and soothing and relaxing messages can help reduce irritation. He also notes the problem of 'absorption potential' of messages and this is realised by gratifications expected by the receiver. Zillman recognises that this is problematic and that there needs to be a 'semantic affinity' between mood and the message. He notes that 'hedonic valence' of messages is important to bring about certain moods, that stressful messages could perpetuate stress. He found, however, that when respondents were placed under pressure and stress they actively selected exciting material over and above relaxing material. Equally respondents who were placed under boring conditions overwhelmingly selected exciting material. Zillman states 'it can be suggested that exciting programs are capable of calming hyperexcited persons because their distraction effect may outweigh opposing forces' (ibid.:335). Where individuals find it difficult to escape dissonance and where social and physical constraints prevent this, the role television can play is important. Gratifications described as 'hedonistic consumption choices' are employed when real life situations cannot be resolved.

Much of the work on mood management that has followed Zillman is summarised as three broad categories; *loneliness and isolation*, *depression and stress* and *anger and irritation*. In addition the role and functionality of television with respect to mood management also links to personality traits such as addiction and provides a mechanism for managing and enhancing quality of life.

4.3.1 Loneliness and social isolation

Studies into loneliness and television use (Perse and Rubin 1990) and social isolation (Finn and Gorr 1988) consider how the 'locus of control' (Rotter 1954) is managed by individuals. It was noted by Rotter that internal control means that an individual believes they can control events that ultimately pay dividends for them, external controls means that others influence outcomes for them. Loneliness can lead to boredom, passivity, helplessness and depression. Withdrawal from social interaction may be an outcome of loneliness due to circumstances such as being housebound, out of work, ill or lacking in social confidence and self-esteem. Research shows that chronic loneliness is not always resolved by media use, as other factors such as age also impact on television use in these circumstances. Perse and Rubin found that the chronically lonely engage and interact less with friends and family and social activities, and that television served to pass the time (1990:47). Finn and Gorr's study on social isolation and support found that 'once the gratification obtained is identified, it is relatively easy to trace the causal chain to its psychological and social origins' (1988:153). As a result television viewing is deemed as 'social compensation'.

Rubin (1993) examined the effect of individuals' locus of control on communication selection, feelings of anxiety and levels of satisfaction. He found that 'external control signifies ritualistic communication motivation, interaction avoidance, and communication dissatisfaction. Internal control means finding interaction rewarding and satisfying' (1993:168).

Locus of control is therefore instrumental in identifying different kinds of rewards individuals seek from communication outlets. Rubin argues that 'because internals and externals believe differently in the efficacy of one's effort to alter outcomes, communication motivation and levels of anxiety and satisfaction should differ for internals and externals' (ibid.:163).

4.3.2 Stress and depression

Anderson et al. (1996) found that women showed levels of television addiction in relation to stressful situations. They also found that stress was associated with an increased selection of comedy and the avoidance of news programming. Stressed women watched game shows and men chose action and violent programmes. Stressed men increased the amount of time of overall television consumption. They state that 'people use media to replace thoughts that might produce dysphoric moods and choose media content that induces positive mood states' (1996:257). They argue that, 'TV viewing may be an appropriate and positive coping strategy to temporarily reduce stress and anxiety' (ibid.:257). Bryant and Zillman's study highlights that bored individuals are not necessarily seeking excitement or high levels of arousal (1984:4). This also convenes with Klapp's (1986) thesis that information-led societies result in individuals becoming overloaded with material, which can create boredom.

Potts and Sanchez examined television viewing in relation to depressive moods and found that selections were made as a route for escaping these feelings. In particular news programmes were found to increase the intensity of depressive moods. They examined 'enduring negative mood state[s]' (1994:80) in relation to television viewing motives and outcomes. These negative mood states occur in different degrees of intensity, but intensity does not necessarily equate to clinical depression. For negative moods television has been found as a suitable distraction enabling temporary relief. The intensity of depressive moods was also negatively correlated to news viewing, especially for men (1994:86). They also warn of 'stimuli that could potentially exacerbate those feelings' (ibid.:87) and that are not helpful for people experiencing intense depressive moods or clinical depression. Instead programme selection is 'more likely [to] represent management of a limited set of mild "everyday" moods and psychological states such as boredom or stress...depression was not related to heavy TV use or increased importance of TV in the lives of persons in this sample' (ibid.:88).

4.3.3   Anger and irritation

Concerns about viewing certain types of material, especially violence, have a long history (see Bandura and Huston 1961) and television can often be demonised as a corruptor of moral values and negative audience behaviours, particularly in relation to groups deemed vulnerable such as children and the poorly educated (Jewkes 2011:15). Atkin et al.'s study involved children and their parents and found there was a 'significant relationship...between prior orientations and subsequent program choices' (1979:11). The study emphasises that selection of programmes according to mood overrides the notion of 'viewing-causes-aggression sequence' or effects model (ibid.:11). Age and gender were found to be influential in the types of content preferred and parents limit their children's choices based on their own attitudes and values, rather than their children's own choices (ibid.:12).

Peck (1995:59) found that audiences' consumption of television 'talk-shows' which include crisis, conflict and social problems can help audiences to seek routes for conflict resolution. Boyanowsky argues that the prospect of threat results in some viewers expressing the preference for violent mediated content (1977:134). He found that 'in the low and high threat conditions [they] indicated greater preference than non-aroused controls only for film clips depicting male against male violence' (ibid.:140). He concludes that 'overall, subjects in the low threat condition were most affected by the content of all films viewed, as evidenced by significant changes on ten mood scales' (ibid.:142).

4.3.4   Quality of life with television

Kubey's (1990) study into the quality of family life and television found that television does bring families together. Yet conversation during television viewing can be limited compared to other non-mediated activities (1990:316 – see also Lull 1990). Kubey noted increased states of relaxation compared to situated forms of interaction; however, they were less cheerful and less socially interactive (ibid.:317). Watching together was noted as being more positive than watching alone; however, interaction away from television was overall recorded more positively. Kubey also acknowledged the diversity of family life and the dynamic effect this has on reception. For example, single, divorced or separated viewers sought companionship and time filling qualities of television, compared to married couples, who sometimes used television to bring together the unit or family or as a mechanism for avoiding conflict or confrontation.

Moskalenko and Heine (2003) found that television viewing is a potential route for 'watching your troubles away' and that television use increased if these problems were not resolved. Self-awareness was identified as a key factor for permitting the success of these kinds of activities (2003:76). In particular they frame their study based on Baumeister's (1991) notion of 'escaping the self' (ibid.:76). In particular the desire to seek 'dramatic experience' 'presents an opportunity for people to take on the role of observer instead of being observed' (ibid.:77). In summary, being an observer is considered easier than being observed (ibid.:78). Television viewing and more specifically positive-mood-enhancing television content is a distractive mechanism from themselves. This study failed to account for group viewing or acknowledge the context of reception.

Frey et al. (2007) considered the question 'does watching TV make us happy?' and found that 'heavy TV viewers, and in particular those with significant opportunity cost of time, report lower life satisfaction. Long TV hours are also linked to higher material aspirations and anxiety' (2007:283). They found that 'heavy TV viewers report lower satisfaction with their financial situation, place more importance on affluence, feel less safe, trust other people less and think they are involved in less social activities than their peers' (ibid.:302). These characteristics are synonymous with people who have large amounts of time at their disposal such as the elderly, housebound, unemployed and even prisoners. They suggest that lengthy 'TV viewing may indicate imperfect self-control, as well as misprediction of the long-term costs of TV consumption, reducing individuals' well-being' (ibid.:305). People who are time-poor might assess their time more closely and strive hard to manage their levels of satisfaction. Thus their television viewing may be less, but the quality of satisfaction is greater than those who watch more. Sirgy et al. examined the perceptions of the quality of life and television viewing and found particularly in the USA that television can make people unhappy (1998:125). Corneo's economic analysis of time spent watching television is positively correlated to the amount of time spent at work (2005:100), since television viewing is a 'solitary leisure' activity (ibid.:101). They explain that 'individuals who work a lot have already consumed most of their energy endowment…they thus turn to activities that do not require much individual energy' (ibid.:111). Putnam (2000) however suggests there is a direct decline of civic engagement as a result of television viewing and the proliferation that it has in everyday life.

The prevalence and abundance of television is heavily embroiled in most people's lives. The behaviours and outputs of this kind of affiliation have often raised concerns about the dependency of television for audiences, and it is not unpopular to claim that television viewing and consumption is addictive (McLuhan 1964). For example Kubey (1994) aligns behaviours and responses associated with television viewing with substance dependence and that withdrawal symptoms can be experienced if this is reduced or removed. Kubey and Csikszentmihalyi (1990) account for the relaxing and sedative effects viewers can experience and note that withdrawal and guilt were described. McIlwraith found in his research that television addiction is not a clinical fact (1998:372). He found that self-identified television addicts were conscious of their addiction and 'they were more generally unhappy, anxious, and withdrawn than other viewers…generally more emotionally unstable…have trouble tolerating boredom or idle time and are sensation seekers' (1998:376). He also argues that 'television dependence may be a symptom of, and a way of coping with, depression and anxiety rather than a problem in its own right' (ibid.:382).

This body of research, although limited in its scope to locate more fully the conditions of the sites of reception provides empirical insight for examining the ways in which social agents' affective circumstances interplay with the ways in which television is employed.

4.4   Putting television into prison

The previous chapters have discussed the body of prisoner audience research with respect to prison and prisoner perspectives. All of the research draws upon uses and gratifications approaches. The studies are fundamentally sociological, yet some also employ psychological theory to inform their analysis (Lindlof 1985; Vandebosch 2000).

4.4.1 Impact on social relations

The introduction of mass communications to prisons has extended the nature of social relations. The traditional view that prison institutions are effectively quarantined and sealed societies (Goffman 1991) is challenged by the expansion of interactive opportunities. As outlined earlier in this chapter, media use offers audiences alternative routes for social interaction; 'mediated quasi-interaction' (Thompson 2005). This enables individuals to 'reach' or extend their contact beyond their immediate locale (Moores 1995a), and has heightened significance for prisoners because it provides legitimate routes to 'escape' the prison. As Bonini and Perrotta (2007:186) and Jewkes (2000a, 2000b) found the use of electronic media permits a legitimate separation from prison life and provides prisoners with some privacy, which is in short supply. Vandebosch (2000:535) found that prisoners use large quantities of television partly due to the lack of activity in prison; yet the compelling features of media use enable prisoners to legitimately disappear into their cells and retreat from the public life of prison (Lindlof 1986:191 see also Harrison et al. 2004). Lindlof (1986:353) suggests that relationships and social relations become displaced, or as Jewkes (2000b:212) explains, it permits integration as well as disengagement. Conversely, Ribbens and Malliet's (2015) research on digital gaming highlights the importance of interactivity with other users, albeit with their cellmates and not across larger networks as it can work in wider society.

With respect to integration, the theme of surveillance (see Chapter 2) is commonly reported across this body of research. Media consumption for many prisoners allows them to remain *connected* to the broader social structures as well as provide material to stay close to local and personal interests. Jewkes (2000b:215) and Lindlof (1985:188) for example found that news (print and broadcast) provides an important role in sustaining citizenship. Jewkes noted that male prisoners were compelled to watch factual programmes, such as wildlife documentaries, in an attempt to improve or enhance their learning. Knight (2000) and Gersch (2003) found that media use, particularly television and music, enabled prisoners to feel closer to family such as children or friends on the outside. They could relive domestic scenarios of watching together, for example, or provide symbolic material for talk and conversation with family and friends. Media can provide a mechanism for prisoner audiences to transport from the temporal and spatial constraints of the prison setting. This was also found to be important for prisoners to connect to their own sense of self (Jewkes 2002a). Jewkes emphasises that media is a valuable source of empowerment for prisoners. Incarceration deprives prisoners of autonomy, and their ability to make choices is routinely denied. Media use is one of the few opportunities prisoners have to make choices for themselves in order to sustain their identity and ontological security (2002b:211). Gersch (2007:9) corroborates this, but unlike the position in the UK where viewing now occurs inside cells, prisons in North America are organised differently and viewing mainly occurs in groups. Gersch found that individual prisoners were often coerced into viewing material that was not necessarily aligned to their own personal choices (ibid.:19). This accentuated and continued to divide prisoners largely based on race and thus the rules of viewing were tacitly governed by different ethnic groups within the prison (Gersch 2004:11). Like Jewkes (2002a, 2002b), Vandebosch (2000:40) also reported that media use was important for sustaining sub-cultural identities. These of course are broad and diverse, yet for Vandebosch prisoners were motivated to watch crime news or fiction which she aligned with their criminal identities (ibid.).

Lindlof (1986:353) found that using television was the best medium for prisoners to displace relationships and withdraw to the privacy of their cells and thus disengage from social relations. Jewkes (2002b:222) found that the introduction of television resulted in a settling effect observed by prisoners and staff; prisons had become much 'quieter' whereby television provides prison staff with a tool to pacify and distract prisoners relatively easily and thus locking prisoners in their cells became effortlessly ratified. Harrison et al. (2004) also found that interaction between staff and prisoners reduced and respondents believed this to be directly attributed to the introduction of in-cell television. The negative effects of television use were also noted by prisoners, and according to Jewkes (2002b:222), they feared passivity and idleness. Yet some prisoner audiences were happy to be distracted from both the world of the prison and from their own thoughts (Jewkes 2002a:98). If carefully used, media can divert them from 'introspection' (ibid.) (see also Bonini and Perrotta 2007:189). With respect to selection of mediated material, it has been found that prisoners make choices in order to resist dominant or even pro-prison or anti-criminal agendas. Jewkes (ibid.:124) found that some prisoners selected texts that 'highlight injustice or discrimination', which enables a mechanism for resistance (ibid.:145). Lindlof (1985, 1986) also found that the choices prisoners make with respect to their inmate career are intrinsically bound up with the ways in which prisoners access, choose and consume media.

4.4.2 Constructing and managing daily life

With social relations being stretched and modified, prisoners are also able to both subscribe and disconnect from the temporal and spatial structures of everyday life. The need to escape or survive the physical conditions of incarceration is also an important feature of adaptation (Martel 2006). This section reports what prisoner audience research has documented with respect to *time* and *space*.

Time

Achieving 'good' times can be enhanced by media use, for example by recreating domestic routines, rituals and social occasions that are punctuated and shaped by media events or markers, particularly in broadcast schedules (Jewkes 2002a:100). As a result, pleasure in planning viewing or listening to broadcasts gave prisoners a tangible temporal structure to look forward to. The mundane and repetitive nature of the prison routine is further amplified by the limited opportunity to engage in purposeful activity. This can amplify boredom (Lindlof 1985; Knight 2000; Gersch 2004). Media use therefore enables prisoners to fill time by offering an activity in order to cope with the dichotomies of time: highly structured regime and unstructured time (Jewkes 2002a:111). Prisoners are able to actively 'dissolve the structural shackles and barriers that hold them' by using media (ibid.:114). Bonini and Perrotta (2007:190) found that the use of radio can alter time and accompany other activities; this was also important for securing private times as well as keeping up to date with the broader social structures. This, they found, was important for minimising 'cultural jet-lag'; the fear of losing touch with social and cultural progress (ibid.:191). Moreover they found that it helps prisoners to distinguish different parts of the day, week or seasons and thus not become victims of the monotony of time (ibid.:190).

However the gains of media use are also undermined. The passing of time for some prisoners is painful, as Jewkes (2002a:98) found the dailiness of broadcasts and print media, although providing important markers, can accentuate separation from the outside world or even slow down time. Jewkes found that prisoners were often frustrated at their inability to contribute to public life that many broadcasts instigate (ibid.:108). Moreover, their use of media was limited to the 'traditional' or 'chronological' time and prisoners were unable to time-shift using VCRs or other recording equipment (ibid.:112). Seasonal markers in the annual calendar such as Christmas were also sometimes painful for prisoners, and some television content amplified the nature of time passing and reinforced their absence. The fear of aging and stagnating whilst in prison was sometimes a dilemma prisoners reported to Jewkes (ibid.:98). In managing daily life the introduction of electronic media into cells means that most prisoners cannot independently organise their 'own' routines. The coerced living arrangements of prisoners mean that the organisation of time requires negotiation (Lindlof 1986:353). He argued that television is best suited to single cells, as those that share cells are unable to fully benefit from the positive qualities television can offer. The need to negotiate viewing is often fraught with difficulty and can create conflict based on taste and levels of control (ibid.). Media content for prisoners was also viewed by some as boring (Vandebosch 2000:533).

Space

The impact of media use on the temporal features of everyday life in prison is also connected to the spatial features, and similar senses of separation it can enhance or even improve can also be attributed to space. Jewkes (2002a:91) remarked on the distance media use can evoke and in some instances this distancing only served to amplify disconnection from public life. In attempting to achieve control over the space they inhabit, Jewkes (ibid.) and Knight (2000) found that prisoners actively try to recreate a 'sense of home' (Jewkes 2002a:93). The ways in which prisoners negotiate space, as they do with time, is dichotomous. In some instances prisoners wish to create distance between themselves and the prison setting and connect to public and private life beyond the prison. Equally prisoners wish to withdraw and distance themselves from public life; there is a 'declining significance of physically bounded space' as media provide a route for prisoners to travel beyond the confines of the prison space (ibid.:108). Bonini and Perrotta (2007:191) explain that this modification is not necessarily 'escape' but a means of survival. Gersch (2007) asserts that television particularly is placed inappropriately into the physical conditions of the prison; it is communal rather than in-cell. Gersch found that the nature of public viewing served to reinforce division amongst prisoners and thus most prisoners were unable to use television in meaningful ways (2007:13). Due to constraints of access defined by the privilege system, prisoners' opportunities to fully employ television and other media can enhance 'communication poverty' (Knight 2000). This only serves to remind and reinforce their status as prisoners and hampers their ability to completely transcend time and space through their media use in the same way as non-prisoners audiences are claimed to do.

Care-giving qualities of television

Prisoner audience research captures the significance and amplified value of media use for prisoners. Despite some of the dilemmas prisoners are presented with through using media, the care-giving qualities of television are evidenced in this body of work, yet remain underdeveloped. These are related to the 'deprivation' model of incarceration (see Chapter 3) and prisoners are mostly active in the ways in which media use can reduce the pains of imprisonment (Sykes 1999). In relating this to media theory the cognitive and social outcomes of media use in this setting are not dissimilar to non-prisoner audiences. However, prisoners have reported that they changed their 'consumption to attune to circumstances' (Jewkes 2002b:213). This does not necessarily mean that their consuming behaviour is distinctly practiced in different ways from non-prison audiences, but modifications and motivations to access certain media texts for example are in direct response to the conditions of the prison.

Making autonomous selections where possible to cope with everyday life is evidenced also in prisoner audiences, for example Harrison et al. (2004:13) reported the relaxant qualities of television, Jewkes (2002b) noted the importance of media use on striving for ontological security. She also found that overcoming deprivation of heterosexual relationships can in part be satisfied by the pleasure and companionship of media personas (ibid.:218). Gersch (2004:14) found that some of her female respondents described how certain programmes such as reality shows or dramas enabled the women to look at their own selves in terms of their circumstances and identity. They reported that these programmes facilitated learning about oneself and thus working towards self-improvement. Knight (2000) and Harrison et al. (2004) also emphasised the importance of media in enhancing a sense of safety and security. Knight particularly noted that the chronic levels of boredom bring about detrimental assaults to the self and thus respondents frame the provision as an important mechanism for minimising self-harm. As with non-prisoner audiences, the flow of television particularly can assist in reducing social isolation and loneliness (Finn and Gorr 1988; Perse and

Rubin 1990). Like parents with children, staff could pacify prisoners reliably since viewers' attachments to television are perceived to be intense and reliable (Silverstone 1999a). The relationship between media use and harm minimisation is evidenced but significantly remains underdeveloped in this field of inquiry. Vandebosch (2000:529) describes this relationship as 'therapeutic' but unsuccessfully articulates the nature of this particular function. Gersch's (2003) thesis discusses sensitively the emotive structure of everyday life with mass communications but she underplays the importance of this with respect to the range of social domains, that is, psychobiography, situated activity and contextual resources. The psychological and cognitive strength media use also gives to Jewkes's (2002a) respondents is widely documented in her work, and facets of explicit emotive dimensions such as boredom and frustrations are regularly overlooked. My earlier work (Knight 2000) includes boredom, but falls short of relating this to other emotive states and the direct influence of the material and symbolic conditions of life in prison.

Overall this body of research is extensive and work by Jewkes (2002) and Gersch (2003) provide an in-depth sociological examination of the complex role of mass communications within prison settings. Gersch's examination of the living conditions of prisoners is useful, but these conditions in the USA do not easily contrast with the arrangements in place in the UK; in the USA television is watched communally. In line with broader media theory, particularly in relation to television studies, prison audience research would benefit from a closer examination of the direct living conditions in which television has now been placed, that is, the prison cell.

Summary

This chapter has outlined how television has brought about an expansion of social relations (temporal and spatial) by extending the potential reach of its audiences, which is mediated activity. The uses and gratifications model has begun to demonstrate how media can offer nourishing and reparative outlets for audiences. It is evident that domestication of television has focused predominantly on the household as a site of reception. Prisoner audience research has begun to offer additional insights into the nature of viewing, with researchers recommending modification of some media theory to account for the conditions of incarceration.

This review has identified gaps in prisoner audience research, which also corroborate in very similar ways those identified in the previous literature (Chapters 2 and 3). Across this broad field of study, emotion is largely absent both in discussion of the prison, the prisoner and audience of television. There are also unanswered questions about the place in which television is now placed in prison: the cell. The following chapters outline the key findings of the study drawing on an ethnographic strategy.

5
Making Room for In-Cell Television: Access, Availability and Points of Use

This chapter provides contextual background to the introduction of in-cell television to prison. This discussion draws upon data from interviews with prisoners and staff together with data from the television-use diaries. The first part of this chapter charts how in-cell television is accessed and made available to prisoners in line with the behaviour management policy framed fundamentally by the IEP system; the final part reports on the habitual use of television recorded in the television diaries collected from prisoners.

5.1 Access and availability of in-cell television

> And then what you can do is providing on you being how you are as a person they use the TV as a carrot. It's a known fact, they use the TV and your regime as a carrot, but the main carrot out of it all is the TV.
>
> (Ned – prisoner)

As Ned suggests, television in prison is regulated; its provision is conditional and not without constraint or cost: emotional, social, psychological and economic. The prison apparatus operates on a timetable where policy provides prison staff with the 'contextual resources' to control and regulate this environment (Layder 2004). This section maps the introduction of in-cell television, the ways in which television access is secured through a contractual agreement and the extent to which in-cell television is incentivised.

5.1.1 The birth of television in prison
Television use goes unnoticed.

Routine events such as television viewing are part of the often invisible history of everyday life, a history that was not recorded by the people who lived it at the time.

(Spigel 1992:2)

The cultural impact of television's introduction to prison cells captures personal insights and provides indications of how the environment of the prison began to welcome (and resist) television. Theories of punishment readily remark on transformations of control within the penal system (Foucault 1991; Garland 1991); equally media scholars account for the adjustments of cultural life as a result of the omnipresence of television in domestic life (Spigel 1992; Silverstone 1999a; Moores 1988, 1996). The concept and practice of control in prison extends beyond what Layder (2004) defines as 'situated' to include 'mediated' interactions. This section and those that follow present the experiences of these interactions as they are remembered, and how they continue to feature as a negotiation within and across these types of interactions within the prison.

Television was not initially introduced to individual cells but to 'association' spaces, where prisoners could spend leisure time playing games like pool, interacting and watching television in this communal area (Gersch 2003). Communal television became available in the 1970s, but this provision was patchy.[1] Before this time, films were periodically aired to large groups of prisoners in prison chapels. Like the national television broadcast service, its availability was initially uneven and rollout occurred relatively slowly (Spigel 1992:32). There are no national statistics available to outline the reception of television in prisons in England and Wales, but this transition did not occur in line with national household uptake of television.

Respondents report that access to television was in the past strictly controlled and limited in terms of location. Times were often dedicated in the regime to viewing (Knight 2001; Gersch 2003). Paul explains,

A long time ago, many years ago, prisoners' access to any form of media was on a Saturday morning where they used to attend the chapel for a video. And the video would be played and then you'd bring them back and that would be the only thing they had, they had in cell radios and that was it. So the onset of the televisions as we brought televisions into association areas which was not so long ago, maybe in the last 10 years or so.

(Paul – senior prison officer)

Visual forms of media were therefore initially scarce and served as a formal activity; it is something prisoners were offered to *do*,

> But going back to days when you had film shows and big TV screens where everybody sat watching Top of the Pops or Coronation Street or whatever, it was the highlight of their week to be able to do that. Obviously now things have moved on.
>
> (Tony – senior management)

Physically 'going to' television was the only way provision could be made. As Silverstone (1999a) reports, television was initially placed within the formal and most public space in households; the 'front room' where guests were received. At this point television had begun its transformation into what Silverstone (1999a:98) defines as 'domesticated' or 'bringing things under control' (see also Berker et al. 2006:2). These ideas provide insights into forms of control such as paternalism. In much the same way, television enables primary care-givers an opportunity to continue with domestic chores whilst their children are occupied with watching. The provision of television in prison also sought to occupy prisoners in similar ways. These parallels provide important evidence of the forms of control television assisted with in its earliest form within prison and the kinds of political positioning of prisoners that the uses of punishment ultimately seek to achieve (Bosworth 2007).

One important transition is that television found 'a place within the moral economy' in prison (Silverstone 1999a:129); the routine in prison became intertwined with broadcasting. Time and space was made for television and it began to have currency in the prison culture. The regime and requirements for staff to ensure prisoners adhered to the strict prison routine, often resulted in communal viewing being disrupted. Tim recalls these kinds of tensions,

> Sport events were generally, would always be on. So if you were going through a major football championships, the FA cup or something like that, then yes, it would be football on. What I would say is, the problem we had is, at that time if there was a football match on, generally association would finish half way through the game or half an hour before the end of the game, so we had major problems getting prisoners away. Everybody would come out, so association would be full, nobody wanted to go back in, so it was a real problem time. Half the other landing wouldn't be watching the television but they would want to watch it so it had to be taped and then we'd have the

next day going through the whole scenario again of watching the identical football match and having the identical issues of trying to get the prisoners away.

(Tim – prison officer)

This highlights the value placed on the medium of television by its viewers and the meanings and attachments prisoners have with television (Vandebosch 2000). Acknowledging these attachments and possibly for the sake of order and control, the prison officers saw to it that desired television events like football were made available. Using a VCR to accommodate these requests was not an uncommon method of managing the broadcast schedules. Fran recalls how this was also the case in a women's prison she worked at,

It was all Coronation Street or EastEnders and they never clashed. And you all sat down... and that was their only access. The orderly, the cleaner, would then put the tape on to tape the things that the girls wanted to watch later on because they didn't have access to it... then they would watch them the next night.

(Fran – prison officer)

In effect, these prisoners Fran refers to never watched their selected programmes in broadcast time. Instead, time-shifting accommodated the taste of these audiences.

Eventually the prospect of in-cell television was raised on policy agendas and the era of scarcity was waning (see Chapter 2). Staff talked about the dilemmas of deciding who should receive television in their cells first and how could they maintain a functioning prison amidst the disruption of major re-wiring. Tim remembers what happened,

I mean the staff had a long time to get used to it. The in-cell electric programme took the best part of 18 months to two years and they did a quarter of a landing at a time, so they perhaps did 15 cells at a time. So there was a lot of work, so if you imagine that the televisions were drip fed into the prison, so by the time that we'd finished doing the project, they were used to it because it was 18 months down the line. But initially, it did cause a few concerns with the staff and the prisoners, in respect of who's going to be the first to get the televisions.

(Tim – prison officer)

At this site, 'enhanced' prisoners were the first to enjoy in-cell television.[2] This programme slowly extended to 'standard' prisoners and in this establishment, all cells were able to receive in-cell television by 2004, six years after its official introduction in 1998. Tim also observed the effect that television had on a prisoner's status,

> ...enhanced prisoners were the only ones with televisions. Enhanced status appeared to have a lot more status, if you like, prisoners were more keen to get onto enhanced because there was a perception that there was more to offer on enhanced than standard or basic.
>
> (Tim – prison officer)

This meant that there was a flurry of applications from standard prisoners to achieve enhanced status, as the prospect of in-cell television for prisoners was attractive. As Will describes, enhanced status not only offers additional goods and services but also an important label or a heightened status.

> The IEP regime does affect me; I can access everything. I feel trusted. I've earned the trust though.
>
> (Will – prisoner)

Carlton was also keen to do well in prison,

> I think what I've got to do to get my life back in order...to live comfortably and try and get through, doing prison time, get things sorted.
>
> (Carlton – prisoner)

The novelty and 'luxury' of in-cell television brought about increased motivation from some prisoners to comply and benefit from access to in-cell television. Thus, in many instances the intended effects of the in-cell television project were actually working. Some of the prisoners described their motivation to have an in-cell television,

> Your TV can be took off you in here and the kettle can go too. That is another reason to keep your nose clean; you can lose out on everything.
>
> (Malcolm – prisoner)

Malcolm and Will represent themselves as high-status prisoners, although Malcolm was a 'standard' prisoner when interviewed, identifiable by what Irwin (1970) defined as 'gleaners'. Both respondents were looking to glean as much from their incarceration as possible and comply with prison rules in order to minimise the risk of further deprivation. Lindlof (1986:344) highlights that gleaners are highly motivated media consumers, in pursuit of the educative and moral material. If the introduction of in-cell television saw an increase in 'gleaners' who benefit from the privileged ownership of television, then new tacit forms of control emerge in the form of self-governance and regulation (Rose 1999; Bosworth 2009) to sustain access.

Controlling prisoners and essentially creating an environment in which prisoners are willing to progress towards a 'gleaner' status caused some staff to become anxious of these kinds of effects. These anxieties were also captured with the introduction to television in national households; as Spigel (1992:3) reports there were mixed feelings about television coming into the home.

Utopian statements that idealized the new medium as an ultimate expression of technological and social progress were met by equally dystopian discourses that warned of television's devastating effects on family relationships and the efficient functioning of the household.

Brian explains why television made staff anxious,

I think the staff were suspicious at the start, me included. I think it was a way, we believed it was a way of cutting back on staff because obviously if prisoners got in-cell television. I mean it was a massive, massive step, so staff thought that they could keep them locked up longer, they'd be happy because they had a television. But then obviously they wouldn't need as many prison staff because it was a way of cutting back. I still think, you know, I think that's what happened. I think they got used to it and realising that it was actually a good thing because it reduced a lot of problems.

(Brian – prison officer)

Staff were fearful that television would replace the work that they do with prisoners if control was achieved by a technological medium, rather than through direct contact. A panoptic goal to achieve control via surveillance is modified; instead control is achieved through prisoners watching television and their 'work' is replaced by a machine (Spigel 1992). In particular, the erosion of social enterprises and pursuits meant that some worried about the moral decline of social values, cohesion and sacred family life (Spigel 1992). These fears relate to concerns about the intrusion of mediated forms of interaction which some respondents (prisoners and staff) describe (Jewkes 2002b).

Television could operate, as Silverstone (1999a) suggests, as 'care-giver' or technological parent to occupy prisoners and minimise problematic behaviour. Paul recognised that prior to the introduction of mass communications like television, he functioned as a source of knowledge, as informant or teacher to the prisoners in his care.

> [in] local jails where you grow up with the population, over a period of time you get to know them as well as your own family in some ways. And so conversations are like everyday conversations, what's going on out there, we've heard on the radio that this has happened, we've heard on the radio that's happened. So you fill in on the news, yes there was an incident here, there was bad weather there or whatever. You are joining the dots for them, they have a communication process, i.e. the radio or visits or whatever, so you're filling in the dots and making the picture for them ... as television has come in and the access to television and phones has come in then we don't have to fill in the dots so much.
>
> (Paul – senior prison officer)

For Stuart, the availability of in-cell television brought about interesting effects on the ways prisoners conversed with each other. He refers to his viewing of soap operas in the prison context,

> I get into the story lines that becomes part of your life, you hear lads on the landings talking about it. You wouldn't think lads would watch these things, I wouldn't on the out, it is the last thing I would watch.
>
> (Stuart – prisoner)

These shifts in forms of interaction and dialogue mean that situated activity, especially between prisoners and staff, may have become distanced and fragmented. The introduction of television had allowed different forms of sociability to become feasible, based on mediated encounters (Jewkes 2002a:222). Some of the staff appeared sad at the interactive losses in-cell television has brought about. In-cell television has helped to tame resistance from prisoners, by occupying them (Berker et al. 2006). Prisoners were also attuned to this prospect,

> TV are in pads because it makes life easier for staff. In this day and age there is more trouble in prison. So if they are behind their doors and say can't read and write, bored they are going to fight. I suppose it is a privilege. On basic it is taken off you, on standard you've got telly. If it wasn't what is the point of basic. Going behind your door is basically go and watch your telly. It is classed as control I suppose, a bit harsh. A chap in healthcare was offered telly, he said he doesn't watch telly, so he put himself on basic, he must have had a reason, was he in control? He has just done their job.
>
> (Pete – prisoner)

For Pete, television helps staff to help prisoners manage their 'life situation' (Layder 2006). Tim confirms that managing prisoners has become easier,

> I think the main difference for staff with prisoners having their own in-cell televisions, they're a lot easier to put away behind the doors. They appear to be happier behind the doors because they're occupied. And because they're occupied, they're far less likely to be on the cell bells requesting telephone calls or for any other reason that they may want to be coming out their cells. Funnily enough, if there's something important on the television that they want to watch, they generally don't come out to association. If there's football on television, they'll not come out on association. So the management of prisoners, particularly on the evening, is far, far easier.
>
> (Tim – prison officer)

The differences in interaction present a dilemma for prison staff. Prisoners are choosing to stay in their cells and not interacting in prison life. This kind of withdrawal from the immediate public life in prison is like the changes Silverstone (1999a:54) charts with the centring of television in private domestic life. In-cell television, like television within the home, 'became fundamentally dependent on a whole network of technologically derived services' and consequently the processes and cultural practices within these spheres adapt to embrace the control technologies demand, as well as how social agents can exploit control (Layder 2004). The positioning of television in the cell has contributed to the process of entering the moral economy. Others suggest that communal television placed in the exterior (communal settings) of the prison have not essentially permitted entrance into the moral economy; it didn't fit well there (Lindlof 1987b; Gersch 2003). Claire noticed how the public spheres within the prison environment such as association areas were accessed and used less frequently.

> Certainly when I first worked here, when I was an officer up on the landing, at association everybody came out and there was a big television on and they all sat and watched the television. And now they don't do that, they really come out for their phone calls; some of them will play pool and do a bit of interaction.
>
> (Claire – Governor)

One benefit of this is that overall the establishment became more 'settled', a term routinely used by staff respondents. This outcome echoed the original rationale of in-cell television's introduction, 'as a means of contributing to good order in a prison' (Hansard 1998). A less chaotic environment is much easier to manage and the inclusion of in-cell television into the privilege system can ensure much more compliance (Liebling et al. 1999). The calming effects of in-cell television have contributed to a decrease in problems related to disorder. Overall, television has provided a technological mechanism for sustaining control and order,

> The purpose, I know we said the original purpose was to keep the prisoner in the cell, but to me the purpose to having it in cell is appeasement more than anything else. And also it's what people are used to.
>
> (Paul – senior prison officer)

As in-cell television became embedded into the routine practice of everyday life at this prison, all 'standard' prisoners began to expect a television in their cells. Television has therefore been scaled down the privilege system from enhanced to standard, and 'normalisation' of its provision 'is entirely consistent with normal life' (Jewkes 2002a:172). In keeping with the notion of incentivising prisoners, prison establishments were therefore looking to add additional incentives. These have over time, but not exclusively, included DVD players, Freeview boxes, Sky television (for a very short time), toasters, more time out of cells, wearing own clothes instead of prison issue, and so on.[3] Brian explains

Enhanced, which it won't be long now before everybody gets a DVD because it started off for enhanced with TVs anyway and now everybody gets TVs, so the feeling is that that's the way it will go.

(Brian – prison officer)

Attempts to maintain a level of deprivation of goods and services (Sykes 1999) is therefore perceived important in establishing control. By not providing certain goods and services wholesale, prisoners are kept deprived. In escaping deprivation, prisoners are required to focus on their own behaviour in an attempt to 'glean' access to goods like television. By exploiting deprivations, prisoners are directed towards dependence of the institution much like a child is dependent on its care-givers (Silverstone 1999a; Sykes 1999). This type of control relies on a concept which Layder refers to as 'positional appeals' where rules have to be learnt and there are consequences or sanctions if these are rejected (2004:31). This is neither straightforward nor entirely effective. Some prisoners, as we will see in Chapter 7 are certain that deprivation in prison is not necessarily that difficult to bear, particularly in relation to in-cell television. Being a prisoner, in essence has traditionally being conceptualised by levels of deprivation and the kinds of methods prisoners employ to adapt to and cope with prison life (Cohen and Taylor 1972; Jewkes 2002a). The potential to withhold and control access to television and other technologies is a defining feature of the domestication of television in prison.

5.1.2   Signing the contract: Incentivising television

TV is a privilege; they can take them away from you if you get a nicking.

(Ryan – prisoner)

In-cell television is provided as a basis of standard care in prison. On entering prison, a prisoner is identified as an 'entry' prisoner (progressing to 'standard' on review and with that package comes an in-cell television. Upon reception and induction to the prison the rules and regulations are delivered to prisoners; included in this process is a contract outlining the provision of an in-cell television, as a result prisoners are co-opted into self-inspection. This 'contract' stipulates that the prison owns the television and it can be withdrawn at the discretion of prison staff. The payment for hire was something prisoner respondents were keen to explain; they thought that the public's perception of prisoners' access to television was that it was essentially free for prisoners and provided at the expense of the taxpayer. As Simon explains,

I pay £1 per week for the TV, I've paid for that, over 10 years that is a hell of a lot of money.

(Simon – prisoner)

Joshua also added,

We're paying for it. There have been times where, alright then, there's been times where I've been in my cell for a month but like I said then I've gone to the seg, that one pound is still coming off my money while I'm down the seg and I ain't got a telly. So it all differs. If they were giving it us without us paying for it then I suppose they could say, yes, it's a privilege, but at the moment I don't think it is. I think it's something we're paying for and therefore we should have a right for it.

(Joshua – prisoner)

Contrary to Joshua's insistence that it should be a 'right', the Home Affairs Committee in 1997 stipulated that 'the availability of television in this way is clearly an earned privilege rather than a right' (Hansard 1998). It is rare to find a prisoner who refuses to have an in-cell television.[4] However, Mick talked about how he had witnessed some prisoners return their television sets,

... no one would say TV is crap in here. It can do your bird for you. There's a lot of bang up here ... TV is all about control. If you did an experiment and took the TV away for two hours it wouldn't last. I've seen people give their TVs back; young one's wouldn't do it. Some people tell lies and say they would. It is more the older types that give it back.

(Mick – prisoner)

Mick believes that most prisoners are dependent on television. Wanting to accomplish personal control could explain why some, according to Mick's testimony, hand their sets back to the prison. Ned however talked about his experience in another prison at the time when televisions were not yet standard provision and were exclusive to enhanced prisoners,

I didn't have a TV when I was in jail in 2001–2002; even though there were wings with TVs I opted to stay on a wing without a TV because staff seemed to use it as a carrot, as a privilege to take away from you. So I opted to stay on the wing, it might sound a bit silly, but I stayed

on the wing where they couldn't take it off you. And then basically
you knew where you stood so I stayed on . . . .

(Ned – prisoner)

Ned actively resisted engaging in the 'game' (McDermott and King
1988). Refusing to enter the contract meant that Ned did not have to
engage fully in the IEP system. By his refusal to have television, Ned
had some semblance of control, and by choosing this he avoided threats
to his basic security and refusing to have his emotionality traded by
the prison (Layder 2004:32). Imposing self-deprivation, as in Ned's case,
is a powerful statement and also evidence of self-directed restraint and
resistance.

In-cell television is constantly under threat of removal. Will for
example talked about a situation he found himself in with a cell-mate
and he was fearful of the consequences it would have for him. This
perpetual fear of getting into trouble and having your access to goods
and services limited and controlled must make ontological security
difficult to achieve,

No-one is a true friend, you have to be self-orientated and you can
easily be guilty by association. Like drugs and phones. One time a
bloke took something [drugs]. I was going to ring the bell, but I
don't want to be perceived as that kind of person. It was scary . . . . He
was tempted to ring the bell, jail doesn't allow you to do that; what
should I do? They see him laid out [on his bed] and they say it is
alright.

(Will – prisoner)

For Will, becoming embroiled in 'incidents' such as he describes means
that he becomes the focus of scrutiny and observation by prison staff.
Scrutiny adversely means that his character and conduct may be called
into question and privileges like television could be removed and
curtailed.

In contrast to the standard regime, basic equates to a loss of privileges.
Overall, this means that basic prisoners spent a large amount of time in
their cells. Steve describes at length the principles of the basic regime,

They know the process because if they get three behavioural warnings
then they do get IEP regime reviews. And they are warned when they
are given the first behavioural, if you get another two of these you
are on basic and you explain to them what a basic prisoner is. And

to some people that's a shock enough, others its two fingers up at the system and they think they can flaunt and win the system. You tend to find a lot of these young ones, the ones that have just come from [other] establishments, they think they can beat the system. Whereas if you talk to the lifers, the ones that have been in the system for a long time, they know you can't beat the system, you will probably win the odd battle but you will never win the war. So going back to it, yes you do inform them that you could potentially lose your television, you will lose your kettle, you will lose a lot of what you are entitled to. Yes you are entitled to go to the gym but you will only go to the gym once, whereas at the moment you get two or three times a day a week, so you will lose that facility. You only get to use the library once a week. But everything has to be done by application so it's a real strict regime for them. And when they get onto basic they are the last one who are fed. And if they don't follow the protocols of the basic regime like putting applications in, they will get nothing. It usually takes a couple of weeks, especially for the young ones, to realise well hold on a second I'm not getting anything, and then they start toeing the line, they are thinking well yes I need this. Television is a good bargaining chip but sometimes when they have got the stereo they don't use the television.

(Steve – prison officer)

Basic prisoners are heavily monitored and their status is systematically reviewed by officers. They require extra input and monitoring and some staff commented on both the value of the basic regime and its influence on behaviour, and the overall effectiveness of the IEP system altogether (Liebling et al. 2011). The system encourages these basic prisoners to understand principles of conformity and this requires them to take responsibility for governing themselves (Rose 1999). It is not until they can display forms of control that can they be promoted from basic status. The IEP framework shapes the work of staff and lives of prisoners, and the provision of and access to television is inherent in this form of governance.

5.2   Valuing television: Mechanisms for control

Incentives like television require the individual to examine and scrutinise themselves, and this is routinely assisted by staff as facilitators and experts in self-help; Shaun, a prisoner for example said 'I'm constantly analysing myself'. The IEP system offers staff a method to work consistently as Liebling et al. (2011:105) suggest, Paul believes this facilitates *fairness*,

> I genuinely think it's the fair application of the basic process. I think the way staff on our floor deal with prisoners is consistent. I think the way the prisoners perception of how they are dealt with is consistent. I think the IEP application is consistent. And I think the prisoners suddenly realise well basic isn't as good as it's cracked up to be, they don't need to be the hard man who can run the jail or cause uproar because they are actually losing out. And the families are getting affected as well; they're not seeing their children, they're not seeing their families who are restricted to visits. So I think right across the board the application of the IEP process is consistent and that demonstrates to the prisoners that their standard of behaviour is needed.
>
> (Paul – senior prison officer)

Operationalising the IEP system through consistency brings a framework that is essentially transparent to staff and supposedly for prisoners (Liebling et al. 2011:107). Prisoner respondents were knowledgeable about the system and readily offered lists of their entitlements. Staff were sensitive to the deprivation prisoners experience and were able to emotionally connect to their losses. As Paul described, these losses extend beyond the prisoner and can affect the ways in which the prisoner can routinely connect with his family, for example. Paul continued to explain that,

> ... if we take that facility away it's a punishment, and therefore it's a punishment that they will struggle with.
>
> (Paul – senior prison officer)

Other staff recognised the potential losses prisoners could experience without television, and staff recognised that this can make prisoners vulnerable, and thus difficult to manage. The paradox of care and control is evident here, as officers act as both carers and controllers. Brian explains that in-cell television can help to prevent problems arising and be used as leverage to explain the consequences of their actions,

> So it can be used to control the problems that you have and if you've got a circle of violence or a circle of, you know, misbehaviour, then you can actually stop that. And you can say to them, look, you know,

you've gone three weeks now without getting into trouble, isn't it much better?

(Brian – prison officer)

Claire noticed a difference that in-cell television had made since leaving the establishment and returning,

There is a marked difference I think, I left X [prison] 10 years ago and I came back; when I left it had no in-cell TV and obviously since having the in-cell TV the prison is cleaner because there are no t-shirts hanging out the windows. They used to spend a lot of their time at windows shouting out windows, throwing stuff out windows.

(Claire – Governor)

Claire's observations show an important feature in the ways prisoners interact. Before in-cell television, situated forms of communication, for example shouting out of windows, seemed to occupy periods of bang-up. The introduction of in-cell television, for Claire has seen a reduction in this form of interaction, which has been displaced by mediated forms of interaction. The decline in situated interaction has therefore brought about significant 'improvements' in the ways prisoners occupy the time spent in their cells. Mediated interaction has enabled the establishment to function in a controlled fashion (Layder 2004). These kinds of constraint contribute to what Silverstone (1999a) described as 'domestication' of private life, and the introduction of television has served to cultivate prisoners' obedience. The civilising effects of in-cell television are related to the curtailment and containment of emotive responses and its outcomes (Elias 2010). The moral and visible hygiene of the prison has, as Claire identifies, changed since the introduction of in-cell television.

The staff also showed extensive understanding of the kinds of attachments prisoners and audiences generally have with television; therefore the rationale to incentivise television is based on 'transitional' attachments that individuals have with television (Silverstone 1999a:14),

I think in general people like television, they like watching it, they like their football or their soaps or 'This Morning'... all that. I think it is a motivator for prisoners because I think they feel quite lost without it.

(Claire – Governor)

Staff also recognised the implications of boredom in prison settings acknowledging it as a potentially dangerous emotive state,

> ...prisoners can become very bored, and when they become bored they become mischievous. So by installing in-cell television I believe it prevents a lot of that mischievousness, it's allowed them to be less bored.
>
> (Paul – senior prison officer)

By introducing television into this controlled environment, staff are able to manage some emotive dissonance with almost instantaneous effect. Managing increasingly large numbers of individuals is made possible by its introduction. In Paul's view, in-cell television reduces problematic behaviour. Fran also noticed that prisoners who are punished and have their privileges removed are visible to other prisoners,

> ...you are all being constantly observed by each other. If somebody is in need and they look desperate they know that everyone else can see them looking desperate or needing help. Or if they are not coming out of their cell people can visibly see that they are not coming out of their cell.
>
> (Fran – prison officer)

The witnessing of punishment serves as an important reminder of the deprivations the prison can impose, and can function as a stark reminder to prisoners. Stigma and shame operate here and compliance can follow (Scheff 1988; Garland 1991; Pratt 2000). Maintaining order is not necessarily straightforward, as accounts from prisoners in this study suggest, with some admitting to creating or witnessing violence, bullying and extortion. Steve explains that despite the mechanisms to maintain order, these are constantly challenged in their everyday work and forms of resistance routinely manifest (Liebling et al. 2011:122),

> You get the innocent ones, but then you get the ones that are at it, and no matter which way you do it they will get passed from cell to cell to cell. And when you have got 110 prisoners and three officers on a landing you can only police so much. And it's a shame but it gets into the prisons, you get mobile and contraband brought in...yes we know phones are in there at some point but its catching them....And

it's the same with the drugs, we've had a load that's come over the walls but you can only stop so much. People will try to flout the system and try their best and some get away with it and some don't, but it's a game.

(Steve – prison officer)

The occupying nature of in-cell television allows staff to manage a large volume of prisoners, as Steve describes. McDermott and King (1988:360) explain that games are 'to gain control over the meaning of a situation ... they are competitions about power'. Alan suggests,

It is a luxury item, the regime tries to get you in on it. But then it gives you some borderline for you.

(Alan – prisoner)

Alan suggests that prisoners are encouraged to participate in the IEP regime as long as the rules to this 'game' are understood by its participants. The day-to-day work for officers working on prison landings predominantly involves dealing with the domestic upkeep of the prison and its prisoners. Steve, for example, disclosed precise details of his daily routine at work and was able to define almost every minute of his working day. Steve stressed how much of his time is taken up with dealing with requests from prisoners, which are recorded through a formal and written application process. McDermott and King highlight that this kind of work is not dissimilar to childcare or parenting: successful parenting requires control, but also discretion (Liebling et al. 2011:121). The discretion of the officer is based on power and it is not surprising that 'tit for tat' games evolve in a competition for power. However, as Liebling et al. highlight, organisational policy is sometimes confusing and disorientating (2011:125) and the prison service has been criticised for being 'vague' (Bottoms 1990). Tony also explained that the in-cell electrics could be turned off if required. Tony did not intend this to mean that this was done in reality, but hypothetically they have the power to do so. Staff hold a significant level of power to control what prisoners do and when they do it, as Liebling et al. (2011:126) suggest 'discretion ... is inevitable .... Wherever there are rules, there will be discretion. In the prison context, this is especially true'.

Despite the incentives, disorder still arises. One of the challenges staff respondents discussed was that they thought that television did not carry as much value to motivate prisoners as it did when it was first introduced. This decrease in value presents a threat to the IEP system that frames so much of their work. This can weaken the control that staff are trying to achieve and 'weaken this already fractured monolith of power' (Liebling et al. 2011:131). Being able to 'disconnect' prisoners from mediated forms of interaction is a powerful act, as Tim describes,

> I mean for an example, if a prisoner is, at the moment if he attracts an IEP review, we can take his television off him. So, bearing in mind that they don't have any other forms of communication anymore in respect of newspapers, prisoners used to have stage papers where we used to give papers out, now the televisions are there, their contact with the outside world and news and all the rest of it can only be achieved through the television. So they're not quite so isolated with the television. Once the television's withdrawn, then their contact with the outside world becomes withdrawn, other than their normal royal mail to friends and family.
>
> (Tim – prison officer)

As Tim continued to assert, television is an important tool in prison-craft, 'another piece of the jigsaw that we can use to control the prisoner'. Challenges to these levels of control are continually evolving; Brian is critical of the value in-cell television now has,

> ... it's easier. At the start it could be used as an incentive, so we will take that off them. That's dried up now because we don't take it off them no matter what, and we've moved on to another level whereas the in-cell television was something that was great at the start and the prisoners thought that once you give them something then that's it, it became the norm and that was expected. So then Freeview and then DVD, well actually DVDs then Freeview.
>
> (Brian – prison officer)

Tim also noticed this decrease in value, 'once the televisions got bedded in ... the novelty had worn off'. In effect, the control staff initially had with television positioned as a luxury item was in their view decreasing, as it has in wider society (Ellis 2000). The additional challenge to maintain control has meant that supplementary television related hardware like DVD players and Freeview were added to the privilege list and rolled out as incentives under the discretion of the Governor, in the same way that that in-cell television was initially introduced. Other digital technologies are also being lined up in the same ways too (see Chapter 7). For now these are exclusive items intended for enhanced prisoners, yet some staff predict that this will also become standard issue, just like television. Tony and Paul considered how the advancements in technology and the inevitable digital switchover would require television provision to align with these advancements. Tony was worried that current provision appeared 'old fashioned', and that the challenge for bringing the establishment's provision in line with the digital revolution would need addressing. As O'Sullivan (1991:166) reports, television can symbolise 'a sign of progress' and discourses on consumption regularly return to this theme (Moores 1993:89). This again would entail additional investment and expenditure and likely disruption to the current service provision. Owing to the evolving nature of technology, the prison service is also seeking to maintain television as a leading object across the prison culture.

5.3   Mediated routines: Television-use diaries

The final part of this chapter documents the findings from nine 14-day television-use diaries completed by prisoner participants. In order to appreciate the viewing experiences of prisoners and what these audiences *do* with television it was necessary to record and observe the ways in which television is watched and how prisoners are able to do this. In order to get closer to the 'meanings and motivations' of prisoners (Jewkes 2002a) viewing television, it is necessary to locate this audience within the prison context. The routine of prison life collides with broadcast life. The trends mapped provide temporal and spatial features relating to use of television. These can also begin to outline the kind of movements prisoners make between mediated and situated 'places' (Moores 2006) and review how prisoners are 'anchored' to time (Martel 2006:606).

5.3.1   Time use and television

Periods of unlock and lock-up are significant factors which can influence television viewing. The periods of lock-up are potentially where prisoners consolidate most of their viewing, and conversely periods of unlock influence a reduction in television viewing since prisoners have opportunities to work, receive visits, attend treatments (medical) and attend to domestic needs. Time and space are therefore 'heavily

Table 5.1 The routine: Typical periods of lock-up and unlock in prison site for weekdays and weekends[5]

	7am	8am	9am	10am	11am	12pm	1pm	2pm	3pm	4pm	5pm	6pm	7pm	8pm–6am
Weekday (Mon–Fri)		Work, education, gym, visits, treatments						Work, education, gym, visits, treatments				Association[6]		
Weekend (Sat–Sun)			Visits, exercise, treatments, worship (Sun)					Visits, treatments[7]						

Locked-up in-cells   Unlocked

scripted' for prisoners (ibid.:595). Table 5.1 captures these periods in this particular site.

The sample of diarists included in this study do not necessarily represent the typical prisoner population, since six (out of nine) of the diarists were on enhanced privilege status and three were on standard status. These differences are relevant for achieving access to employment, goods and services[8] and time out of cell such as association, visits and leisure opportunities. Enhanced prisoners will experience less 'bang-up' time than standard and basic prisoners and are therefore unlocked more. Standard prisoners would experience less time out of cells than enhanced, particularly for leisure opportunities such as association. These factors influence the amounts of time prisoners are in cells. Overall, this sample typically over-represents the enhanced status group.[9]

According to the Broadcasters' Audience Research Board (BARB 2011), the national average viewing times for UK households for the same period as diary completion were 26.63 per week; an average of 3.8 hours per day.[10] Prisoners watch on average 61.39 hours of television (see Appendix 3) over the course of one week (seven days Mon–Sun) equating to 8.77 hours per day. During the weekend this increases slightly to 9.1 hours per day or 18.2 hours over the course of a weekend. This is more than reported by Vandebosch (2000) in her study in Belgian prisons at 6.6 hours per day at the weekend. Periods of unlock and opportunities to leave their cells are generally much more limited during weekends. Most forms of paid employment, visits, education and gym for prisoners operate on a Monday–Friday schedule: these are significantly reduced during the weekend. However this pattern of viewing is also a feature of television audience behaviour across the UK, with weekends seeing an increase in numbers of people watching, but also increases in the numbers watching earlier in the day (OFCOM 2010). Opportunities to access broadcast media in non-linear ways are limited to what is available through Freeview channels, for example repeated programmes at different times.[11] Prisoners are therefore unable to record or download (time-shift) material for television or other formats[12] and the audiences in this site are locked into broadcast schedules or the linear flow of television. However, there are pockets of movement towards digitisation whereby prisoners use electronic tablets to access applications and downloads to reach television programmes and films as well as self-service applications (see Chapter 8).

Variation in viewing times across this sample does occur. For example, Diarist G (highest in the sample) watches 100.5 hours of television per week and Diarist C (lowest in the sample) watches 16.5 hours per week. Their cases explain this:

Diarist G (interviewee – Malcolm) completed his diary whilst spending time in the healthcare facility (prison hospital) and was therefore temporarily unemployed during this period. As a standard (IEP) prisoner Malcolm's viewing generally commenced from 7am and generally continued until 11pm with few blank entries in his diary. Where they did occur this was usually between 9am and 11am or between 2pm to 4pm. These coincide with times of unlock for association and visits. Malcolm watched the most television on Fridays with entries totalling 11 and 13 hours. Malcolm shared a cell during these 14 days and watched some of the programmes with his cell-mate. Overall he viewed 61% of his total television consumption with his cell-mate and 39% alone. Access to DVD players and Freeview in the healthcare is a standard facility, despite them being only available to enhanced prisoners on normal location.[13]

Diarist C is an enhanced prisoner employed in the prison serving a ten-year IPP sentence. As well as access to in-cell TV he also had an in-cell radio, DVD and CD player. On three of the days Diarist C did not watch any television (0 hours). On the first occasion, which was a weekday, he was transferred to another prison. The second and third occasions were Saturdays. On Sundays the same and only entry was made for the same period, *Countryfile* at 11am for one hour. He completed the diary in the study site for three days before being transferred to a Category B closed training prison.[14] (See Appendix 4.)

This participant watched 57% of the programmes with his cell-mate and 43% alone; for example he watched a film on his own, *The Island on Bird Street* broadcast at 11am on a weekday. Upon transfer his viewing hours significantly reduced from six to seven hours per day to two hours. For every single day apart from weekends he watched BBC1 news in the morning for two hours and no other programmes were entered in the diary. Settling into a new prison does demand more time of prisoners such as induction to the prison and screening and assessments. Training prisons normally have more opportunities available to work and be engaged in purposeful activity compared to local prisons, and the 'core' day or periods of unlock should be longer.

These variations are important and the differences between the two prisons as outlined in Diarist C's case are something that is commonly observed. Prisoners are able to note differences in routines across different prisons. However, it is difficult to measure the impact of these differences and much of the prison literature generally asserts that the impact of incarceration is homogenously painful and the core aims of imprisonment like separation, deprivation and incapacitation are universal, no matter what kind of regime is experienced. Adjustments to time out of cell and bang-up for instance can impact on the intensity of these pains. Experiencing 'hard' or 'easy' jail time could be directly influenced by these factors (Wacquant 2002).

5.3.2   Viewing with other prisoners

None of the diarists indicated that they watched television outside their cells, and all entries indicate they were viewed *inside* prison cells. Communal and association areas do have televisions and they are sometimes switched on. Diarist B is the only prisoner in this diary sample who inhabited a cell alone. The rest of the diarists shared a cell with another prisoner. From the entries made, most of the viewing occurs with a prisoner's cell-mate at a sample average of 75% of all viewing. The remaining proportion at 25% is where respondents declared they either viewed television either alone or that their cell-mate was not watching. Based on this detail there is reduced opportunity to view television alone.

Diarists A, F and I viewed all of their television over the 14-day period with their cell-mate. Diarists D (93%) and E (84%) watched the majority of in-cell television with their cell-mates. Diarist D watched 7% alone and diarist E watched 16% alone. Diarists C and G watched the most television alone; for diarist C this constituted 43% of viewing and for diarist G 39%. Most prisoners in England and Wales today are required to share a cell with another prisoner, unless there are identified risks based on the Cell Sharing Risk Assessments (CSRA) procedure.

5.3.3 Prison routine

Prison routines are considered all-encompassing or 'total' (Goffman 1991) and the business of prison operates predominantly on a strict timetable. Equally, broadcasting is also framed within a timetable (Scannell 1996). By observing the entries in the television diaries it is possible to identify how the prison routine impacts on the viewing routines of prisoners, but also how the routine of broadcasting impacts on shaping everyday patterns of time in prison. Despite the fixed routine of both prison and broadcasting, prisoners *are* regularly negotiating between the two timetables; as Layder (2004:15) describes, there is an 'interplay between the creative inputs of individuals and the pre-existing social resources they draw upon to help formulate their behaviour'. Given the limitations of the prison environment and opportunities to spend time out of cell and/or be in 'purposeful activity', television and its content can evolve into the prisoner's 'own' timetable; no single diary entry is the same across this sample. Differences occur in length of time spent watching (or not) and the types of content selected. Opportunities to view alone are more restricted due to the likelihood of double occupancy of cells. This could also impact on the kinds of selections made by prisoners (Lull 1990) as they require negotiation, compromise and bargaining with others sharing the cell (see Chapter 6) (Figure 5.1).

The viewing routines remain reasonably similar with one visible contrast between the weekday and weekend. Fewer prisoners in this sample watch in-cell TV between 9am and 11am during weekdays. This is a period when prisoners are typically unlocked to attend work and education or exercise. At the weekends however prisoners remain locked in their cells during this time, unless they have visits booked, treatments or exercise. Four prisoners recorded that they spend the entire morning viewing during the weekend and more begin their viewing later, 8am rather than 7am. Eight of the prisoners in this sample are employed in the prison and one is unemployed. Therefore during weekdays most prisoners in this sample are not watching TV during 9am–11am due to their work or training obligations. One prisoner who was unemployed at the time of reporting continues to watch through the morning. Viewing increases for weekdays and weekends during the lunch period. Lunch is served and collected by prisoners between 11.45pm and 12.15pm, after which they are locked into their cells to eat their meals. This time also coincides with the broadcast of national and local news on television, considered one of the peak viewing times during weekdays (OFCOM 2010). A sharp decrease coincides with unlock between 2pm and 4pm on weekdays and weekends, usually for work or education on weekdays

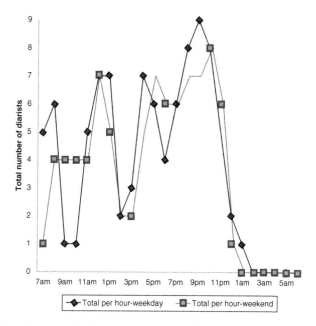

Figure 5.1 Number of diarists viewing in-cell television for weekday and weekend (Saturday)

and association at weekends. From 4pm a sharp increase in viewing occurs especially during weekdays, this increase occurs later, at weekends (5pm). For weekdays, a small reduction in viewing occurs at 6pm, a typical time for association and using the gym. However four prisoners continue to view during these times. This time also coincides with peak national TV viewing periods for weekday evenings, when popular broadcasts like news, soaps and dramas are routinely broadcast.[15]

Summary

Television's entrance into the deep 'interior' of the prison cell has brought about transformations to social relations in prison. Television now fixed in its place means that television and the act of watching television is away from public view, and this has become for many prisoners a habitual activity. Unlike communal viewing, in-cell viewing means that television has entered (sometimes haphazardly and not without effect) the moral economy. Permitting television into the deep interior of prison life has seen a shift not only in the ways prisoners can spend their time locked up in their cells, but also the kinds of choices they make with respect to engaging with prison life. Making room for television has meant time and space has also been carved out to welcome it. This shift from scarcity to plenty is not neutral and its impact, according to respondents, is that prisoners now interact between situated and mediated forms. The prison institution has deliberately taken television and used it to tame and 'domesticate' prisoners. By adopting a paternal approach to behaviour management (IEP), prison organisations are looking for ways to control by occupation. Deserving prisoners are rewarded with access to television as long as compliance is sustained. Those who 'glean' their time in prison modify and adapt their behaviour to achieve and sustain access. The IEP framework signals an important progression towards self-inspection. Rose (1999:127) suggests that the process of governmentality exploits privacy, and that the social enterprise 'used this privacy as the justification for its non-intervention'. The object now strategically placed in the prison cell is a symbolic indication of the very privacy that legitimises a distancing between prisoner and traditional forms of control.

Overwhelmingly all of the staff respondents did not consider television as a privilege despite the fact the IEP system dictates and professes this, and yet they work mostly without question within this framework. Staff continually stress that television is a significant instrument for care. Instead of disconnecting prisoners from television, enabling connection is an important priority to facilitate care and control. As a result, there is a shift in emphasis away from the incentivising of television to it being a normalising (Jewkes 2002a; Gersch 2003) feature, and this is especially grounded by staff respondents' perceptions noting improvements to the moral and visible or material hygiene of the prison. Television is the 'leading object' (Silverstone 1999a), yet this for the most part is invisible across large sections of policy. A technology review by Ministry of Justice (2012) fails to mention television at all. As this chapter has begun to show, television plays a significant and even leading role as a feature of control, impacting on forms of interaction and engagement with prison life.

6
Personal Control: Television, Emotion and Prison Life

Television has had a taming effect on prisoners,[1] with implications for social relations within the prison. This chapter outlines the precarious and sensitive relationship prisoners have with television; it focuses exclusively on the voices of male prisoners to identify how they relate to television. By foregrounding emotion, a closer examination of the forms of control at work in the prison setting can be illuminated, and the ways in which television may or may not serve as a 'protective device' (Layder 2004:26). Layder's discussion on 'the need for personal control' signifies how social agents are continually attempting 'to cater for emotional needs and desires...while maintaining good mental health' (ibid.:34). This chapter discusses emotions which feature most forcefully in the data; boredom, frustration, ambivalence, happiness and joy. The evidence presented here outlines how 'care and maintenance of the social self' is accomplished with television (ibid.:19). The chapter ends by examining the participants' fears of watching television in prison.

6.1 Boredom and television

Boredom is poisonous, it is mental poison. You can easily get distressed and suicidal in here. TV keeps you occupied. Even just changing the channels using the remote, it keeps you focused.

(Leon – prisoner)

Boredom is considered a feature of everyday life in prison which can in some circumstances develop and evolve into deep anxiety and disorientation for some serving prisoners (Liebling 1999a; Vandebosch 2001). No studies have focused on boredom in prison. However, boredom is routinely cited as a causal feature in offending behaviour and crime (Ferrell 2004). Most studies on boredom more generally have been led by psychologists in either laboratory conditions or working environments, particularly industrial and manual labour settings (McBain 1970). Several characteristics of boredom have been identified, such as the experience of monotony, the lack of novelty, the absence of meaning and constraint which lead to sleepiness, restlessness, anxiety and hostility to the environment (Smith 1981; Barbalet 1999). Others have noted that differences occur across different groups: for example those most prone to boredom are men (Zuckerman 1979), people with lower intelligence (Robinson 1975), those with poor mental health (Caplan et al. 1975) and extroverts (Kagan and Rosman 1964). Most importantly boredom is considered unpleasant and unsettling and emotive responses like frustration and anger often follow (O'Hanlon 1981). Levin and Brown (1975) also found that prisoners experience more boredom than prison staff. Furthermore dissatisfaction with their circumstances has been correlated with boredom leading to pervasive attitudes towards the establishment or institution in which they are constrained, such as workplace or school (ibid.). Given these characteristics, it is probably no surprise that boredom was mentioned by all of the interviews.

Alleviating boredom was repeatedly related to their direct use of television. The strict prison routine brings no opportunities for prisoners to experience deviations from the routine shaped by the timetabling of unlock and bang-up with activities restricted to work, education, gym and visits. Given these contextual constraints, boredom, and the fear of it, has an important impact on how television consumption is managed by the individual. Equally, boredom itself was not just a situational outcome of the immediate prison experience, but was also described as a product of prisoners' mediated encounters; watching television for some was also considered boring (Klapp 1986; Jewkes 2002a).

The television diaries (see Chapter 5) outline how prisoners regularly negotiate between the schedules of the prison and broadcasting, with many prisoners watching large quantities of television each week. Only a small proportion of the prison day is potentially 'occupied' with activity, with most of the day spent locked behind their cell doors as Simon described,

> Nowadays they keep you locked up longer, now the workshops have gone, that cured some boredom.
>
> (Simon – prisoner)

The freedom to access activity inside prison cells is extremely limited. Prisoners report that time spent locked up in their cells is increasing.

Even when activity is available, such as work or education, prisoners also report the tedious nature of the kinds of activities they are allowed to do, which therefore feature as meaningless and monotonous (Cohen and Taylor 1972; Hughes 2004). Consequently, prisoners are further challenged in their quest to avoid 'helplessness' (Layder 2004:30). Boredom is not necessarily an exclusive feature of 'bang-up', for some it can be a permanent and 'total' experience; 'hyper-boredom' (Healy 1984). Bang-up is a hotspot for boredom to manifest, hence becoming mindful of boredom is a consequence of options available to Ned.

> ...when I am sat in my cell there is either three things I can do, you can either watch TV or listen to a CD or something like that, or I could exercise or I could be reading or writing.... There is nothing much really you can do in a cell.
>
> (Ned – prisoner)

As in many accounts of boredom, Ned identifies that constraint and opportunities for arousal remain constantly and perpetually limited. As Barbalet (1999:631) asserts, boredom 'emotionally registers an absence of meaning', and seeking out television highlights his need to find something meaningful. To achieve this Barbalet suggests that 'meaning both requires and constitutes sociality' (ibid.). Mediated encounters can supply intimacy to a world beyond one's own immediate spatial context (Moores 1993). Being able to stretch and reach social relations and interaction via television may have important positive effects on well-being and improved mental health (Seeman 1996). Moores (1996:49) suggests that television provides a ' "permeable" external boundary', which otherwise would be closed off from the outside world. The public world is permitted to enter via technologies like television, radio and, under more controlled conditions, the telephone and letters. As Moores (ibid.:54) continues to suggest, 'viewers remain physically rooted in the domestic [prison] realm...these "excursions" are acts of imagination...provides a "technological extension" of human reach across situational boundaries'. This enabling feature of television provides prisoner audiences with the psychological capacity to 'escape' from their harsh conditions and seek out social relations in order to counter debilitating emotions like boredom. Moreover, attempts to make the cell their 'own' place can also be ratified when taking these movements through television (Moores 2006).

Cell-sharing also brings its challenges and adds further constraints to the ability to make their own kinds of choices and seek out activity or material that *they* find meaningful. All the prisoners in this sample were mindful of boredom and most associate it with a series of harms or risks such as depression, self-harm, suicide and stress (Liebling 1999a). Boredom, for them, is therefore dangerous; their relationship with television becomes a viable route to minimise this emotive response (Zillman 1988). Television, amongst other things, (like sleep and time out of cells and drug use) is desired to counter boredom. The interviews also highlight that boredom accentuates other unpleasant emotions and feelings, such as frustration, fear and sadness. In these instances television use helps them to achieve 'personal control' (Layder 2004). It can serve as an antidote to boredom and its associated consequences, as Carlton describes,

> It feeds your brain, just a little. It is occupying boredom.
>
> (Carlton – prisoner)

The need to stay mentally agile and alert was commonly associated with the potential role that television has in the prison context (Cohen and Taylor 1972; Johnson and Toch 1982; Zamble and Porporino 1985). Stuart, for example, was increasingly fearful of psychological deterioration related to boredom, explaining to me that 'you become *cabbaged* here with the boredom and depression'. He talked about the dangers of boredom.

> I find that if I'm left alone, that's when I get bored my mind goes, it is why I am in here, it pisses me off it gets me thinking and that is not a good thing to do.
>
> (Stuart – prisoner)

Being incapacitated by boredom brought on by isolation and loneliness and lack of activity can act as a trigger for 'thinking time', something some of the respondents were actively trying to avoid. These moments are not necessarily boring, but the amplification of thinking about one's self, circumstances and people within their immediate surroundings can manifest itself as distress. This is considered dangerous, as Ned explains that watching television serves as an activity that offers a useful distraction from thinking and focusing on the conditions of incarceration.

> I would say that the TV would help you cope with boredom because you get to watch something to take your mind off. Because when

you're watching something you tend to focus on what you're doing. It's like when you're writing a letter you tend to focus on things that you want to talk about, a conversation. And when you're watching the TV you're not thinking about your toilet being near you, or you're not thinking about being locked in that room for the time being. You are channelled on watching a programme. So if it's exciting I think you forget about all those things. Whereas probably it's not as exciting for you, you probably wouldn't, you wouldn't relax as much.

(Ned – prisoner)

For Ned, excitement through television content is purposeful (Zillman 1988). Others describe the relaxant qualities of television in this context. In particular, some associated relaxing as a break from their immediate spatial encounters.

... helps me to chill out and relax. It does help boredom and aggression. I let steam off through nature programmes; I've got to watch it in an evening. Nature is soothing, a calming programme. You feel you are there with them; it is relaxing and chilled and you forget where you are.

(Malcolm – prisoner)

Other mechanisms to aid relaxation were reported by the significance of sleep, as Ryan explains '*I get bored and go to sleep. I sleep my sentence away*' and Simon describes sleep as a 'bird killer'. Television for some was considered to have soporific qualities as Stuart says '*I watch DVDs, they put me to sleep*'. Yet Malcolm observes,

I think TV can take your life over. It is necessary to stop the boredom. I do a lot of sitting watching TV and playing cards sometimes. Some sleep their sentences away and don't come out of their cells.

(Malcolm – prisoner)

The ways in which prisoners manage their time and the kinds of values they express about their time in prison are diverse. The experiences of time in prison have been previously reported as different from time experienced outside prison (Sykes 1958; Cohen and Taylor 1972; Jewkes 2002a; Cope 2003), and invariably time in prison is routinely 'problematised' or 'alienating' (Martel 2006:596). In relation to boredom, the accounts from the interviewees highlight two aspects of spending time in prison. First, prisoners experience a routine which is essentially fixed and rigid, which they have no power to change within the prison itself (situated). Broadcasting schedules (mediated) also operate on a timetable. Second, they experience unstructured and empty time. The sensation of boredom can make 'time appear to stand still' (Barbalet 1999:637), or as Anderson describes a 'stilling and slowing' can be experienced (2004:743). Television can fill this void and lessen the stillness boredom can reproduce. The television-use diaries highlight that time is regularly filled with television programmes, but this does not mean that television itself can lessen the stillness of time and boredom. Filling time with television also has its costs and risks. Klapp (1986:3), for example, takes the view that information society brings about degradation resulting in boredom. Exposure to information at high speed means that the 'slow horse of meaning is unable to keep up with the fast horse of mere information'. Thus, meaning can be lost and the information consumed can become redundant and dilute into 'noise', resulting in what Klapp terms 'banalization' of modern life (ibid.:2). There is little said about the impact of space on boredom, yet the data here suggests that the 'excursions' through television are not only important to bend time, but also to alter space in attempts to find a place in which boredom doesn't feature.

Feeling disorientated was also common. Mick was unemployed and in a single cell and television provided him with a structure. Planned and unexpected television events can sharpen his mood.

> Here I have no structure or routine and I get bored, so I get in bed and fall asleep. But then no sleep all night. On Tuesdays there is nothing on, but oh there is Shameless which is brilliant, then there is soaps oh and that Holloway thing [prison documentary].
>
> (Mick – prisoner)

Mick found he was watching a lot of television, especially at night, and his routine began to move away from the routine established in the prison and was instead directed by broadcasting schedules. He began to distance himself from the prison schedule. Unlike many of the respondents, Mick felt he didn't need to plan and organise his viewing.

> I watch that much I don't need a TV mag. On BBC there is always a film at 11.10pm, it is on and is predictable. Basically I know what the schedule is. I know what they are and it bores you. It plans it for you. It is a break from the routine when I'm not watching. You get

set in your ways, being like this in jail, it breaks up routine. A routine round the TV routine.

(Mick – prisoner)

Mick suggests that broadcast schedules can be monotonous and this is especially heightened by imprisonment. Television viewing becomes habitual, which soon can be translated into feelings of boredom. The 'rituals' (Scannell 1996) of broadcasting therefore generate unconstructive emotive responses and in particular predictability reinforces these sentiments. This subverts Silverstone's (1999a) premise that ontological security is in part secured by the ritual nature of broadcasting and everyday life. Instead predictability is considered a risk of television viewing.

> Bill – On an evening I won't watch soaps. I am not a soap man. I didn't watch it before prison and I'm not watching it now. They are boring and predictable. But I do watch The Bill, Casualty and Holby City.
>
> VK – Aren't they soaps?
>
> Bill – They are but they are not, there is not always a follow on, it is separate for each episode. Follow-ons are predictable which makes them boring.

In overcoming predictability, Bill avoids certain types of programming. Furthermore, predictability may still be a feature but as long as a programme can deliver antidotes to boredom through entertainment, excitement and relaxant qualities, prisoners may still choose to watch these types of programmes, because they can introduce meaning into an otherwise meaningless situation. Pete talks about these paradoxes in relation to the popular game show *Deal or No Deal*.

> I can do without it but it is on, it does get monotonous, same old thing but there is entertainment value.

(Pete – prisoner)

The lack of novelty for Pete is tempered by the entertaining value this programme can offer him. Accessing novelty is a way of reducing boredom (Klapp 1986), in particular the evolving conditions of leisure, work and domesticity have according to some changed the emotional landscape with respect to boredom (Klapp 1986; Anderson 2004). However, boredom can arise in encounters of over-stimulation, where meanings can become disordered. The quest for excitement in viewing is also important, but this is unreliable.

> Television can be boring sometimes, like I said Saturday nights are swings and roundabouts sometimes it is really exciting. Sometimes I watch 'X-Factor' and it drives me crazy and I think that's crap but that's just my personal opinion.
>
> (Ned – prisoner)

For Ned, exposure to large doses of television in the hope of finding novelty is symptomatic of his need to overcome boredom. His dissatisfaction with Saturday night viewing occurs despite his persistence in watching with the hope of experiencing novelty. As Anderson suggests, 'listening-to-get-through' (2004:748) or watching in the hope that television can deliver, allows viewers to comprehend and make sense of unfolding time. They acknowledge that events within prison will largely remain the same, but having a meaningful mediated encounter can make this prospect more bearable. Excitement is also identifiable in respondents' references to soap operas and sport. For soaps the use of cliff-hangers was important for arousing excitement.

> Soaps and prison go well together. There is something to look forward to until the next time, like the cliff-hangers.
>
> (Pete – prisoner)

The diaries show that soaps are regularly consumed in large quantities. The interviewees were able to offer intricate descriptions of the soap story lines and characters. Soaps provide substance and material for conversation with fellow prisoners, staff and their family (Lull 1990).

> I get very excited and say to my family 'did you see ... ?'
>
> (Sunny – prisoner)

These 'did you see' moments provide meaning to the act of watching television. Soaps and sport were also reported as helpful in minimising isolation and providing content for talk (Wood 2009:57). The temporal and spatial qualities of mediated content helped create a sense of intimacy by bringing people close (Horton and Wohl 1956), also an opportunity to witness events that others are also witnessing at the same time (Meyrowitz 1985). These effects can be important for increasing excitement. For example if a 'big' soap storyline is resolved or an important high profile football match is being broadcast, there will often be verbal and physical outbursts such as shouting and banging on doors (Gersch 2003, 2004).

Boredom signals and triggers the need for action. As Layder (2004:27) describes, emotions appear in a queue and a social agent's 'need claims' orders how these should be dealt with. Techniques cited as useful ways of dissipating boredom include indulging in fantasy, play and also conflict (Roy 1960; Barbalet 2004) because they can help to locate meaning. By cross-referencing the accounts of boredom in this data set it can be identified that television is used in similar ways. Television serves important para-social interactive opportunities (Horton and Wohl 1956; Meyrowitz 1985) or 'sociability' (Scannell 1996) and the textual content of television provides substance for its regulative uses (Lull 1990) such as talk and interaction. Furthermore, other correlations appear in relation to the deprivation effect of incarceration, with boredom signalling the desire for activity (Layder 2004). For example, the use of DVDs by enhanced prisoners can offer additional choice and variety, providing respite from broadcasting schedules. Boredom can also amplify other emotive responses.

6.2   Frustration and television

It is hard been locked up in a cell, bloody hard.

(Ned – prisoner)

Like boredom, frustration is an unpleasant sensation and leads to emotions like anger and fear. Irwin and Owen (2005:104) describe the 'arbitrary' and disorientating nature of prison rules and frustration and expressions of anger as well as acts of violence are densely populated in accounts of penal research (Snacken 2005:306). Frustration can evolve from boredom and again signals the need for action (Layder 2004). Observations of frustration indicate that incarceration manifests deep anxiety brought on by deprivation, particularly related to the restriction of autonomy (Irwin and Owen 2005; Sykes 1999). Television use, therefore, can serve as an outlet to channel frustration, but in some instances can also be the cause of it. The demands on a person's internal locus of control (Rotter 1954) can be assisted through watching television, especially given the kinds of long-term 'transitional' attachments (Silverstone 1999a) these individuals would have formed with television. Going to television to receive 'care' is a method to soothe their angst. When television fails to offer a resolution to these feelings, they can be compounded (Layder 2004). Fear of violence in prison is common (Sykes 1999; Snacken 2005). 'Keeping your head down' is common argot amongst prisoners and was repeatedly described by the interviewees. This is a way of explaining the social and psychological techniques required to govern themselves to avoid unwanted risks. Television viewing can sometimes provide essential respite and restoration from disorientating and debilitating circumstances. Viewing can provide a legitimate withdrawal into the privacy of one's cell and thus reduce the risk of contamination from prison culture (Jewkes 2002a; Crewe 2006; Bonini and Perrotta 2007).

Some respondents were clear about the 'therapeutic' role television can have for reducing frustration. They acknowledged that life in prison without television would probably increase their frustrations. For Carlton, it would be 'long and frustrating. I've never not had TV...In Gambia I didn't watch TV, but I had chance to walk around in the sun'. In contrast his outside experiences permit other options. Television can provide a space to eliminate frustration and find 'security' (Moores 1996:48; Silverstone 1999a:19). Carlton continued to explain that 'you dispose your frustrations through TV. It occupies the mind enough to take away bad feelings as well'. These 'bad feelings' were regularly reported and respondents recognised the danger they could pose.

> But if they take that away from you boredom will drive you to do things that you wouldn't even consider doing.
>
> (Ned – prisoner)

Conflict can be a consequence of boredom and thus risk-taking behaviour can generate meaning (Roy 1960; Barbalet 2004). Yet these can be particularly dangerous, especially in a volatile context like prison. Ned continued to explain that,

> I won't let myself get in that state. I'll go and say something to someone, some people don't; there is a lot of pent up frustration.
>
> (Ned – prisoner)

For Ned, taking responsibility for his emotions and well-being was important for staying in control, yet he was unable to accomplish 'interpersonal control' (Layder 2004:13) of other people in the same way. Taking responsibility for one's own emotional needs demonstrates the 'regulative technology of expertise' and the 'tightening of ego controls over inner conflict' (Rose 1999:220). Stuart also exhibits this expertise to achieve 'some sort of psychic peace' (ibid.:219).

Mind you if you didn't have TV I'd find it stressful. I'd be plotting and it would lead to depression. I now see why they say this now; without TV we'd all just be plotting and they'd be saying I'm gonna do this.

(Stuart – prisoner)

The value of television is attributed here to the role it has in reducing stress (Anderson et al. 1996). Finding a rational rather than emotional route is something that men in particular are expected to conform to, as Williams (2001:96) notes there are 'cultural prescriptions' concerning the emotional 'styles of both men and women' and men in particular are expected to have 'mastery of unruly bodily passions and 'irrational corporeal impulses' and adhere to 'feeling rules' (Hochschild 1983). The examples suggest that men are attempting to find a rational way through their experience. Paradoxically, these disclosures also signalled degrees of reflexivity. They acknowledge their emotions and find ways (sometimes with television) to heal the harmful effects of emotions like frustration, anger and fear. As Williams (2001:109) notes, this kind of reflexivity could be interpreted as a 'so-called "crisis" of masculinity'. The disclosures of stress were also commonplace and respondents described how they avoided certain mediated encounters, for example Ned and Shaun are news avoiders;

I find news rather boring, I do personally, but other people watch the news to find out what's going on in the world and I have got more things on my plate....

(Ned – prisoner)

I don't watch news, who wants to listen to news? I don't care what's going on out there, I just don't care. I sometimes read a newspaper like [local], Inside Time is better for in here. Like the Michael Jackson death, it is a big thing in the media and on the front cover of the newspapers, so my girlfriend tells me. I am in a way disconnected and media still allows me to interact.... But I don't care at present, as soon as you come through those gates the world has ended.

(Shaun – prisoner)

Other research has also indicated that people who are stressed and depressed avoid news to evade conflict (Anderson et al. 1996). Carlton explains why he doesn't like soap operas, yet likes to watch spin-off sports programmes about fighting and boxing. He also avoids watching television news.

Carlton – So sad all the time, always conflict in them. I think to myself if I watch it affects the way I see things. It affects you, all the conflict. It sounds bad cos I watch all the fighting (laughs)...

VK – Yes I was going to ask you about that...

Carlton – It's the fighting instead of looking at it, it is the tension release, it's not going to affect my life the same way.

VK – So what about TV news?

Carlton – Yeah they tell you all the bad stuff in the world.

Making the right television selections is therefore an opportunity for respondents to manage their emotions, by directly avoiding or extracting what they consider to be the nourishing qualities of television broadcasts. For Carlton, watching conflict through sport rather than news enabled personal control. As Zillman (1988) found, people who experience stressful situations are more likely to seek out 'exciting' material from television. Sunny stated that he recommends television to other prisoners as a therapeutic mechanism for resolving distress.

> ...if it is their first time experience it can be very hard for them. I tell them not to worry and watch TV to help them be distracted.
>
> (Sunny – prisoner)

Rose (1999:218) suggests that therapy 'has become the staple fare of mass media communication'. The inculcation of the 'psy' sciences into everyday life can be extended to mediated texts in which many types of programmes, like talk and lifestyle shows, that profess the 'rites of...self-examination bring the soul's moral disorder and danger to bitter consciousness, achieving detachment from sinful inclination' (ibid.:223). Therefore self-regulation appears along a continuum and the negotiation between mediated and situated encounters induces personal scrutiny and observation which are key qualities to therapy.

Frustration was also expressed towards the provision of television. During the fieldwork stages of the research, Freeview boxes were made available to enhanced prisoners as an additional reward for their compliance and good behaviour. I witnessed the removal of these boxes for all prisoners on an occasion when I visited to carry out an interview. Officers walked down the landing, entering the cells, filling black bin-liners with the digital boxes as I and prisoners looked on. Some prisoners questioned the officers, but most remained quiet and acquiesced. The rationale provided at the time was related to 'security' in that the boxes were considered unfit to maintain a secure prison.[2] Questions around fairness appeared in some of the interviews with prisoners, most expressing frustration at the ways in which television and its associated products like Freeview are provided or not (Irwin and Owen 2005). Leon, who had also witnessed this incident at the same time, described that television

> ... solves loads of problems. They cost £50 say and it saves you hundreds more such as staff, paperwork, suicides. It is a well meaningful privilege. It is better to be proactive than reactive. People just don't realise. All the people involved in helping people it saves money from all angles. It is integral and essential; there is a large amount of good for prison and inmates. The IEP system here is rubbish, there is no incentive to be enhanced here, look at what happened today. I've been to HMP X and HMP Y, they gave you incentives. There are so many fights, bells ringing, people on roofs, suicide attempts. I was listening to a chap on FNC [first night centre] and what I realised was he didn't have a TV. I couldn't believe it, how could they do that to someone who just came in. So I spoke to the officer to try and get him a TV. How ridiculous is it?
>
> (Leon – prisoner)

Discrepancies and reliability of broadcast services made available were also mentioned; Stuart was irritated with the bad reception and Alan, Pete and Will couldn't always tune in to terrestrial channels either.

> I am blessed for our BBC1 is tuned in, we pay 50p for a TV each week, but you rarely get BBC1 and 2 in here. All they need to do is press the reset button to change it. Just get someone to fix it. It's fuck you jack. I'll watch TV.
>
> (Will – prisoner)

Frustration mounts for these individuals as a consequence of not been able to resolve the problem themselves; they are not permitted to do this, but instead have to rely on staff to resolve technical issues. As frustration mounts, so does hostility towards their keepers, particularly when discrepancies arise. The desire to take control of these kinds of situations reminds these individuals of the constraints in which they are placed. The extent to which prisoners can achieve personal control is regularly denied. In these instances where access to television is limited by technical difficulties, emotional responses such as anger and frustration cannot necessarily help with coping with prison life.

6.2.1 Cell-sharing: Modus vivendi

The diaries suggest that most television in prison is viewed with another prisoner and scope for carving out their own viewing schedules is limited.[3] Little is known about the cell-sharing experience and this is an unexplored feature of prison life. Most spoke about compromise or the need to accommodate viewing preferences, which often meant that not all of their viewing needs were met. Instead, a *modus vivendi* evolves in order for life to go on and avoid a stalemate situation. Some talked about conflict over viewing schedules and the ways in which these differences are resolved (Gersch 2003). Barry and Will, who shared a cell together (interviewed separately[4]), disclosed their frustration with each other over viewing preferences and their domestic habits. Barry was not as keen as Will on sporting events. Will did not like Barry's choice of action movies and the lead actors in them, thus as Hobson (1980:109) describes, they operate in this confined area in largely 'two worlds'; separated by their different tastes in television. Both disclosures outline an insight into their living arrangements:

> Barry – I've been having rows with pad mate cos the athletics is on, he's not bad but don't tell him. It was on all day yesterday. Last week I watched what I wanted with a view to him watching the athletics and 'Match of the Day'. I don't want to watch it, especially after five hours, I'm climbing the walls. He ain't bothered though. He hates Steven Seagal and Jean Claude van Damme. He hates it; I know it winds him up. I leave the toilet seat up too. We get on alright. I know him from in here. We also like the same curry house.

Barry suggests they have little in common and their tastes are mostly different. Within this confined space two separate cultures evolve and do not always nestle well together. The few things they share are the experiences of being in prison. Learning to compromise and be tolerant of each other requires personal control and a willingness to ratify a treaty or surrender. Layder's application of Goffman's 'interaction order' can account for how individuals find ways to look after their 'social self' and dealing with problems in social life results in 'mutual moral obligations' (2004:18) in this context being readily foregrounded and omnipresent. Will confirms what Barry states about their planned viewing and that occasionally viewing together is achieved. Will's interest in sport enabled a sustained sacrifice of his viewing preferences in order to 'bank' television time with his cell-mate.

Will – Like in the last two weeks I told him to watch what he wanted cos I knew sport was on. He enjoys football I think, he does get into it. We have a cup of tea and sit on the bed and watch it.

Barry describes how planning together helps to establish a shared television routine in which a rhythm of mutual viewing can evolve. This assists in cohesion or *modus vivendi*.

Barry – I plan TV and mark it down; we also plan it together. He is the DVD orderly: I tell him what I fancy and he brings it. We have as many as we like really. Tonight we've got 'Shooting Gallery'. We'll watch a DVD at bang up between 12–2pm and on Saturdays and Sundays we can do three DVDs back to back.

By having a shared ritual they develop their own social rules, and these become ratified as time spent with each other in these circumstances goes on (Layder 2004:18). However, this is not always a seamless or innocent negotiation. Will admits that he will deliberately select programmes which challenge Barry's taste.

Will – Sometimes I do the opposite to him. I can't stand Jean Claude Van Damme and Steven Seagal or crime and 'The Bill'. I like 'Panorama', 'Dispatches', News on ITV, but not regional. 'The Bill' is most frustrating, it is police orientated, a warped perspective of what police do.

The game-playing (McDermott and King 1988) can in part help to temper their own frustrations and manage a situation which most find intolerable. Moreover, in a climate in which boredom is commonplace, conflict can emerge as a response to these conditions (Barbalet 1999). Furthermore, finding and sustaining power within the cell requires focus, and the playful nature they describe underlies their attempts to sustain personal control (Layder 2004:17). On the surface, Barry and Will wanted to present an egalitarian version of their domestic circumstances, yet Barry's description describes how his own power could not be fully realised with Will, due to a prisoner code (Sykes 1999; Crewe 2005).

Barry – We have a remote each now, we normally pass it to each other. My pad mate was in his cell before me so it is his pad, when he moves out it then becomes mine. Mind you I moved into a cell and there was a young lad and I told him to shift. I didn't bully him, I just told him. I don't like to associate with people in here; some are nasty, but I know who is good. My pad mate is not bad but he is never wrong. He has a way of saying stuff. We like 'Star Trek', when we were kids, our era. We just like it. You see things in 'Star Trek' and 'Star Wars'.

Finding common ground and the ability to relax in these awkward circumstances is important to make the situation bearable and meaningful. Sharing and liking programmes that they both enjoy provides respite from potential tension and conflict. In maintaining the 'self as a finely tuned security system' (Layder 2004), they can function with less effort as they become united (Kubey 1990).

Will – My pad mate's choice 'Big, Bigger and Biggest', I enjoy that. He sometimes says 'that's amazing' but we don't normally talk, that is a sign of a good pad mate: if you can sit in silence. I remember this chap, one of the bully boys, like making demands; I think it was a lack of education to deal with problems; there are arguments sometimes. Like my pad mate we have arguments sometimes; his hygiene levels, he smokes and the toilet. You have got to respect each other and he snores. TV is great for your mental health, but you need ear plugs for your sanity, but it is more to do with his snoring. In daytime I might watch 'Countdown' or sports. My pad mate watches 'Murder She Wrote' and 'Heartbeat'! I'd murder that Angela Lansbury. Curtain twitchers watch that stuff; it reminds me of my Nan.

Will explains that television provides an escape from his environment and the people within it. Will may worry about the potential risk his pad mate could pose, as he knows about the way the prison had managed Barry as a high-risk prisoner. This must mean Will would need to tread carefully. Barry described the violent crime he was involved in and the prison will have assessed this as a factor of significant risk. Inadvertently, these kinds of actuarial assessments can highlight and perhaps inflame the pathological label. Will therefore may be worried about the contaminating effects Barry could have on him, and experiencing large quantities of time in a confined space with a 'dangerous' prisoner can induce fear. Television, if handled and negotiated properly, can provide respite from these tensions. Striving for ontological security using television can offer protective factors against unsettling and distressing emotions like frustration or fear.

Will – In the evenings TV is separation from my pad mate; I get head space from him. I think he was single cell and high risk, so I need head space from him. I'm a private person. I enjoy my own company. My pad mate is a big kid; it is frustrating. In here sometimes you are forced into violent situations. It is divide and conquer with other prisoners; it is much easier to control and we become products of our environment.

Their relationship requires 'a rational plan' in order for them to co-exist in the same cell without conflict (Layder 2004:27). Planning television viewing and bargaining are techniques which help to maintain an amicable relationship, sharing the remote control for example and Will providing Barry with DVDs help to temper conflict. Will has clear distaste for Barry's television choices and Barry finds Will's love of sport tedious: both manifesting as frustration. Despite these differences some common ground was achievable and Barry's testimony in relation to sci-fi was an opportunity for these individuals to identify a bond or intimacy via television, which can bring them together (Lull 1990).

6.3 Happiness and joy

I get great pleasure from watching wildlife.

(Joshua – prisoner)

The salience of emotive responses like happiness and joy rarely feature in the published literature on prison life. I did not therefore expect to come across expressions or descriptions of happiness and joy during this investigation.[5] Despite the condition and experience of incarceration as painful, moments and periods of serving time in prison are sometimes flooded with contentment. Above all, the ways in which the respondents here do their best to avoid 'helplessness' or the sensation of boredom, frustration, anger and fear in striving for ontological security can help to galvanise this further. Achieving happiness, albeit momentarily, could indicate moments when security and assurance are accomplished and identifying these across the data adds value towards understanding the self-directed techniques prisoners adopt to cope and adapt to life in prison. Achieving happiness and joy in these circumstances can be aligned to Layder's theory of personal control.

Personal control is the means through which you make a difference to your world and have some say in the decisions and actions that shape your future life experiences....

(2004:34)

This can also be combined with Csikszentmihalyi's (1999) theory of 'flow', which can assist in describing how happiness is accomplished. For him, this is achieved by self-direction towards this feeling (1999:824). Ritual activities can allow 'flow' to occur. The act of watching television is ritualised and 'one has to be in control of the activity to experience it [flow]' (ibid.:825). The gratification and security one can accomplish from watching television may result in the immediate feedback the activity permits.

With a focus on television, expressions of happiness associated with particular kinds of viewing feature in the data. Unlike the other kinds of emotions described in this chapter, happiness is rarely associated with reference to the experience of incarceration. Instead, fondness for programmes provided a route for identifying happiness. For example, Bill relished a surprising discovery,

> Like last night there was a big game on, Chelsea, but it wasn't in the TV Time's, one of the lads told me, I was really pleased . . . it was a nice surprise, I was very happy about that.
>
> (Bill – prisoner)

Bill was also surprised and relieved to discover that,

> When I first came I was pleasantly surprised that we got TVs and a kettle and a toilet that flushes.
>
> (Bill – prisoner)

This was Bill's first time in prison and he knew little about it. Bill received a lengthy sentence and now in the later stages of his life and struggling with ill health; the likelihood of leaving prison alive looks bleak. The role of relief and surprise in this context means that his basic needs could actually be accommodated. Bill realised that television could provide him with a familiar activity, which also related to his pre-prison circumstances.

Finding ways through incarceration and adapting to prison life and its routine is essentially softened by the kinds of choices prisoners can make by consuming television. 'Good' times are identifiable in the prisoner narratives, as Joshua describes,

> I've watched one documentary on one channel, switched it over, 'Panorama's on, switched it over, 'Dispatches' is on. That's a great night for me; it's like going to a club.
>
> (Joshua – prisoner)

Joshua's comparison to television viewing with a night of clubbing relates to the kinds of social and emotional outcomes this situated activity can evoke, such as sociability, intimacy, thrill, excitement, fantasy and joy. As Moores (2006:7) suggests, 'place gets pluralised' brought about by 'habitual movements' or migrations using media (ibid.:16) Shaun, who at the time of interview didn't have an in-cell television, talked about the same kinds of pleasures derived from reading *Harry Potter* books.

> It takes you away from your cell, she is so descriptive, so brilliant, with twists and turns.... Books create a TV inside your head.
>
> (Shaun – prisoner)

Also for Sunny the same kind of effects can be achieved through television,

> I am not addicted to TV, but sometimes I don't feel like I'm in prison when I'm watching.
>
> (Sunny – prisoner)

Being able to travel without actually physically moving (Moores 1996:54) is a powerful psychological outcome; with the body constrained, the mind can be given an important outlet or 'mind-scape' (Cohen and Taylor 1975), in which the sense of deprivation can at least be postponed. Accessing and finding meaningful television content arouses happiness and sensations for some.

> I like X Factor to watch the singers develop. Like that girl who sang Hallelujah. It was beautiful; it was music I could relate to.
>
> (Bill – prisoner)

For Bill, the emotive responses this event creates allow him to access emotions that are not frequently available to him, nor are expected to be displayed (Hochschild 1983; Crawley 2004). For Leon, some programmes allow a form of intimacy enabling him to remain socially and emotionally connected to his family. Moores (2006:6) explains that 'at-homeness [can] be modified and multiplied'. For example, Leon explained that children's television films help him stay close to his family, despite how painful it is being away from them. The conversation soon turns to the memories of his family.

> He likes 'Thomas' and 'In the Night Garden' so we talk about those programmes. We watch them on the out. After I have finished

cooking we all curl up on the couch with our son, then we might watch a movie. You see there is not much on to watch and film-wise it varies, so sometimes it is refreshing when something does come on. I have the same sort of interest about films as I do other things: family stuff.

(Leon – prison)

Recalling these types of moments was common among the respondents, and that the habitual nature of viewing in domestic settings brings a sense of intimacy that can affirm contentment and the comfort that life is still ongoing outside. However, some respondents were cautious about how much of this kind of activity could be useful to them in this environment, and were careful to note how these kinds of pleasures from television should be handled. Happiness can soon turn sour and lead to frustration, anger and sadness. Being close to others through the facilitative effect of television is welcome respite from negative emotional states such as boredom and frustration. The danger of doing this, though, is that it also makes some mindful of isolation and separation from the outside world. By delaying gratification, despite the pains it may bring in the short term, avoiding certain television content can defer a monopoly of pathological emotions (Csikszentmihalyi 1999:821). Mastery over all emotions does not necessarily mean that happiness is the ultimate panacea. Williams (2001:118) suggests that 'to manage our emotional life with *intelligence*' or the 'application of expertise' (Rose 1999:258) can define the feeling rules for one's own self and maintain control, so happiness may have to be stifled.

Ron described his fondness of sport, particularly boxing, cage fighting and football. Searching out and consuming sports programmes serves important references in terms of his own identity. Ron was coming to the end of a long sentence. Finding ways to prepare for his release and re-entry into the community means that his only access to his preferred resources, that is, cage fighting and boxing, is through television and occasionally through friends and family on the telephone. Unable to participate, as he used to before prison, television intermittently provides him with important routes to affirm his identity. This provides Ron with contentment but also some frustration that he can't access more cage fighting through television.

... it sort of came on for a couple of weeks and then it stopped. This is over the last couple of months, it came on and there was me thinking, I would sit there and watch that every week quite happily.

(Ron – prisoner)

In order for Ron to sustain his expertise in this area, he spends time combing newspapers for information. Others also reported fandom in similar ways by making adjustments to their viewing routines to fulfil their interests whilst in prison. For example, Joshua takes radical action to watch the documentary, *FBI Files*.

> Joshua – That's on Channel 5. I may sound a bit of a saddo here but it comes on here, usually it comes on at about 11 o'clock at night but recently it's been starting to come on, they've been starting to put it on at 4 o'clock in the morning.
> VK – So what have you done?
> Joshua – So I wake up at 4 o'clock in the morning to watch it.

Unable to time-shift using other forms of technology, like digital recorders and downloads, results in adjustments to viewing. Striving for pleasure by using television is a powerful technique to manage his life situation and Joshua's adjustment to satisfy these needs is a stark example of this (Layder 2006:29).

Similarly, outlets for laughter provide an important cathartic response to the restrictions placed on the individual. Crawley observed that humour and laughter play an important role in facilitating communication and uniting people in particular circumstances, especially those that present threat or danger (2004:50). She also observed that humour plays a significant role in adapting to difficult circumstances by providing a mechanism of defence against distress and disorientation (ibid.:87). Laughter and humour therefore are preferred to crying and breaking down, which can be considered weaknesses. The 'feeling rules' professed by Crawley (2004) and Hochschild (1983) emphasise how certain emotions receive more credence than others.

Comedy programmes and comic features of some programmes provide meaningful benefits to counter deterioration of the self. Leon explained that much of his viewing included comedy because they 'bring you laughter; that makes you younger'. Leon dedicated much of his time in his cell to his own strict timetable, punctuated and marked by television viewing. Leon described an extensive exercise regime that he followed each day whilst watching situation comedies during the lunchtime bang-up period. Attention to his physical well-being was important for Leon to cope with prison life and securing a healthy lifestyle would help him to see himself through his long sentence. The physiological sensations of fitness and laughter have important outcomes for self-directing and governing Leon's mood.

... like exercise it releases endorphins, like hormones, and TV does that for you sometimes too. It releases your mind. Like the gym it does three things, physical release, looking good gives you gratification and a mental release. TV is working you out mentally, it stops letting the memories get to you. With TV I am in another world. It is mental torture in here, so you need somewhere else to escape, to cope and not breakdown. If you don't have TV in these cells, the walls talk to you; we need external input; we are social beings; we need this.

(Leon – prisoner)

Leon, as Rose (1999) suggests, knows what is good for himself; he is an 'expert' on himself and by acting upon his own needs, television can provide a route for him to stay healthy. This form of self-governance is also echoed by Malcolm.

I like comedy and have a good laugh; it does you good and sets you up for the next day to face the next hurdle.

(Malcolm – prisoner)

Satire allows some respondents to take on 'oppositional' readings (Hall 1980) of mediated texts and position themselves against established and dominant agendas. Drawing on Irwin's (1970) typology of prisoners' adaptation; the 'deviant' may resist certain ideologies through mediated routes and thus enjoy these kinds of pleasures (Lindlof 1987). In addition, laughing *at* events on television as opposed to *with* the narrative can bring small pockets of power to these kinds of audiences; this was especially pertinent in relation to talk shows like *Jeremy Kyle* and *Trisha*. Malcolm enjoyed *The Simpsons* because he liked the ways in which 'they take the mickey out of them [characters]'. Finding subversive or deviant routes through television texts could be considered destructive, yet principles of 'flow' (Csikszentmihalyi 1999) can still evolve. Enjoyment of tragedy and other people's demise is also relevant and akin to the kinds of pleasure Ang's (1993:6) female viewers of the soap *Dallas* described as the 'tragic structure of feeling', in which happiness can only ever be fleeting and witnessing problems becomes pleasurable. Soaps and reality television were useful for prisoners to engage with tragedy. As Malcolm explained, he enjoyed the 'bitchiness of the contestants' in *Dragon's Den* and the hardships of the participants in *Wife Swap*. Male characters in soaps were often addressed with fondness, particularly the central villain or rogue.

I like Phil Mitchell: the way he carries himself, all the wheeling and dealing.

(Mick – prisoner)

I've always watched Hollyoaks; it is a soap for my era. It relates to things I know about. Like Warren, he's a local gangster; he's upset people and he murdered someone, his wife's ex-boyfriend. And then he killed her on their wedding day; he was standing at the altar and she didn't turn up: he'd killed her! But everything came back to haunt him. Claire then killed him; there was blackmail and more.

(Shaun – prisoner)

The Bill is realistic; there is something going on; there are a few storylines in one episode, but it is not a soap. There's cops and basically not EastEnders there is more things happening. I have no favourite characters, but I want all crims to get away with. But a rapist got caught and then was dead. But mostly I wouldn't want them to get caught.

(Lee – prisoner)

Personal identification and fondness of criminal characters and crime fiction through television provides direct access to contextual resources (Layder 2004). These audiences are able to draw on cultural references and knowledge which help to confirm their own social positions. For Lee taking an oppositional reading to the police soap/drama is important for his own identity as a criminal and prisoner. Taking on the dominant reading of *The Bill* and being in support of the successes of the police could, in his view, be seen as being disloyal to the criminal community. Adopting this code means that some prisoners may orientate themselves towards values of a criminal hierarchy (Clemmer 1958; Irwin and Cressey 1962; Crewe 2006).

6.4   Ambivalence and coping

The range and spread of emotions described by the respondents also presents conflict and mixtures of feelings towards television in prison. These may appear as contradictions in the prisoner narratives, but on closer reading the interviewees describe ambivalence, and this helps them to acquiesce to imprisonment. Ambivalence can highlight how resolving and tending to the emotional well-being can also be a disorientating experience. Moreover, it can also begin to highlight that individuals' emotional lives are not necessarily permanently polarised by traditional positive or negative emotions, for example, happiness or sadness. Ambivalence, although considered by some (Harreveld et al. 2007) as unpleasant, features for these respondents as a middle-ground where individuals can 'keep their head down'. Ambivalence also helps to identify moments of resignation to their incarceration but at the same time resistance.

> It [TV] helps some things; some people can't do it; some people can. There are the strong minded and the weak. Some are copers and some are strong minded. You are still in jail; if they take the telly it doesn't matter. If you are sat in your cell with no TV it is the same as the day before, exactly the same as yesterday. Days, weeks and months go by, they are taken. It does for me sometimes; it depends what's on.
>
> (Alan – prisoner)

Despite expressions concerning the therapeutic role television can play, some also expressed ambivalence towards it. For Alan, prison time will always be there and if television were taken away it would make little difference to the fact that he has to serve time. The 'carceral schedule' is vital for prisoners to sustain access to goods and services, yet at the same time it is frustrating (Martel 2006:5). To hold these conflicting views helps prisoners cope. Bill talked about how he couldn't be 'bothered' anymore and yet was passionate about media events. Despite his ability to talk enthusiastically about television in prison and also his love of radio and music, he had become ambivalent.

> The digi-box has a radio. But I have this music thing now…I can't be bothered with it now…. When I think about what I miss, TV isn't one of them.
>
> (Bill – prisoner)

Letting go of consumables was also a common response amongst the prisoners as Bill and Mick describe,

> I've never missed a canteen [prison shop] but I did last week. I didn't need anything; material things aren't important.
>
> (Bill – prisoner)

> I will and do help others in here. This morning I gave my last fag [cigarette] away. I can do without it. I get used to it.
>
> (Mick – prisoner)

Mick also said, 'I can do bird without TV. Don't bother me. Course it is easy with TV'. He went on to explain that he had experienced prison before in-cell televisions were introduced and like others he believed time would pass quicker without television.

> I have experienced jail with and without TV. Time went quicker without TV; we were tucked up in bed early. Now we are up all night and it is doubling our sentence.
>
> (Simon – prisoner)

> In the 1990s there were no TVs and it was 23 hour bang up, it seems to fly quicker then than it does now.
>
> (Ryan – prisoner)

These respondents wish to present themselves as prison copers. The ability to project these kinds of attitudes towards prison conditions can highlight 'hegemonic masculinity' (Jewkes 2002a, 2005a; Karp 2010). Being able to cope with the pains of incarceration establishes a shared kudos among male prisoners. Experiencing 'hard' jail as opposed to 'easy' jail is considered important argot and to register ambivalent descriptions of this kind asserts and presents a number of social and cultural characteristics like power, control and knowledge. Here the 'feeling rules' towards incarceration are maintained and upheld by some.

> This is a little holiday in here, long enough though, but it is not exactly hard. I suppose you can do without TV for a few weeks.
>
> (Alan – prisoner)

Ambivalence is also useful for justifying their own values and personal circumstances and at the same time ward off frustration and anger. Pete, an enhanced prisoner, would have been entitled to Freeview television at the time of interview, but due to his location in the prison this was not feasible.

> I don't miss it down here, there are lots of repeats, there are films on but it is no chore. There are music channels, good for young people, but I'm not a music person; it didn't bother me.
>
> (Pete – prisoner)

Ambivalence provides Pete with a way to make sense of the discrepancies in the provision of television in this particular prison. By suggesting that there is no hardship to him he is maintaining important control over his emotional well-being. Getting too frustrated and angry is dangerous and being completely resigned to the situation could signal surrender. By holding these opposing feelings Pete maintains personal control, even though it is unpleasant.

Ambivalence is an important emotional state to facilitate the ongoing coping and adapting journey through prison. It also permits individuals to strive for ontological security and conform to the demands of the public stage in prison life (Goffman 1990). Ambivalence is therefore an important defence and operates within the suffocating 'hegemonic social order' of the prison (Martel 2006:608). This is a mechanism to ensure that other emotions do not monopolise the soul, which 'creates relative order out of the potential chaos of feeling responses that threaten to swamp action...' (Layder 2004:27). These techniques can enable 'successful implementation of action plans [which] has the effect of draining tension...' (ibid.).

6.5 Fears of watching television in prison

I watch TV sometimes and wonder what an earth I'm watching.

(Stuart – prisoner)

As already suggested, prisoners' relationships with television are not always objective, and encounters with television in prison do lead prisoners to concerns about their own well-being. Despite the reflective benefits of television in managing emotion, the lure of television can be met with suspicion, guilt and also shame. Becoming lazy and as some suggest 'addicted' to television whilst in prison is not considered a healthy route to choose. Avoiding laziness or 'addiction' requires personal control to prevent psychological and physiological deterioration. Some respondents can restrain their viewing, whereas some remain resigned to the dominance of television in their daily life and are apprehensive of it (Jewkes 2002a). Resistance to the 'hegemonic social order' emerges in diverse forms.

The restrictive nature of prison is such that the availability and choice of activity remains perpetually limited, especially during bang-up. Simon believes 'all you can do is make three cups of tea, so you are gonna watch TV' and Pete explains 'I have to [watch TV]; there is nothing to do'. The desire to do other things with their time was also salient.

TV can take your life over, but there is nothing to do; sometimes I'd like to do other things.

(Malcolm – prisoner)

It is here where interviewees began to realise and understand the gravity of television whilst in prison and the dominance television exerts over their everyday lives. By contrast, not watching any television for some would be unbearable, and so there is a paradox. Carlton described himself as a controlled viewer and could find other activities to do such as writing or listening to music, much like Bill who would switch off. Sunny, however, felt compelled to watch most of the time and was unable to find other ways to occupy his time. Sunny's diary entries showed that he watched an average of 44.25 hours of television per week or 6.3 hours per day, and said that he wanted to reduce this. Some were able to describe with pride that they considered their viewing to be healthy, whereas others aspired a healthier relationship with television. Thus, personal control of television use is variable and diverse, and discrepancies between healthy and unhealthy forms of control exist amongst prisoner audiences' perceptions (Layder 2004:87).

Carlton, for example, watched an average of 5.25[6] hours of television each day and described,

> ...some pad mates I have had religiously watch five hours of telly in a row like Hollyoaks, Emmerdale and all that rubbish. I do a lot of writing instead.
>
> (Carlton – prisoner)

Carlton's diary does confirm that he does not watch television in large continuous blocks, as he asserts. His viewing is interspersed with listening to music (which he entered) and empty slots in the diary. Carlton developed 'strategies to control time' (Cope 2003:159) by using a range of media and activity. Despite this, he planned to adjust his viewing,

> But I can tell you when I am getting out I won't be watching that much... I'm staying away from TV, but I will play my console Xbox.
>
> (Carlton – prisoner)

This was not uncommon, and Shaun and Lee (who both shared a cell) talked about their plans for a television 'diet' when their set would be returned. Once they had behaved in line with the IEP, a television could be returned to their cell. At the time of interview, Shaun and Lee were subject to basic conditions and had had their television removed for bad behaviour. This meant that time out of cell, visits and access to goods and services were limited, resulting in extended periods of bang-up. In the absence of television, Shaun found he read and wrote more, something he got great pleasure from. Lee enjoyed dance music, which Shaun also liked. Unlike Barry and Will, described earlier in this chapter, Shaun and Lee's relationship appeared more settled; they shared similar taste in music, shared a past before prison and also liked crime novels and similar programmes. Shaun's taste appeared more diverse than Lee's; he also liked wildlife programmes, rock and pop music. Both were very familiar with popular soap storylines and characters. They were concerned about boredom and the impact that certain kinds of broadcasts would have on their well-being,

> Lee – My typical day is in a morning if I had TV I'd turn on 'Jeremy Kyle' then get lunch and sit there all day until dinner. I get bored of watching it; it is the same every day. It makes time drag with telly. You know how long they are on for and then it is dinner time. It is one big time game here. Time flies with me and him [Shaun]. We get up and clean pad and we jump up and do something. But cos TV might be on you're just lying on your bed. I go to sleep at lunch and we have a messy pad. I clean in evenings all the time.
>
> Shaun – There is crap on TV. TV in your cell is ok like if you weren't working and nothing to do. But in the day it is rubbish like 'Build a House in the Country', 'Trisha', 'Wright Stuff': crappy, shitty, rubbish. But then TV is something to look at, something to stare at. Day time fries your head, scrambled brain; it makes people anti-social; no one talks when the telly is on. You talk, but it is not a conversation, like saying 'Oh she's fit', 'yeah' it is not a proper conversation. There is no danger with TV in prison; it entertains people, keeps people quiet, good for reducing suicides, but it gives people a lot of power, even the prisoners. Like some folks can't read, folks haven't got a stereo, so TV helps. But without it for me it is easy, I can read and write.

Given their attitude towards the dominance that television can have in their lives in prison, their current experience on the basic regime without television has begun to highlight how getting by and doing their time can essentially be experienced more positively. Shaun especially felt more motivated and compelled to read and write.

> Shaun – I've been three weeks without TV cos I am on basic. It is much better, I feel more motivated to do things such as cell workouts, read books, write more like poetry, a book. If I had TV I'd only just be starting.... But I don't miss them. I suppose if I had a TV that magically came on and then switched off that would be good,

but it is too tempting to leave on and then you become a bed spud: it becomes the be all and end all of your life in here. If my pad mate watches 'Emmerdale', I'll write a letter.

They also show 'sensitivity to spatiality' which is accentuated by their segregation from the standard regime (Martel 2006:600). Television, for Shaun, is a distraction, something that gets in the way of what he considers to be more purposeful. Shaun realises that reading and writing was something that was out of his focus, until he encountered prison without television. Shaun does recognise the pleasures of television, but like many respondents finds it hard to switch off and regulate viewing quantities. Lee is less confident about the absence of television. For Lee, music (which is permitted on basic regime) can provide sufficient stimulation, but he struggles more than Shaun with bang-up time.

> Lee – Music makes you think about other things so you can go behind your door and get away and stay behind your door. I'm alright to talk but it does wind you up also behind your door... it deads my head in this shit. I just cope with it really, but it does wind me up. It is a joke with the staff. My cell mate helps.

Tolerance of isolation and exposure to unstructured time can differ, and coping and adaptation to the conditions of incarceration is variable. Their friendship helps Lee handle these conditions. Under the basic regime, contact with others would be minimal and therefore interaction between themselves in their cells becomes increasingly significant. Lee and Shaun share a common ground, which can make their experience easier. The solidarity they have can be evidenced in how they plan to manage television once it is re-introduced.

> Lee – We've planned a routine with telly; it was his [Shaun] idea; I ain't bothered. I'm getting lazy just lying in bed watching TV all night. I don't like being lazy. I like to get up and be out there and be busy. But here I don't want to do anything; it is a waste of time doing nothing.

Shaun fears idleness and the intrusion of the outside world once television enters his life again.

> Shaun – Prison is depressing, nothing happens and to have the outside shoved in your face is hard. I don't want to think about it whilst

I am here. I'm in my cell all day. I need a certain level of exercise; it lets off steam and you are then not thinking and things playing on your mind. I manage to block it out all day and then it all just hits you all before you go to sleep. I struggle with sleep in here and suppose TV can help with that. Like when I couldn't get to sleep and find myself watching Big Brother and then lay in bed until 11am the next morning.

Despite the benefits Shaun describes, contact with the outside world is too painful. Withdrawal from public life is not an uncommon response amongst prisoners, especially long-termers (Cohen and Taylor 1972; Sapsford 1978). Shaun was a remand prisoner and explained he was probably going to get a life sentence for his crime. Being able to comprehend, witness and be intimate with a world in which he cannot participate may explain his need to disconnect. This is the same world that has confined him to prison and put him in social care as a child. The visual qualities of television for Shaun are an intrusion into his life and therefore do not suit Shaun's needs at this time. He is grateful to spend time without television and escape the punctuated nature of broadcasts (Scannell 1996).

Shaun – I thank them for putting me on basic, I love it. I don't want my TV back, but I do want visits and associations. They don't like that, that I don't want a TV. I'm not in cell crying. I have a choice you see. Time goes quicker this way, I suppose you analyse yourself. I like TV on at certain times and not having a clock. Like the adverts, they come on roughly every 15 minutes and so on, so you get the time all the time. Without a stereo it is hard. You have a 45 minute tape I suppose, but there isn't a constant tab on time. I don't want to know what time it is.

Lee on the other hand imagines a routine in which television would feature in his 'own' schedule rather than he being dominated by television all of the time (Silverstone 1999a). Lee also described how he had struggled to overcome drug addiction, and finding techniques to control his drug use could also be extended to his use of television.

Lee – ... the punishment doesn't bother me. I just take it. I could leave the TV on the doorstep when they move me to level 2. They are winding me up saying I could have a telly. If they offered me a telly

I'd turn on in the morning for the news then keep it off. I'd have it on in the lunch hour and in the afternoon it would be off. It would be on in the evening for the soaps. Then I would do a pad workout to music, switch it back on to fall asleep.

Television helps Lee to punctuate his daily life in prison and he actively aligns television to certain activities. The combination of imprisonment and television accentuates the fears of becoming idle, akin to addiction (Jewkes 2002a). Becoming dependent on television is something the respondents were conscious of and where media dependency (Vandebosch 2000) reaches a level that they considered to be unhealthy, television could become dissatisfactory. This draining effect of television steals important energy and by becoming lazy, prisoners' attempts to remain ontologically secure can be thwarted. As Rubin (1993) found, those individuals with internal locus of control were less likely to be susceptible to these kinds of effects, whereas individuals with an external locus of control and are more likely to take up more television are more likely to be dissatisfied with the activity. Taking responsibility for their viewing is a mechanism for resolving pervasive attitudes, which can be destructive. Avoiding the 'docile' (Foucault 1991) aspect of incarceration serves to ensure that their personal control remains functioning. Losing control by becoming docile can weaken their ability to govern themselves and thus they may become susceptible to subordination of the situated or mediated encounters. The techniques outlined by Shaun and Lee enabled them to secure meaning and control in their disorientating circumstances. The re-introduction of television presents a threat to the equilibrium they have managed to achieve in its absence.

6.5.1 Summary

Taking 'excursions' with television can provide a 'protective device' (Layder 2004:26) against the emotive responses of prison life. The dominant and hegemonic prison culture perpetuates the feeling rules (Hochschild 1983) which magnify emotional resonance. Prisoners are caught between a rock and a hard place, and alleviating unwanted feelings requires constant self-inspection. Fear of psychological deterioration is paramount and boredom especially is over-bearing. Mediated encounters are risky and productive. Prisoners demonstrate competence in self-governance with respect to the selective nature of their viewing. Prisoners' attempts to re-create and establish a place that can bring comfort and security are reliably satisfied by television. The problem is not just of *time* as much of the literature purports, but also of *place*. Onto-logical security requires time and place to be controlled in order for the prisoner to achieve personal control, and television can provide a safe place, like being at home.

Yet the environment presents challenges to sustaining personal control. Cell-sharing is one challenge and finding your own time and space with another prisoner is not achieved without effort. Broadcasts also disappoint some prisoners by failing to deliver much needed emotive responses like happiness; other prisoners, however manage to achieve emotional satisfaction. Layder's (2004:27) notion of the 'emotion queue' reminds the prisoner to achieve personal control. Prisoners in the sample are active in working on their emotive 'need claims' (ibid.:27). Television can in some instances assist in prisoners' quests to stay psychologically agile. If they fail to do so, emotions cannot be successfully handled and dealt with as they appear. Part of adapting to the pains of incarceration is learning to look inwards and self-inspect and develop techniques with or without television to minimise harm (Rose 1999). Conversely, restoration and respite from the situated culture means that some prisoners are highly selective in their viewing; for example, avoiding news broadcasts. Others use television to legitimise their retreat from the public face of prison life. The act of viewing itself is also beneficial in allowing an activity in which 'flow' can be re-produced and being able to draw people closer brings important comfort.

This chapter has provided an extended discussion of the range of emotions prisoners experience in direct response to the harms of incarceration. The ways in which the respondents described and expressed their emotional lives and the strategies they develop point towards forms of governance. Yet governance is fragile and not always achieved. Prison life is not empty of emotion and prisoners are active in their responses towards themselves. Yet what does the prison, its staff and prisoners do with these emotions? Chapter 7 will address this and highlight the techniques and strategies developed within the situated and mediated environments by prisoners and staff to attempt to bring under control the emotional lives of prisoners.

7
Situated and Mediated Control: Managing Souls with In-Cell Television

This chapter will continue to report the voices of prisoners, but will also reintroduce staff perspectives in order to present four concepts relating to in-cell television; *therapy and rationalisation*, the *civilising effects of television, watching and surveillance* and *censorship and prisoners' communicative rights*.

7.1 Managing souls with in-cell television

As reported in Chapter 5, in-cell television has become part of the 'moral economy', and its provision 'does not come neutral' (Silverstone 1999a:79). The projects of rationalisation (Garland 1991) and governmentality (Rose 1999) have collided with the social structures of the prison, and stakeholders have become 'technicians' of the soul. Concurrent to the practice, the mediated landscape has also become a 'psy shaped space' (Rose 1999:266) in which access to experts, narratives and disclosures are considered to dominate broadcasts (Shattuc 1997; Rose 1999:261; Wood 2005). This section examines how staff use television in their practice of prisoner management.

7.1.1 Techno-therapy
The provision of television extends the remit of behaviour management (IEP) and is a mechanism for assisting therapeutic care. Therapy is the process which seeks to change the conditions of maladaptive behaviour. Indeed some prisons establish 'therapeutic communities', whereby the work conducted by staff is 'treatment orientated' (Genders and Player 1995). Rose suggests that the 'gaze of the psychologist' has been instrumental in the discourse of therapy, whereby experts are 'grasping and

153

calibrating the sickness of the soul' (1999:138) in order to govern the individual. This is visible in current prison policy.

The current PSI 11/2011 (HMPS 211) stipulates that in-cell television is an 'earnable privilege', yet the needs of a prisoner can permit extended provision of in-cell television, particularly for those at risk of self-harm and suicide (2006:15). Staff were keen to emphasise that safer custody remits took priority when managing prisoners, and were inclined to take this position in favour of the privilege status that was formerly awarded to television. This resulted from the sensitivity of staff respondents to the degradations experienced by prisoners (Crewe 2009); however, it may not entirely be neutral. Garland (1991:182) highlights that criminal justice professionals are keen to 'represent themselves in a positive, utilitarian way… carrying out a useful social task… as technicians of reform, as social work professionals'. This does not necessarily mean that their sentiments are inauthentic. The culture of punishment has become extensively embroiled in actuarial and target driven outcomes, and the ethos of care has become 'rationalised' (Garland 1991). Moreover, as Sparks et al. observed, the 'problem of order' impacts on the ways in which staff particularly implement and manage control in prison settings. The employment of discretion and the ways in which control is practiced mean that the provision of material goods like television contribute to what they call 'soft policing' (1996:108). The provision of television therefore symbolically represents care. As Silverstone (1999a) suggests, television is a care-giver, and staff talked about this function of television.

> Prisoners who have got issues around self-harm, distressed, vulnerable, isolation, keeping awake at night, we all know the worst place in the world when you are awake at night and you can't sleep and you have got all this stuff going round in your head, at least they have got a television and can watch something.
>
> (Claire – Governor)

Positioning television as 'care giver' (Silverstone 1999a) instead of reward marks an important shift in the rhetoric about in-cell television, as Fran explains,

> People get upset because they have mental health issues and it's beyond their control. People get upset because they have issues and concerns out of the establishment; people get upset for lots of different reasons. And if the only thing that is going to keep you calm is

to engage with a TV event, or having a hot drink, why should those things be taken away?

(Fran – prison officer)

In these kinds of circumstances, staff perceive television as a form of therapy. Television is actively 'prescribed' in order to manage and control adverse situations. Prescribing television, as an antidote or even as 'medicine', can help to sedate and control emotions and people's actions.

I think it's a good distraction technique, a television. I think if a prisoner who is particularly feeling low or perhaps has self-harmed in the past, I think a television can be used to occupy his time. It's about keeping him busy and keeping his mind active.

(Tim – prison officer)

Tim suggests television is a form of stimulation which conveniently fills unstructured time. As Jewkes highlights, the metaphor of drug use has similarities with media use and the

...presence of television can normalize or readjust time...Like drugs...television can provide refuge from the harsh realities of life, filling large amounts of self-time which otherwise might be given over to introspection.

(2002:102)

Staff also understand that television can provide respite from prisoners' experience of prison, as reported in Chapter 6. Even when television is rejected by prisoners, some staff would be concerned about the challenges this may bring to the prison. As Claire questioned, 'hang on a minute, don't you think this might be useful, and maybe suggesting certain times they use it'. The prescribing of television is therefore a viable and accustomed ritual in their practice. Moreover the kinds of expertise the respondents may be demonstrating here relate to what Rose (1999:233) defines as a therapist. These experts stress to individuals 'their potential for enhancing skills of "self-management" and helping clients gain control of their feelings'. The staff also reiterate these characteristics in their descriptions of their contact with prisoners (Bosworth 2007). Ann was very clear how the content she watched on television assisted her in her practice as chaplain. She explained that she watched popular television shows like *Strictly Come Dancing, X Factor, Big Brother* and news to enable her to get closer to her ministry at the prison: 'that helps in the pastoral care of prisoners and sometimes opens up doors that you wouldn't have'. She recognised and reflected on how her own viewing had changed since working in prison to enable her to find connections or 'reach' to prisoners.

> It allows prisoners to engage with a chaplain on a human level...I think it enable some realness. And when you are playing pool with a prisoner, or when you're just sat chatting if they start talking about a TV programme and you just say oh yes, it brings a connection at a different level, still a professional level, but different from the chaplain/prisoner level...it is a very human conversation, and therefore quite helpful. And you can draw analogies from how people are feeling with experiences they have seen which enable them to understand themselves in a different way because you provided a different insight.
>
> (Ann – chaplain)

These comments are not unusual and most staff commented on how mediated events and narratives serve an important function in establishing healthy and meaningful situated forms of interaction (Lull 1990). Paul explained how interacting with prisoners was an important aspect of their work and this for them was the most 'technical' part of their job.

> But what we do make a difference in is we take people who are severely damaged and make them more socially acceptable in as much as you talk to them, you can sit down and make them understand, you can change their views on the way the prison service staff work with prisoners.
>
> (Paul – senior officer)

Rose (1999:251) suggests 'with the aid of experts, [prisoners] can act upon their bodies, their emotions, their beliefs, and their forms of conduct in order to transform themselves, in order to achieve autonomous selfhood'. Steve also described a situation where two prisoners under his care could not read or write. They explained they didn't like going on association and preferred to stay in their cells. Another prisoner offered to help them to read and write and Steve, with support from his line-manager, arranged for the three prisoners to spend time in one cell. Steve saw to it that weekends and evenings could be spent learning;

'I put him in there...and they actually started to read and write...to them it was such a big step...they used their time in there very wisely'. Steve deviated from normal standards to facilitate this outcome; he took a risk by employing discretion. Steve did not 'suspend moral judgment' in carrying out his duties (Garland 1991:183), as he emotionally connected empathetically to the situation. Control, as Layder (2004:17) suggests, is not devoid of emotion, and is a 'constant companion to power'. In the absence of formal routes to therapy, the expert comes to represent a form of psychic control as Rose (1999:144) argues: 'a science of the soul [has] combined with a strategy for the government of the individual'.

7.1.2   Rationalisation and disconnection

The management of emotion is tacit and yet the enterprise of punishment is in itself emotive (Garland 1991; Crawley 2004). Therapeutic control contributes silently to the rationalisation project and this endeavour is paradoxical. Staff are sensitive to the deprivations experienced in prison and the effects of these on prisoners; this in itself requires an emotive connection with people in their care. The provision of television as an antidote to manage risk related emotions such as boredom and anger has shifted the kinds of relationships and interactions staff have with prisoners (see Chapter 5). Spigel (1992:65) reports there were similar impacts reported within the home, 'television threatened to drive a wedge between family members and as a result a "discourse on divided spaces"' (ibid.:67) developed in relation to television in the home. Harmony and unity of household or family togetherness was therefore challenged and spaces within households became distinctive for different household members. For prison staff, this resulted in their grasp and understanding of the prisoners in their care being compromised because of television, and has given prisoners the opportunity to vanish from their view into the deep interior; the cell. Conversely, Moores (1988:25) observed that families were adopting radio to discourage movement in exterior spaces and bring people into the interior; people were coming under control. Yet staff believe, with fewer interactive encounters, their ability to assist in the interpersonal control of prisoners is weakened. Despite the controlling effects of prisoners viewing television, the ability of staff to fully control prisoners is not entirely determined by the work that they do; it relies on 'psychological power' (Crewe 2009:121). Instead, time spent watching television results in control being split across these two spaces. To some extent this legitimises a disconnection from situated interaction,

It is quite important that you get interaction in prison if you really want to tackle re-offending because a prison officer's job should be that you'll sit talking and sit and say, this is not the way to go, there is a different way of life, there is this, you can do that, you know and I don't think we do that, I don't think we do that at all. I think it's reduced it down to virtually nil, if I'm honest.

(Brian – prison officer)

Fran also says, 'I think it's removed staff from prisoners...I think we conversed more before in-cell television. I think prisoners were probably more eager to engage with staff without in-cell TV'. These changes have not necessarily relieved staff of their duties, as some believed it might have done when in-cell televisions were first introduced. As Fran highlighted, their work has shifted away from direct face-to-face work with prisoners towards an administrative role; 'we are more office based'. Paul is also concerned how these changes are directly impacting on the prisoners and the ways he now works with his colleagues.

I think that the art of communication has been taken away from us...you will desensitise or dehumanise prisoners because they won't know how to talk to people...they don't have the social skills. So I think technology isn't always the best thing.

(Paul – senior prison officer)

With this kind of distancing and the increase in administrative tasks, the mission for staff to fully enable rehabilitation is stifled (ibid.:111). Will, a prisoner, was also attuned to these effects and he noticed that

...my diction has changed, it is more forceful. They shout at each other rather than listen. There is lots of repetition, my pad mate tells the same jokes.

(Will – prisoner)

Brian also felt that the separating effect generated by television has brought about a reduction in the kinds of surveillance prison officers are encouraged to achieve,

Dynamic security is prison officers walking around, talking and listening, listening to what happens...now what we do is as soon as somebody says, I'm gonna kill myself or they self harm, we fill one of these forms in and we spend so long filling in this form in … we should go and talk to prisoners, sod the paperwork.

(Brian – prison officer)

Tim, however, believes that interaction with prisoners can be assisted by television's role of providing routes into conversation and agenda for talk (Lull 1990).

… prisoners will talk about what they watched on television last night and I think it's important for the staff to interact with that and pick up on what they are saying, you know, on a wider security issue, it does build up dynamic security. It's important the staff are talking to the prisoners to see what's going on because by having a two-way conversation with the prisoners, it's rapport building and then prisoners start giving you information, it links to other things.

(Tim – prison officer)

The authenticity of these conversations serves to sustain control in prison. These 'innocent' conversations condition prisoners to trust staff and make headway in relationships between staff and prisoners (Sparks et al. 1996; Liebling et al. 2010). Brian, however, does not acknowledge that these conversations about television are genuine.

… conversation is OK when you're talking about what happened on the TV but realistically that's not a conversation that is aimed towards rehabilitating somebody; it's just passing comments.

(Brian prison officer)

Prisoners were also attuned to these television-orientated conversations.

TV is important here; it is a topic of conversation we relate to and share things. Like 90% people here watch EastEnders and football, we can chat about it. Like Big Brother it gives people stuff to converse about.

(Stuart – prisoner)

These conversations amongst prisoners provide a safe 'script' (Cohen and Taylor 1975) in which utterances about cultural life can be framed (Lull 1990; Wood 2009). For Stuart, the purpose of television allows for valid connections and sharing of experiences. However, Leon offers a different perspective.

There are two types of personalities in prison, those that mingle and chat and those that don't engage and get involved in the unnecessary bits of prison life. What have you gotta talk about in here? I suppose TV is a good socialising factor like someone might say 'you looked like that geezer on.' Ha, ha, ha. But it is nothing productive really; it is more productive to learn not that this geezer did this crime etc. I learn more from TV than from folks in here, it is more accessible.

(Leon – prisoner)

For Leon, the outcomes of social relations cannot compete with mediated encounters. Leon is looking to 'glean' from his prison experience and his interview is full of examples that assert dedication to his family and enhancing his opportunities for desistance. Furthermore, the risk of contamination from other prisoners is reduced.

Ron is contemplative about the effects of incarceration on his ability to interact. His time in prison has potentially repressed his ability to interact in day-to-day situations. The disconnection and separation that incarceration brings about doesn't allow him to rehearse situated encounters or have an opportunity to carry out 'impression management' (Goffman 1990; Layder 2004). Ron fears he is not prepared for situated activity for his transition into the community,

I do wonder how I will be around my kids and my wife when I go home because I have spent so long away from them. It does worry me a little bit, will I be alright? I think I need to go away to another country and sort my head out for a month or so, try and get used to having people around me.

(Ron – prisoner)

Mediated encounters are probably the most trustworthy interactions that exist for many of these respondents. Silverstone (1999a:16) stresses 'the creation of trust – which over-determines television as a transitional object, particularly for adult viewers'. Accounts from staff and prisoners highlight a complex picture of the forms of interaction taking place in prison. Staff are anxious about the depletion of situated activity, especially between staff and prisoners. Yet it seems prisoners are happy and trusting of mediated encounters and retreat to their cells. This distancing creates a partial disconnection from situated forms of interaction and mediated forms of interaction proceed. Rationalisation is therefore even more achievable and with the help of in-cell television the emotional life of prisoners become invisible and hidden (Martel 2006). The emotional lives of prisoners are being ratified and articulated with in-cell television. Thus emotions are still there, yet obscured from view. Staff, therefore, struggle to reach prisoners. However, television is not the sole cause of the decline in situated forms of interaction; rationalisation, and attempts to restrain the emotive character of social agents, has been tempered across the social enterprise since the onset of modernity (Garland 1991). Studies like Crewe's (2009) and Sparks et al.'s (1996) acknowledge in detail the ways in which social relations manifest in prison setting; however, forms of mediated interaction are absent in both of these important studies. As a result, staff's anxieties, which are also supported in both Crewe and Sparks et al.'s work, are based on ideological frameworks and the losses they fear were never actually there in the first place.

7.2   A civilised medium

This analysis provides evidence to support the contribution of television to wider discussions about the 'civilised' status of modern prisons. According to Elias (2010), a 'civilised' society is fundamentally coalesced by features of self-regulation and the forms of control. Moreover, the ways in which prisoners and staff have described television's role also links with this insight. The data presented in this section demonstrate how prisoners attempt to make best use of television and in some instances as 'purposeful' described some of the ways prisoners framed their relationship with television. Prisoners are cautious about their viewing and actively seek out programmes that they consider valuable for their well-being. Conversely, staff were less clear about the usefulness of television, especially in line with policy such as 'purposeful activity' targets.[1] This section distinguishes three concepts; *learning from television*, *engaging in public life* and *organising daily life* which further extrapolates the civilising processes.

7.2.1   Learning from television

As described in Chapter 4, uses and gratification models can exemplify prisoners' motivations to consume television (Jewkes 2002a). All of the prisoners in this sample made reference to television's potential to provide them with opportunities to learn. Their motivations to learn from television whilst in prison were directly related to fears of psychological deterioration (Cohen and Taylor 1972; Zamble and Porporino 1988). In order to diminish these fears, self-inspection encourages social agents to seek out improvements (Rose 1999). This coincides with rehabilitative agendas such as the seven pathways out of crime, which includes an educative strand (Home Office 2004). Therefore prisons are expected to exploit as many opportunities as they can to enhance the learning and skills of prisoners in their care. This however is, problematic as prisons struggle to deliver meaningful education, training and employment (Knight and Hine 2009). Many prisoners watch television with intentions to learn but these do not coincide with formal learning remits. This is because learning through television in their circumstances assists in wider social and psychological outcomes. The television use-diaries confirmed that documentaries, quiz shows and in some cases news programmes were watched frequently and in large quantities.[2] Carlton craved more access to opportunities to learn through television.

> There's a lot of things you can learn. I like to watch nature documentaries, you can learn from them... I suppose if you are going to watch it have it teach you something... In my view prisons should have TV but they should play more documentaries to learn things, like university programmes, give them something to learn from, an opportunity. They used to play DVDs at night, put on documentaries or even quizzes. That's what I think.
>
> (Carlton – prisoner)

Maalik had just come to prison for the first time and he spoke about how many of his preconceptions of prison and the justice system had been ratified but also challenged. Maalik demonstrated how his adaption to prison life was still evolving and essentially he was continuing to learn how to be a prisoner (Jones and Schmid 2000). Television helped him to orientate and make sense of prison life. By engaging with material, especially through documentaries, Maalik had points of reference with the wider social world. This provided him with some semblance of normalcy and justification for his punitive experience.

> For me it's more knowledge. It's more knowledgeable because stuff which you experience out there, once you watch it and then you understand it better. Because I've never had a time on my own to watch a documentary out there but once you're in here you've got so much time where you can sit and watch that documentary and understand that documentary.... There's a lot of knowledge that has concerned me because when I was out there I knew of things but it didn't happen to me so I wasn't taking any notice of it but now

because I read about it and watch it and I've experienced it myself personally so it has actually affected me a lot.

(Maalik – prisoner)

Carlton also identified how the experience of prison combined with watching certain material on television revealed some important lessons about social life: 'TV shows people's differences to stop bullying. I didn't know this before I came to prison.' This was also noted by staff.

A more informed prisoner is a less volatile prisoner because they are making informed choices then. So when they contact partners and the partner says look we are really struggling for money, because he is saying he wants money sent in, they can see through the media exactly how bad it's affected families. So it's about a window to the world that they can access freely.

(Paul – senior prison officer)

Acquiring knowledge and being 'informed' assist in the control of prisoners. Furthermore, television provides resources for staff to carry out their work. Brian highlights that the medium of television can assist those prisoners that struggle with literacy.

It can be used for prisoners to be educated; we've got prisoners who can't read and write and television can be used for educational purposes.

(Brian – prison officer)

Pete also recognised the potential effects that different types of programmes would have on the diverse prison population.

I like Countdown; that is educational, like quiz shows. It is good for people who can't read and write, got to put something in their brain; it is teaching them, like the Weakest Link. I suppose you can learn from soaps sometimes, like not to do things, so I suppose it is educational. I learnt they serve water in the Rover's Return!

(Pete – prisoner)

The 'meanings and motivations' (Jewkes 2002a:116) described by prisoners show that they are compelled to acquire knowledge from their experiences of watching television. Like Carlton, some were frustrated at the limited availability of documentaries available on broadcast television and craved access to more documentary programmes and quiz shows. Prisoners appreciate the cognitive benefits of such material.

> Other things I watch religiously is Dragon's Den; it is good TV. I'm interested in other people's ideas and how to make money, if you see something and you think that would be handy! It gets your mind active.
>
> (Stuart – prisoner)

Pete, Bill and Sunny also spoke extensively about their personal interests and enjoyed the process of being informed.

> I only watch nature in here too. There was one about Yellowstone. I take much more notice of it in here. I wouldn't watch them on the out. I just get into it in here. I'd flick over out there. If there is nothing else on I start watching, it is interesting. There was one called the Hottest Place on Earth I think, it was a geology programme; they visited the desert; the place was horrendous. Loads of volcanic rock and a guy went down and did a gas test; it was fascinating to watch. I can concentrate on them in here.
>
> (Pete – prisoner)

> I like things like with Michael Palin, like travel programmes and like the faith programmes on at the minute. There is one on tonight I think about Muslim religion; I find it fascinating.
>
> (Bill – prisoner)

> I like documentaries especially on BBC 1 and 2. I like global things like global warming and sometimes I like travel, especially all over the world.
>
> (Sunny – prisoner)

Here, watching television extends their immediate surroundings and access to information that is unavailable to them in prison; television permits reach (Meyrowitz 1985; Silverstone 1999a; Moores 2006). However, this concept of 'escape' from prison was not entirely ratified by Pete. He was quite clear that this was not directly related to loss of freedom; 'I don't want to fly away like a bird'. For him the ability to focus on the detail in the broadcasts was an influencing factor, because prison has few distractions compared to his life on the outside.

In addition choice of crime documentaries was popular as Jewkes explains,

> ...whatever gratifications we seek from media content they are not divorced from our environment...It is therefore unsurprising that it is very often violent or criminal media figures that provide identification for prisoners.

(2002a:144)

For Barry, documentaries about crime were a source of important information. The process of becoming informed and up-to-date with latest forensic technologies enabled him to make assessments about potential future offending. Barry had been in prison a few times before and offending was a significant part of his lifestyle outside prison.

> NCIS is a crime thing insight into forensic technology what crimes are really about; soon it will be impossible to commit a crime. It won't affect me; you can't beat a bit of fraud, so you don't have to hurt. 'Panorama' is good for scams, which I've been involved in. That Crimewatch, there is a lot of scary people.

(Barry – prisoner)

The ways in which Barry lists the purpose of the programmes enable him to establish 'expert' status in relation to crime. Simon also acknowledges the purpose of these kinds of programmes.

> I learn from them programmes; it is the criminology, not to leave DNA, all the forensics, so I watch that.

(Simon – prisoner)

Barry and Simon subvert the 'gleaner' mode and favour the 'jailing' mode (Irwin 1970). They are not necessarily looking to change their behaviour as they are active in sustaining their criminal identities and television offers them access to contextual resources (Jewkes 2002:144). Prison is a disruption in their offender lifestyle. Equally, accessing these kinds of programmes provides them with authentic material to inform their criminal occupations and classify themselves as 'experts'. Others, although they watched similar material were less likely to assert the same kinds of identification with these programmes.

Instead, crime documentaries offer prisoners forms of identification that are not necessarily related to their criminal identities but their prisoner identities. Jewkes (2002:211) adds that these selections allow prisoners to 'engage with the public side of prison', especially hegemonic and dominant aspects of prison culture. As prisoners, they all have a shared experience of crime and prison brings them together; the experience of their incarceration defines their current position within a given culture, yet at the same time widening and bringing close the 'imagined community' (Williams 1974; Moores 1988) of the criminal world. It also provides a direct reference point to the kinds of individuals prisoners are likely to come across in their time in prison. Prisoners are unsurprisingly compelled to learn about the kinds of people they could experience prison with. Therefore, learning about criminal cultures assists individuals in being able to participate, when necessary, in the public life of the prison (Crewe 2009). These technological reference points mark a form of power that enables prisoners to be equipped with knowledge about their immediate community's experience. These are not proportionate either, and the authenticity and value of mediated material of this kind may only serve to perpetuate fears of contamination and brutality from other prisoners. In much the same way, the media are considered to contribute to the fear of crime (Jewkes 2011:155). As many theorists have argued the mass effects of mediated messages serve as important mechanisms for control and order (ibid.:10). There is a range of learning that television can facilitate, most prominently the men in this study are eager to seek out material that enables satisfactory cognitive functioning; others seek to pursue personal interests and some use television to sustain deviant forms of identification.

7.2.2   Engaging in public life

It takes you to different places like jungles and deserts. I'll never be able to go; TV is the next best thing.

(Shaun – prisoner)

It is difficult to suggest that television in prison permits full and extensive access to the 'public sphere' as Habermas et al. (1974) imagined, far from this. But as Shaun suggests, television offers a pragmatic avenue to take imaginative excursions. As commentators like Moores (1988), Spigel (1992) and Silverstone (1999a) suggest, the introduction of technologies essentially transports the 'public' world into the private sphere of the home, bringing the exterior to the interior. To an extent this is duplicated in the prison setting, but there are also peculiarities and departures from these views. The prison space is an unusual construct, essentially private and closed off from community life. Inside the prison, however, enclaves of privacy are essentially difficult to come by.[3] The experience of prison is therefore a public one: it is only since the introduction of mass media that public life has become extended or stretched beyond the confines of the prison. Television and radio have transformed the communicative reach in prisons. This ability to reach, however, does not permit liberated participation in public life and, due to the constraints of imprisonment, is partial. As described in the previous section, mediated encounters are useful in providing access to contextual resources in order to operate within their immediate community; the prison (Layder 2005).

Ned provided an example of how his own experience of prison and his connections to the wider community through television present a series of challenges for him.

> ... for prisoners they charge us £2.09 for a Radox, a shower gel. Now if you watch the TV, because TVs tell you about what is going on, it's 69p in Morrison's. So we earn in jail £8. I am a cleaner and you get £8 a week, but because I have got my qualifications, because I am qualified in industrial cleaning and maintenance, I get an extra £2 because I am qualified, so I get £10 a week. So what I am trying to say is the TV will let us know; you might watch TV to put a complaint in, because I complained about that. Because why should we by paying £2.09 when you can go to Morrison's and pay 69p. And plus then you have got to think about the prisons are buying everything in bulk, so you can buy one for 69p how many could you buy if you bought £3000 worth? I know about these things because I run businesses. Its things like that that can drive you crazy and makes you end up losing your TV because you say something that will get you into bother.
>
> (Ned – prisoner)

As Ned highlights, the direct access to public life via television inspired him to try and resolve the market forces at work within the context of the prison. The frustration Ned expresses here relates to his immediate experience as a prisoner. The disparity in prices and the income he receives from his work remind him of his deprivations in prison and the exploitation he encounters. Ned sought to follow formal routes and it is unlikely this disparity would have been resolved.[4] Participating in public life is not just constrained in economic terms but also in cultural terms. Will is a football fan and enjoys accessing football through television. He acknowledges that television allows him to continue supporting his team. For him his fandom can only be partial as he is not allowed to have a football shirt, as these are considered a potential trigger for antagonism between prisoners.

> I always wait for 'Match of the Day' on TV; I'm a Liverpool fan. When I go to Liverpool it feels like home. Scousers get a bad rep. We are not allowed football shirts in here. We could get them brought in but it might be an issue.
>
> (Will – prisoner)

Local news was also considered an important source of information as Maalik describes,

> Yes, everybody watches the local news because what it is you tend to know what's happening as well and plus you know people that's come in, in the local news. It's just a thing of prison that everyone watches the local news because they all know what's going to happen and who's here .... And the local prison newspapers, because you hear stories from other prisoners themselves, so watching documentaries, you know, it reflects a lot so you understand it more better.
>
> (Maalik – prisoner)

Maalik draws attention to the connection between local news and its relevance to the people in prison. Local news features crime-related stories and subsequent outcomes of justice. In these ways television news provides a route for acquiring up-to-date knowledge of convictions. In the same way, Barry wants to scour television items to find people he knows (Gersch 2003). Barry wants to witness events that may directly impact on the setting in which he is placed,

> I'll watch 'Car Crime UK' on ITV to see if I know anyone... There was that 'Panorama' about bent officers, name and shame them, they were gonna knock it off. I've been in before when they bang it off. This bloke molested someone with kids and the [local newspaper] wasn't allowed in. Like scandals with female officers ....
>
> (Barry – prisoner)

Barry realises that this information is a particular challenge for the establishment and protecting high profile cases such as prisoners or staff could challenge security.

Respondents draw on their own context not only to manage their viewing but also to determine how they interpret these choices. Some of the samples described their desire to engage in wider social affairs that are not necessarily prison/crime related. Sunny, for example, described how certain social, economic and political events presented through television help him to remain connected to the discourses perpetuated across wider culture.

> It gives me fresh words, say, through news such as 'credit crunch'. This is very helpful.
>
> (Sunny – prisoner)

Sunny's fear of losing touch with current social affairs and cultural discourses motivated his selections significantly. As an enhanced prisoner he was able to access DVDs from the library and he selected Indian Bollywood movies. He explained that this was to attempt to stay up to date with the cultural practices in his community. He was also pleased to witness via television the opening of a shopping centre in his local community. Mick also described how, when he left prison on a previous sentence, he was given a mobile phone. He described that 'I didn't know how to send texts'. Ann, the prison's chaplain was also sensitive to the technological deprivations prisoners can encounter and made reference to the absence of light switches in prison cells. Access to technology helps to minimise 'cultural jet-lag' (Bonini and Perrotta 2007).

Bill finds that some television programmes help him to duplicate his pre-prison role.

> However, I do like things like Deal or No Deal, Who Wants to Be a Millionaire. I like learning you see; I don't think you are ever too old. You see lots of different people from lots of different backgrounds on these programmes; I like to see this. You see, it is what I used to do; I employed thousands of people. I suppose I'm following this on in prison, by keeping up with lots of people through television.
>
> (Bill – prisoner)

The exposure to people in this mediated form allows Bill to establish social relations or 'para-social interaction' (Horton and Wohl 1956). Thus television permits him to replicate some of these social practices. Bill also described how he works as an *Insider*, a peer mentor for prisoners whom he advises and guides with their induction to prison life. His imprisonment has prevented him from continuing with his management role, yet Bill has sought outlets through which he can continue to interact with people both through television and in his work at the prison. As Crewe (2009:348) also found, finding connection with

prison life and its people was important for some prisoners' modes of adaptation.
Television provides an additional route to experience social relations.

> We move between public and private spaces. Between local and global ones. We move from sacred to secular spaces from real to fiction to virtual spaces, and back again.
>
> (Silverstone 1999b:7)

7.2.3 Organising daily life

> ...for most of us most of the time, everyday life does go on, and it is sustained through the ordered continuities of language, routine, habit, the taken for granted but essential structures that, in all their contradictions sustain the grounds for our security in our daily lives... Ontological security is sustained through the familiar and the predictable.
>
> (Silverstone 1999a:19)

Imprisonment disrupts time and place (Matthews 1999). Prisoners experience a temporary loss of 'home' and their routines are 'heavily scripted' by the prison (Martel 2006:595). Their forced separation from their own 'home' can be experienced as loss and be disorientating. This forced migration causes prisoners to attempt to attach meanings to places they are confined to and television enables them to develop this sense of place (Moores 2006:10). Prisoners in this sample are 'housebound' and fixed to one place. The role that television has in this kind of situation relates to Meyrowitz's (1985) thesis on home and reach. Here, audiences can not only reach different spaces, but can come together and be united in a temporal and spatial sense. Joshua explained,

> My partner obviously I've been with from school and I've got three kids and basically my partner's kind of like me, we're both Pisces and she likes wildlife a lot, documentaries, but she's more into soaps than I am. So of a night time I will talk to my partner on the phone and she will say what are you watching tonight and I will say I'm watching this and she will watch it at the same time. In a way I feel like I'm with her if you get what I'm saying. I know that sounds a bit strange but telepathically I feel like I'm with her.
>
> (Joshua – prisoner)

In order to emulate this closeness, Joshua and his partner were prepared to synchronise their viewing. The intimacy that Joshua and his partner can achieve is a valid mechanism. The mediated encounters that Joshua and his partner self-select highlight how 'broadcasting mediates *between* these two sites' (Scannell 1996:76): the broadcast event and the place where it is watched. The outcome for Joshua is that broadcasts provide 'a common sociable topical resource' (ibid.:159) in both sense of time and place.

Broadcasts were also evidenced as a mechanism for punctuating or filling time.

> Most of it is shit, but half hour gone; it is passing the time so you watch it. I'll watch Emmerdale sometimes and always Enders; that is two hours done. Mondays you have Gadget Show at 8pm; I might miss first half hour because of EastEnders. I like the Gadget Show.
>
> (Barry – prisoner)

Ryan, like Barry, highlighted how he actively used broadcast time to mark his time spent in prison.

> You sail through with telly. There is always a new series. Like Prison Break that is 6 months gone, a 6 month break and then it is on again. Then there is all season Top Gear, then Formula 1. There is always something new starting. I like Top Gear. It is something to look for-ward to. I go to the F1, as well; I love it, nothing else really. So once a week there is Prison Break for 6 months, a one-hour episode. I just see it advertised. Oh then there is the Sheild, I've seen all of them, all of them inside. Thurs night is 'Prison Break on 4, Friday is The Shield on 5 and Sunday Top Gear on 2. Then Monday to Friday you've got Emmerdale, Corrie and EastEnders.
>
> (Ryan – prisoner)

Ryan conceptualises time using television broadcasts, not just based on times of day but according to broadcast seasons or series (typically weekly broadcasts over a three-month period). Ryan looks forward to new series starting. He has trust and confidence that his programmes are there for him and are there even though he might not need them (ibid.:149). Essentially Ryan's television diet fills the weeks and his evenings spent in his cell are fundamentally framed by television. The role that technology plays in this is crucial, as broadcasts provide him with a reliable calendar thus facilitating a meaningful way for him to do prison time. The serialisation of broadcasts reminds these viewers that life goes on and that time is moving on by providing a 'bio-narrative' to their time and place (Martel 2006:602). This is in stark contrast to common analogies that time in prison is experienced as 'frozen' (Porporino and Zamble 1985). Broadcasts can therefore enliven the self. Ryan's selection of dramas, soaps, sport and special interest programmes like *Top Gear* give him access to narratives that are not cyclical, they are linear in their narrative form. This is a contrast to the experience of prison routine, which is endlessly cyclical. Pete remarked that 'the serials every week help. Soaps are very big in prison'. Seeking out narratives that punctuate time but also provide some sense of time passing can, of course, bring important comfort, especially from boredom and frustration. Scannell's (1996:149) notion of 'dailiness' suggests that 'our sense of days is always already in part determined by the ways in which media contribute to the shaping of our sense of days.'

Malcolm, Mick and Ron all illustrate this concept.

> At 10pm I watch the general news- it keeps me up to date. It is important because it affects us when we do get out or even whilst we are in here, like the trouble with telephone calls in prison it made the news.
>
> (Malcolm – prisoner)

> It doesn't, it tells you the time, you know what time it is like EastEnders is on at 8pm and 7.30pm; it tells you the time.
>
> (Mick – prisoner)

> VK: So after you have done your morning shift, back to your pad.
> Ron: I put the telly straight on.
>
> (Ron – Prisoner)

Television therefore marks, time or as Scannell refers to, 'zoning' (ibid.:150). This is the breaking up of parts of daily life, within which broadcasting operates, and is attuned to 'what people are doing and when' (ibid.). The life of prison also operates within a domestic framework, with usual activities like work assigned during the day, eating times, and leisure time during the evening. There are, however, many prisoners who for many reasons fail to access work and other purposeful activity, and are without situated events to zone and mark their daily lives. Broadcast schedules assist in the zoning or carving up of daily, weekly and seasonal life into meaningful chunks that might otherwise be empty. For Ron, television serves as a marker, the end or break from work and the transition to leisure is secured by putting on the television. Malcolm exploits the television hardware; 'I set the TV as an alarm in here and it comes on ITV in the morning'. Will explains that he doesn't watch much television in the day, due to his work and other commitments.

> Not through the days, it's the evenings. I'm busy in the day such as job, gym, physio and visits. It goes quick when something is on. Ten minutes can feel like an eternity or the weeks can go fast. It is like yesterday was the first day I was here; it is time done.
>
> (Will – prisoner)

Will assigns his evenings as a period to unwind from work.

> TV does help pass time a bit; it is human psychology; it helps to break the day down, morning, afternoon and evening. If something is good on it is another hour gone, it is chewing gum for the eyes.
>
> (Will – prisoner)

Will relies on television to differentiate parts of his daily life in prison. He also seeks reassurance that television will deliver him comfort, and he therefore trusts its provision. Claire is also sensitive to the 'zoning' effect.

> I think television is in blocks, isn't it, and you know the news is on until 9 o'clock, and I don't know, I don't do daytime television but whatever is on for half an hour chunks. And therefore I can imagine that that means it's ... I studied philosophy once and I remember very clearly them saying if we didn't have watches we wouldn't know how long time was. And if sometimes 10 minutes feels like an hour and sometimes an hour feels like 10 minutes. If you didn't have a watch it would be whatever it felt like, and I guess that's the same for prisoners.
>
> (Claire – Governor)

As Jewkes (2002a) found, 'good' and 'bad' times can also be marked by television. Stuart, for example, believes that his life is improved at certain times.

> It is better in the football season.
>
> (Stuart – prisoner)

The seasonal changes in broadcasting bring him valuable mediated content. Equally, his sense of time is shaped by what is fundamentally a culturally constructed and mediated time-frame. The faith and trust Stuart achieves through the broadcasting calendar helps him to look forward to 'better times'. Lee was also frustrated at television.

> My typical day is in a morning if I had TV I'd turn on Jeremy Kyle then get lunch and sit there all day until dinner. I get bored of watching it; it is the same every day. It makes time drag with telly. You know how long they are on for and then it is dinner time. It is one big time game here.
>
> (Lee – prisoner)

This dailiness is not helpful for Lee and he finds it slows down his time and 'shows up as a mild form of dread' (Scannell 1996:173). The stilling effect (Anderson 2004) that Lee experiences is not unusual, and therefore the ability to take control and find broadcasts which can speed up time and counter the totality of the prison routine is essential. Klapp (1986:71) also proposes that 'overload' of mediated information can bring about the redundancy of time and result in boredom. From Klapp's position, mediated encounters as Lee described here are reduced to 'noise' (ibid.:81). Lee, conversely preferred music to television and found this suited his well-being much better than television. Television is redundant for Lee as it fails in its provision as care-giver; his attachment to television is not necessarily secure. As Tester (1998:88) argues, the relevance of mediated forms of communication is 'important only in relation to other things which have happened today'. Maalik observed that prison brings about viewing adjustments.

> I used to watch it at home but it's just in prison I put it in a different way. I know some people and I talk to people they never used to watch EastEnders, they started watching it here because everybody at that time is locked up and everybody at that time watches EastEnders because you know if something happens in EastEnders everyone bangs their doors.
>
> (Maalik – prisoner)

Both Silverstone (1999a) and Scannell (1996) remark on the 'eventfulness' of television which as Maalik describes brings audiences together. Staff were also attuned to this effect and Claire saw this as a positive outcome.

> . . . we would also try and do if possible is to get big screens and still do that. Because there is a sense of community, isn't it? I, for example,

can sit and watch the football in the house or I go to the pub and watch it with a group of people which is preferable. That would be the same; you can watch it in your cell but actually we will put it on the big screen and get you out and have you out watching it as a group, and that's more of a sense of community.

(Claire – Governor)

This sense of community is not always necessarily ratified in the ways that Claire imagines, and some prisoners are sometimes reluctant to engage in public events in prison (Crewe 2009). Some prisoners like to take control of the ways in which their time and space is organised, and their use of broadcasting in these ways allows them to take respite and disconnect from prison routines. Broadcasts help them to reach time and place outside prison, as Scannell (1996:167) describes '[the] world in its availability is within the range of "my" concerns'. Time is therefore organised technologically, allowing prisoners to absorb themselves in the ordering and flow of everyday life beyond the walls of the prison. As Fiddler (2010:6) suggests, prisoners strive to intervene with time and space to 'bend it to their own purpose'. The types of encounters and methods for organising their time are acutely defined by broadcast schedules and this is essentially technological. Technology permits 'my' time, which Scannell (1996:152) refers to as 'experiential time'. This can make prisoners' existence meaningful by defining and ordering everyday life in prison. It also provides a sense of moving through time and alongside timeframes that continue outside prison or '[broadcasting], whose medium is time, articulates our sense of time' (ibid.:152).

7.3 Watching

... surveillance is a posh word for spying.

(Barry – prisoner)

Observation is a fundamental characteristic of prison (Foucault 1991). The act of surveillance is also a compelling feature of media use (Lull 1990; Jewkes 2002a). Moreover, the 'gaze' of the audience satisfies deep psychological needs or scopophilia (Mulvey 1975). The act of watching either via situated or mediated environments means that scrutiny and inspection of other people and the self is a function of control. This section presents two concepts of watching: *the spectacle* and *the panoptic*. This section will argue that the act of watching contributes to the restraint of sensibilities in order to rein in emotive affects and established a rationalised experience of everyday life.

7.3.1 The spectacle of television in prison

The act of watching has become a benign feature of everyday life; as Jewkes (2011:228) highlights, voyeurism has itself become entertainment and 'surveillance has been consistently viewed' by large numbers of audiences. The act of watching television by prisoners is also framed as a spectacle; staff in particular notice the act of watching television and believe it is worthy of assessment and scrutiny. Television viewing assists in the monitoring of prisoners. Conversely, the prison is subject to observation by prisoner audiences and watching 'their' environments has become part of their own viewing repertoires. This 'bottom-up surveillance' (ibid.:230) in the context of the prison is enabled by the television and 'surveillance technologies have inevitably been turned inwards' (ibid.:228).

Many of the respondents watched crime documentaries, reality programmes and dramas. Fuelling these motivations is the acquisition of knowledge, to learn more about the environment they are placed in and the people they could potentially come into contact with. The prison becomes a 'spectacle' in which television transforms the prison into an event. The recording and representation of the prison makes the prison public; it belongs to the world and it has its place in the world. It brings the inside to the outside and validates their existence to a wider non-prisoner audience. Prisoners attempt to reject and refute their 'civic death' (Jewkes 2010:26). Mick was frustrated about a programme about a women's prison.

> ...that Holloway thing. It is realistic but it is not showing you a fraction of it, so yeah right. I've seen slash ups and they walk away. It is like kindergarten sometimes and they get away with the brutality. You get thrown off a landing.
>
> (Mick – prisoner)

Leon also liked a programme about a celebrity who went into a prison to 'uncover' the harms of incarceration. Leon believed that the prison experience in this programme was not sufficient and that it failed to complete the spectacle of the prison; he believed it did not capture the difficulties of incarceration.

> The public can't judge us though; they should educate people on the outside; people don't understand. Let them come in here. Like that programme that took kids inside prison and they were shown what prison was like. Anyone can do three days though; they need the real

impact: that once you are here there is no way out. I don't know how long I am here for.

(Leon – prisoner)

Leon reflects on his own experience and the 'real impact' cannot be reproduced in a television programme. The entertainment values of these programmes override the authenticity of the prison experience. Leon, on this occasion, was frustrated by the missed opportunity for broadcasts like this to educate wider audiences about imprisonment.

Stuart also actively assesses his own experience of programmes about prison, ' "Banged Up Abroad" is quite interesting; I compare it to here'. He went on to say that the prison experiences of British citizens in other countries certainly make his experience of prison seem much easier. He reported how distasteful mechanisms of punishment in other cultures were and that his own experience of prison failed to be a 'spectacle'. Dramatisation of prison and crime enabled Ryan, for example, to access the spectacle.

The Shield is about a bent copper and Prison Break is a US drama about prison. It is gripping, seeing what's next and then it finishes so you tune in the next week; it works! I sit there rocking.

(Ryan – prisoner)

Unlike the authentic and 'real' representations of prison as reported by Stuart and Leon, the dramas Ryan refers to do not represent law enforcement in ideological terms. Jewkes's (2011:162) discussion of mediated representations of policing outlines how the portrayal of police has moved away from the archetypal *Dixon of Dock Green* police officer to a much grittier and problematic police role; 'with all the human flaws and vices that any other section of the population would have'. The appeal of *The Shield* for Ryan he says is that it features a corrupt police officer.

Ron also talked extensively about the US drama *The Wire* and was suspicious how many crime dramas were essentially making crime a 'spectacle'. Ron felt that this was having an effect on real crime and the ways in which crime was being committed by contemporary offenders. He identified himself as belonging to an old breed of criminals, working to a strict code of criminal conduct. Ron identified that the younger criminals in *The Wire* adopted different values.

I am a bit older but these young guys now I think they are totally different; they glorify all the bad stuff that comes up.

(Ron – prisoner)

Ron felt the programme displayed these articulations sensitively and he was able to use *The Wire's* narrative to highlight these tensions. Making these kinds of assertions about their own criminal identity can also be extended to the ways in which they chose to represent their prisoner identities. Malcolm, for example, was a fan of *Big Brother*. He suggests that watching a social construction of a form of incarceration is appealing because of the voyeuristic qualities. As Jewkes (ibid.:226) suggests 'the postmodern quest for the hyper-real, the desire to be part of the "action" may be satisfied by the ability to see it played out as it was caught on camera'. This programme for Malcolm is a cultural analogy to his own experience of prison, and he draws parallels to the kinds of conditions experienced by the 'contestants' on this programme.

> Big Brother – everybody watches that here – I like to watch the characters and see how they get on. They are banged up without TV, music – it is a case of survival. We get more here, they can't get out but they can ask to come out. I have favourite characters – the funny ones. I remember there was an aggressive girl; she had to take courses when she got out.
>
> (Malcolm – prisoner)

Malcolm went on to say that because of his experience of prison he would be able to withstand the conditions in which the *Big Brother* participants endured. He was also attracted to the prospect of being an active participant in the spectacle itself. Like the contestants, Malcolm's life is under observation in prison and his need to have this ratified is exemplified by this programme. Other prisoners however found this kind of participation in the spectacle distasteful, as Alan, for example, remarks,

> There is some right numpties on here [Jeremy Kyle]. How can they humiliate themselves?
>
> (Alan – prisoner)

The confessions and disclosures of ordinary people in these programmes parade human suffering, misery and conflict for audiences to witness. Suffering is commodified and access to suffering through mediated forms is uncomplicated (Gersch 2007:14). Despite Alan's distaste for the ways in which these programmes catapult humanity as a form of spectacle, he feels compelled to watch. Alan did not switch off the television during the interview and the broadcasts provided him with points of reference for discussion (Wood 2009). The act of watching and being the voyeur on people's lives provides some semblance of power. *Jeremy Kyle* is also too authentic or close to the realities of the prison experienced by Alan on a daily basis. The degradations Alan faces as a prisoner and his exposure to vulnerable and pathological people demonstrates how precarious viewing this kind of programme can be. The spectacle of suffering is sometimes too much to stomach and avoiding programmes is necessary for personal control.

High profile crime cases result in prisons having to deal with 'famous' or newsworthy inmates. Staff in this study were sensitive to the effects a high profile prisoner can create for the running of the establishment. Handling these kinds of prisoners requires specialist intervention and often these prisoners are encouraged, or at least given the option, to be segregated from the main prison population.[5] As Tim describes,

> ... if we've got a prisoner that's got quite a high profile, quite a high media interest, there was one yesterday that was on Sky News that's in here, then yes it is a concern because it reflects obviously on his own personal safety, his own self harm issues if he has got any because something might tip him over the edge ... He may not be aware that he's been on television, so we'll speak to him and say, look, you know, you managed to make the headlines yesterday.
>
> (Tim – prison officer)

The staff are required to temper the spectacle that some prisoners bring to this environment and some talked about handling notoriety of high-profile criminals. As Sparks et al. note, maintaining order in prison is a 'matter of concern and debate among staff' (1996:146). The presence and subsequent consumption of television and other media entails the use of additional work and resources when handling the public nature of offenders' lives.

7.3.2   Panoptic

> When we get there first thing in the morning we have the usual morning briefing in the officers' mess. That gives us any details of what things we need to keep an eye on, whether we have got problems ... So it's so we have got a full outlook.
>
> (Steve – prison officer)

The techniques of observation, surveillance, scrutiny and assessment all lead to forms of governance associated with disciplinary and therapeutic control. Television in prison enables all social agents in prison to observe (Bonini and Perrotta 2007:87). Television plays an important role in surveillance, as it supplements the 'inspection [that] functions ceaselessly. The gaze is alert everywhere' (Foucault 1991:195) and now with television in its place it ensures that the 'individual is fixed in his place' (ibid.) even more.

In its traditional form the Panopticon, as Foucault (1991) describes, is intended to keep subjects under perpetual observation, as Stuart acknowledges,

> ... they want you to play on landing, but we are not allowed to take furniture out, they want us to break the rules and play on pool table [cards] but it creates problems.
>
> (Stuart – prisoner)

Like many prisoners, Stuart wants to retreat to his cell when he can, even during association time; he prefers to withdraw to his cell to socialise with some of his peers. He explains how he is encouraged to be in full view of staff, rather than outside their view and so 'visibility is a trap' (ibid.:200). If Stuart retreats to a cell to play card games with other prisoners, the panoptic principle is broken: being out of view of staff results in observation becoming obscured. Sparks et al. (1996:322) add that

> ... situational dimensions of the prison environment could be adapted to reduce opportunities for control problems, without destroying the legitimacy of social relations and trust necessary for effective social control.

Permitting such minor infractions is therefore important to maintaining overall control.

The effect of this kind of panoptic surveillance is wide reaching and in the case of television, many prisoners and staff reported that television can singularly confine activity of prisoners. Sporting events, soaps and quiz shows are popular for creating collective experiences. This form of sociability within the prison creates a sociable occasion and the act of watching is amplified to an event. Audiences come together in one single moment, yet at the same time are physically separated; this is panoptic. The following section of transcription from an interview with Maalik reiterates how this is played out within the prison routine.

Maalik: Then everyone watches Coach Trip.

VK: Oh right, that's Channel 4, is it?

Maalik: That's Channel 4 as well, that's just started, Coach Trip, so everyone talks about Coach Trip. Everyone says this person should be off, that person should be off.

VK: And it's about people going on a holiday, is it?

Maalik: Yes, on a coach trip and then they get red carded off.

VK: For what reason?

Maalik: Because the people don't like them. So the group don't like them so that means the prison don't like them so the prison says they should be off.

VK: So you really tune into the fact that whatever's on, the prison's watching it and so are you?

Maalik: Yes, everybody tends to watch the same thing and it's always talked about afterwards.

Maalik suggests that 'everyone' is watching the same programmes, but although the television-use diaries highlight immense diversity of viewing, some programmes remain popular and watched by many. Foucault's description of the design and purpose of the Panopticon illustrates how television as an object can be compared here.

> By the effect of backlighting, one can observe from the tower, standing out precisely against the light, the small captive shadows in the cells of the periphery. They are like so many cages, so many small theatres, in which each actor is alone, perfectly individualized and constantly visible. The panoptic mechanism arranges spatial unities that make it possible to see constantly and to recognize immediately.
>
> (ibid.:200)

The physical qualities of television, such as the glow and the sound, do light up the darkened cells. Bill, Mick and Malcolm all reported that they liked to sit close to the television. This would mean they would be in direct view of observers looking through the cell door hatch rather than lying on the bed which is off centre view. The light from television enhances observation, as Foucault describes. As Tim and Steve observe,

> ... they'll all be watching the same programme; they'll all be watching Jeremy Kyle.
>
> (Tim – prison officer)

> EastEnders is one of the many soaps they do watch and when the
> channel is down, which has happened in the past, it causes an uproar
> which then makes it more interesting to work on the landing.
>
> (Steve – prison officer)

The television inside the cell faces inwards and, it is therefore not possible to see the content of the programme when looking through cell
hatches, without physically entering the cell. Given the diversity of
the viewing by the small sample of prisoners who completed television
diaries, it is misleading to make assumptions about the range and scope
of viewing.

Tim described a scenario in which a circle of observation occurred.
A staff-prisoner-television cycle of watching took place in the segregation unit. This prisoner was placed on 'constant watch'.[6] This means
the staff have to sit outside a specially designed cell which is made of
bars with covering strengthened plastic instead of a solid door. The staff
are required to record the prisoner's behaviour to enable assessments
and interventions. In this instance, the staff member was watching the
prisoner, who was watching television.

> It's only the other day we had a prisoner on a constant watch and
> he was afforded all these luxuries that they're entitled to upstairs,
> although it was a bit bizarre because he had the officer watching him
> watching telly but it's a means to an end, isn't it? The main thing is
> getting him off his constant watch and getting him in mainstream
> population and over his concerns and worries.
>
> (Tim – prison officer)

In an attempt to 'normalise' the prisoner, television is employed to
provide staff with a structured activity they can observe and make subsequent assessments. Television cannot watch the audience, yet most
significantly the audience can peek into the lives of others and directly
observe representations of social life without fear of violating others'
privacy.

Surveillance also applies to staff. Maintaining control in prison is
the nature of their work. Steve explains why it is important to have a
coherent and attentive team.

> Fortunately I would say on the [wing] we have got a good group
> of officers up there because everybody works in a uniform style so
> everybody knows what everybody else is doing.
>
> (Steve – prison officer)

Monitoring requires transparency of everybody's actions and, as Jewkes (2011:230) remarks, 'the powerful are [not] exempt from the watchful gaze and...that power does not entirely reside in the hands of those near the top of social and occupational hierarchies'. Everybody is watching somebody and this form of technological surveillance extends beyond the situated landscape of the prison; it is also mediated. Prisoners too are watching each other and staff, and this is often through television. For example, Simon is an active observer; he scrutinises and watches everyone and makes assessments, in this case based on their choice of viewing.

> I'm the alpha male here, though I have the bottom bunk. If he wants to watch something I do let him. But it is my remote and my telly; if you don't like it, then get out. There has been loads of arguments, but not with current pad mate. I remember a man wanted to watch a cartoon; I ain't watching that 'Winnie the Pooh'. He got ejected from here. I refuse to live with them...Got to be flexible, like the odd football match, which I'm not bothered about. I let them watch what they want. If I get an awkward pad mate I get him to move out.
>
> (Simon – prisoner)

Simon was aware that he was also subject to observation, and finds ways to avoid this intrusion; 'I disappear and visit my friends' when the cells are unlocked. He was also curious of my level of observation and he worked hard to undermine the interview. Instead, I became his subject of observation and he wanted to experiment with his 'observer' status. The interview broke down and he interviewed me. Compounded with this, his power within the prison was evident. Many prisoners kept coming into the cell and he continued his interview with me in front of an audience of four prisoners. This reinforced his powerful status. I was being watched, assessed and scrutinised. The visit turned out for him and also myself as an 'event'. Simon's thirst for information, especially related to the prison and its people was insatiable.

> ...but you get news first hand in here, what is going on, all the criminals are in here, they are all my neighbours.
>
> (Simon – prisoner)

In maintaining his status, observation of staff was also important in order for him to achieve his own ends.

I've been around hard people; even the staff are hard. When I came to prison I had to survive and learn the hard way; you can select officers out, if you want something. I can't stand anyone; it is human nature. In here, calling them boss and gov is all a game. Some are OK, but 90% are here to pay their bills and some take this work personally; they were probably bullied at school; they couldn't get in the police so they become prison officers.

(Simon – prisoner)

Simon admitted to bullying people to get what he wanted, and not just in prison. By identifying the 'right' staff, punitive responses to his manipulative behaviour could probably be minimised.

Achieving levels of situated control within this environment is fragile and the claims associated with observation are also brittle. Malcolm had a remote control in his possession, and he suggested it was contraband and therefore a secret from staff; however, other prisoners knew about this. The prohibited exchange of goods among prisoners demands acute surveillance because tiers of power manifest routinely across the illegitimate economy in prison (Crewe 2005). The tightening up of observation of prisoners is prized very highly by staff and also prisoners. Prisons today are challenged with over crowding, cost-savings and increasingly more vulnerable prisoners coming in to the establishment; as a result, techniques of observation need to adapt and change to counter these barriers. The panoptic process is therefore left to the prisoner, and the effects of being watched in order to guarantee control, in part relies on this process of self-inspection (Rose 1999; Bosworth 2007; Crewe 2009). Television is embedded predominantly across all individuals' lives and therefore surveillance through these means is continued into the prison landscape, and the principles of subjectivity are 'imported' (Irwin and Cressey 1962) into the prison. The continuity of viewing television from the community to the prison and back to the community is today unlikely to be disrupted. This is because television in this environment enables visibility, which is an important feature of situated and mediated control. These forms of control culminate in personal control.

He who is subjected to a field of visibility for the constraints of power; he makes them play spontaneously upon himself; he inscribes in himself the power in relation ... he becomes the principle of his own subjection.

(Foucault 1991:202)

7.4   Prisoners' communicative rights and censorship

As this book has already outlined, prisoners' access to in-cell television has in many instances nourishing qualities (see Chapter 6). The ways in which this access is orchestrated is underpinned by the privilege system: IEP (PSI 11/2011). What this means is that the paternalistic measures that the IEP system defines highlights a number of key factors relating to the ways in which prisoners are deprived of goods and services. We know that these 'deprivation' modes are symptomatic of incarceration and in essence the regulated access to television reinforces this. Related closely to this are the varying views on how watching television should be managed as a risk related activity – hence censoring prisoners' viewing is considered by some a reasonable adjustment to make. In essence if staff deem television a useful activity for an individual prisoner they will make it available despite the privilege system's entitlement criteria. Prisoners' access to all modes of communication is not straightforward: most are behaviour dependent. Both mediated and situated forms of communication are embroiled within the prison regime and its rules. As a result, the process of incarceration intentionally limits and regulates communication, which creates additional and new pains of incarceration. These feature loss and social exclusion as a result of being subjected to communication and digital poverty (Jewkes and Johnston 2009:135).

7.4.1   A desire for communicative rights

Easton and Piper highlight that prisoners are unable to secure access to 'goods through their own efforts' (2012:309). Therefore some would argue that prisoners should have extended rights to access education, paid work and medical support. As it currently stands, television and other media are not a right: they are a privilege, characterised by the IEP (see Chapter 5). Prisoners' rights in the UK are contentious and only a few cases of litigation have brought about changes to the ways in which punishment is administered. Article 10 of the Universal Declaration of Human Rights emphasises the need to reform and rehabilitate and the European Convention on Human Rights has influenced English law making (ibid.:310). These include improving the management of deaths in custody, decent conditions in prison, treatment of mentally ill prisoners, access to courts and the right to secure a family and private life (ibid.:311). None of these refers directly to the ways in which communicative outlets like television, radio, books and the Internet are framed in prison law as rights. Instead they feature as privileges.

> The Prison Service has resisted rights talk and a rights culture, preferring to use the currency of privileges and incentives which are not legally enforceable entitlements. They can be withdrawn and used as a disciplinary measure to maintain good order and discipline within the prison.
>
> (Easton and Piper 2008:309)

In these ways the Prison Service in England and Wales has avoided developing a rights-based system (Scott and Flynn 2014:120). This has meant that penal power can be maintained using paternal methods which continue to keep prisoners dependent on their captors. Within the UK context, prisoners are denied the right to vote; this is stripped from them once they enter prison. Despite European ruling in support of electoral voting, the law and services have been rejected by the coalition government outright, and a stalemate position has occurred. The rhetoric that surrounded in-cell television's introduction was never framed in line with entitlements – its agenda was to make it a privilege. In contrast, however, evidence collected in this study highlights how important television is for maintaining a civic identity (see Section 7.2). Despite these benefits, television continues to remain a concession to maintain order. The promise of including social and economic rights-based laws for people in prison remains very limited (Easton and Piper 2008:313).

Of course we know that the provision of in-cell television is bounded by the IEP system in the UK, but so are opportunities to access visits, use the telephone and interact with other prisoners. In these ways, limiting communicative opportunities is a defining feature of incarceration and the deprivations espoused by Sykes (1958) and Goffman (1991) have and now continue to have painful consequences. The end of the silent and separation systems defined at the onset of modern imprisonment still lingers today, achieved by limiting the number of occasions prisoners can telephone home, meet in person with their family, read a book and interact with their immediate prison community. These limited opportunities unsettle many of the prisoner respondents that took part in this study. Moreover, the framing of in-cell television as a 'luxury' item alerted both staff and prisoner respondents to a number of paradoxes in relation to their rights and entitlements.

Until 2006, a selection of newspapers was freely available to prisoners. These were purchased at the Prison Service's expense and were available to prisoners on the wings or landings. This resource was stopped as prisoners are able to purchase their own print media using their own funds. It was cut as a cost-saving exercise. In a letter to *The Guardian* an ex-prisoner wrote,

> Like many prisoners I had little or no contact with mainstream society while either in or out of custody. Newspapers were also my way of finding out about the world when I decided to turn my life around. The idea that current affairs are now available via television is ridiculous; there is no comparison, in the variety or news content.
>
> (Anon 2006:23)

Whilst justification to withdraw these newspapers may seem logical, this ex-prisoner believes that breadth of access is important. The solution was that each prison establishment holds an account with local newsagents and prison governors decide what print media should be available for prisoners to purchase; thus prison staff already determines the list of print media they can buy. Prisoners are also permitted to buy their own radio and music systems through authorised suppliers using their own money. There are however strict controls on the types of equipment permitted. This local devolvement to prison governors can be productive, but for many prisoners this can mean they experience different prisons with varying rules of access and engagement. It is these kinds of things that exacerbate unfairness and can thus impact on feelings of trust and safety (Liebling et al. 2001). As outlined in Chapter 6, feelings of frustration towards the prison's rules are commonplace. This also applies to the way television is framed as a privilege.

> ... they say it's a privilege. Me personally I don't think it should be a privilege; I think it should be a standard thing like a kettle, like the use of the telephone; it should be a standard thing. It shouldn't be a privilege because we are paying for it.
>
> (Joshua, prisoner)

For Joshua, renting his television means that his access should be unconditional. The exchange of personal cash for an in-cell set meant that many respondents felt the same way as Joshua. However, others were more particular about who should access and under what conditions. Lee, a prisoner, felt that prisoners' index offences could indicate who should access television and who shouldn't.

VK: Is TV a privilege for prisoners?

Lee: Yeah, for certain prisoners like burglars and thieves. VPs [vulnerable prisoners] shouldn't get it, especially certain VPs. If you're on an ACCT you should get it, if you're vulnerable it takes your mind off killing themselves.

This ranking of access links to broader discourses about criminal hierarchies, whereby sex offenders, for example, receive no or little status with prisoner and criminal subcultures (Irwin and Cressey 1962). In Lee's case his reference to 'VPs' refers directly to this group. As a result, he and others believe the right to access television freely is forfeited through the criminal act. Of course the service doesn't distinguish access to mass communications in these ways but it is fundamentally concerned about regulating risk and normalising prison; which television and other media can amplify (see below). Pete like Lee also subscribes to this tiered approached based on criminal history.

> ... VPUs like sex offenders should be restricted. I heard that at HMP Y [sex offender prison], they watch sex-related crimes and he has seen guys gorging at children on CBBC. But how can you govern that? You can't.
>
> (Pete, prisoner)

The next section extends on Pete's point in more detail. Regulation of television content features significantly in the management of risk.

7.4.2   Managing risk or censorship?

Mechanisms to observe and control prisoners' media choices are in reality unrealistic unless the hardware and information is prohibited completely. The degree to which censorship is actually enacted is difficult to trace. The IEP (PSI11/2011:15) makes reference to censorship of television based on age restrictions and limited access to Freeview channels.[7] Much of the prison policy stipulates the requirement to regulate and control in order to manage a series of risks. As a result, censorship in the context of the prison is used either to reduce harm or as a form of treatment – at best to prevent something getting worse. The flow of media, particularly television and films (DVDs), into prisons creates some anxiety when prisoners, especially 'dangerous' prisoners, access them. More recently the introduction of email in some establishments in varying jurisdictions means that this correspondence is managed closely. Where email is permitted, some penal authorities opt for a censoring package which actively censors specific words. This can be tailored to review content of specific types of prisoners including sex offenders, terrorists and racists. Of particular interest are sex offenders because of the ways in which their behaviour is monitored and treated.

> ... So it would be interesting to say if we give them access to these, will they go and pick up children's books in which case we have got a concern? If there are no children's books to pick up and they can't, we can't monitor their behaviours, so there is that element as well ... I think that the other thing which is an interesting element in the sex offender prison is they will sometimes say let them have access and let them have choice and then we will monitor what they are doing. If you take it all away, then that's no use because we can't tell what they would be doing if they could.
>
> (Claire, Governor)

Hence, opportunities to survey prisoners viewing habits conforms to mechanisms of control (Cohen 2007). Much of the prison legislation in the UK carefully documents where prisoners entitlements start and finish. However, the nature of offending within categories highlights how prisons find it difficult to manage risk effectively as this example highlights,

> They didn't have any children's books in the library; Harry Potter and things were not allowed. They weren't allowed DVDs of cartoons, that kind of thing; Argos catalogues, all the pictures of children were taken out, so it was very, very clear. When we expanded the prison and it was then 50% child sex offenders and 50% adults there was a big issue about you can't blanket ban everything, and why shouldn't we be allowed to read Harry Potter so I can chat to my child about it? And there is a real dilemma between giving people choice, decency, and public and child protection issues.
>
> (Claire, Governor)

Knight (2001) noted that censorship is practiced and this is believed to protect prisoners and also victims of crime. Examples include access to local newspapers, whereby staff may withhold them or remove pages. This is because local press tend to include details of people's criminal investigations and trials and the people who are involved in this tend to be imprisoned within that local area. As Tony, a deputy governor highlights,

...newspapers are fairly easy to manage because you know they are coming. And to be fair often the [newspaper] will phone if they have got something to tell you, especially if they know it's going to be a little, could cause any grief. Local TV, I have known it where prisoners have suddenly appeared, the case has appeared and all of a sudden they are well known and you have got to move them out the prison because of that, I have known that happen. So that just shows the power, doesn't it?

(Tony – Deputy Governor)

Managing high profile cases has a series of resource implications since media, like television, are available in prison. Barry's curiosity of high profile and sensitive cases got him into trouble.

There was that 'Panorama' about bent [prison] officers – name and shame them. They were going to knock it [TV] off. I've been in before when they bang it off. This bloke molested someone with kids and the [newspaper] wasn't allowed in. Like scandals with female prison officers and the Facebook thing... I asked my mum to send me details in and so I got the sack from the job ... proper censorship.

(Barry – prisoner)

Whether or not prisons deliberately switch off televisions, actively censoring the material requires a sophisticated system coordinated centrally, as Claire highlights,

In terms of censoring television, I just think it's really, really difficult.

(Claire – Governor)

Additional interviews with industry professionals outlined that managing and controlling what prisoners access is 'well behind the curve' and that the service 'could be more prescriptive about what prisoners watch' (digital industry interview 3). This interviewee argued that the desire to regulate prisoners viewing is met with the complication of how to do it in reality. The advent of digital technologies means that prescribing access to certain digital media content could be achieved. However, as outlined in Chapter 8, digital media across many prisons in the UK and abroad are not being used to their fullest capacity and the question of censorship is just one small consideration in prison settings. Instead, prison policy is expected to manage these concerns and rely on staff to act as 'human filters' where necessary. Now, digital technologies are becoming increasingly embroiled in this enterprise.

Other types of print media are also censored or made unavailable to prisoners as Knight (2001) also documents that, for example, *The Pink Paper* a national gay editorial is not made available in some prisons. Simon explains how censorship, in his view, is part of wider regulatory control.

> Whatever your choice they are stunting your growth... Censoring is a joke, supposed to have free speech... there is censorship on the outside. TV is always censored. To see certain material you have to go to a shop for a DVD, like porn or even educational stuff that is not on TV.
>
> (Simon – prisoner)

Furthermore, certain prisoners such as those that are separated from association with other prisoners are sometimes subjected to further limitations on their access to mass communications, as well as primary forms of communications such as letters, visits and telephone calls. In particular, opportunities to network with outside links and glean information about victims are scrutinised by the prison establishment in order to protect the public and minimise risk of harm. As a result security departments in prisons managing these types of offenders examine the kinds of communication opportunities. It is these kinds of concerns that magnify any kind of development in other kinds of digital communicative outlets (see Section 8.2.1).

Take PSI06/2011, for example, which outlines prisoner communications and correspondence. In the interest of victims, potential victims and witnesses, the service is obligated to protect them. Here the nature and content of prisoners' letters both incoming and outgoing is deemed as contaminated and thus in order to militate against re-offending, prisons have the legislative powers to open, read and in some instances withhold the letter. This procedure also applies to emails (see Section 8.2.1). Therefore, prisoners do not have the right to receive an unopened private letter, unless it constitutes a legal letter. In all other cases, prisoners receive letters already opened and checked for contraband. In Belgium, however, this is not allowed under statute law.

Prisoners' access to books is also subject to regulation in both the shape of prisoners' privileges and the ways in which prison libraries are resourced. The Howard League for Penal Reform has continued to campaign for prisoners' access to books. Concerns about the kinds of books prisoners can access is a thorny issue, especially those that are deemed risky: pornographic and extremist or radical. The decision to supply women's prisons with the bestselling chick lit novel *50 Shades of Grey* received media attention which demanded a rationale from the Justice Secretary. The book's popularity for its explicit sexual content meant that Chris Grayling had to emphasise how the service is not actively censoring and is instead urging 'women offenders to read more' (BBC News 2014). However, prisoners' access to the prison library is also problematic, with volumetric control in place which means at any one time a prisoner can only have 12 books in their possession and getting time to visit the library is not straightforward. From 2015, a revision to the IEP scheme meant that prisoners' friends and family could purchase books (including audio books in CD format) for prisoners from agreed suppliers. For volumetric reasons the number of books prisoners can have in their cells is restricted to 12. This revision comes as a result of significant campaigns to allow prisoners less restricted access to books.

The risk of permitting unfettered access to a range of media outlets is assumed to mean that incarceration becomes compromised both in terms of physical security and harm. Some of these harms remain unfounded, as outlined in Chapter 4 the psychological effects of media use are mixed and conflicting and reveal very little about causal relationships between the watching and committing a violent act, for example (Atkin et al. 1979). As a result, these harms have become imaginary yet have materialised in the policymaking processes without proper evaluation or evidence. As Tony, a deputy governor, outlined,

> ...there has been a lot of prison publicity about Sky and the public expect prisoners to have absolutely nothing, and if all of a sudden we are providing this, that and the other. At one time prisoners, we had a range of 'PlayStations' and games that prisoners were allowed to earn the right to borrow or use. All that's gone because of the public perception really; they think everybody is playing Grand Theft Auto in their cell, doing this, that and the other.
>
> (Tony – Deputy Governor)

7.4.3   Censoring the prison

There is much more clarity, legislatively speaking, with respect to what the public can see within our prisons. In the UK context there are a number of policies which inhibit prisoners from contacting the media (PSO4440), using interactive digital technologies like the Internet

(PSO 9010) and sending letters deemed inappropriate (PSI06/2011). In 2013, a total of 7,451 mobile phones were recovered across prison establishments in the England and Wales (UK Parliament 2014). This is because the Crime and Security Act 2010 outlines that possessing mobile phones and devices that can store or transmit electronic data within prison is an offence. The Offender Management Act 2007 also stipulates that it is a criminal offence to have equipment that can transmit sound or images from within the prison. As outlined earlier in this section, protecting victims is a priority; however, these acts also make a clear statement about the disclosure of prison life to the public. The availability of contraband technology therefore erodes these barriers and can enable prisoners to share their life experiences behind bars. Some of these 'leaks' reveal aspects of prison life that are unjust, and appear often in the national press as whistleblowing stories. On other occasions, tabloid press use these leaks to reinforce how prison is 'soft' on its criminals. In balancing this national prison newspapers like *Inside Time* offer some balance in centring aspects of prison life within its remit. Prisoners are free to write into this newspaper and also coproduce feature articles as long as they comply with PSO that states they cannot earn money from this enterprise. Other examples see serving prisoners as guest journalists for quality broadsheet newspapers, such as Erwin James, a lifer, who wrote for *The Guardian* newspaper between 1998 and 2004. Other high profile prisoners, like politicians, have shared their prison experience via published books and blogs. More recently The Lifer @Prison_Diaries tweets from jail, having disclosed that his partner had paid an officer to bring in the mobile phone for £500, they disclose 'Keeping this phone hidden is becoming a headache.' (Twitter 21.8.14).

The successful National Prison Radio (NPR), which is co-produced with serving prisoners, is only broadcast within prisons. Despite it being a national service, its audience is serving prisoners and therefore its content never reaches the outside world. As a result NPR's policy outlines that material prepared for broadcast should be compliant with government regulations and guidelines and therefore,

> Judgement – whether on a requirement or editorial issue – should be made from the viewpoint that all audio may be heard by the general public. No system is 100% secure and even material which is not intended for broadcast could find its way into the public domain and therefore should be judged with the general public in mind, including young people, victims of crime, and the media.
>
> (NOMS 2014:1)

Hence any material that prisoners contribute to or produce means that,

> Prisoners must not be given copies of their work following employ-
> ment in a radio project or after taking part in a radio course since this
> risks the recordings coming into the public domain.
>
> (ibid.:4)

Moreover, programmes and material that refer to prisoners do not permit prisoners to be mentioned by their full name. This is to ensure that
they cannot be identified and the 'reputational risks' of disclosing the
full name of a prisoner does not harm the NPR, the offender, the prison
service or the wider criminal justice sector as well as victims of crime.
In line with these, NPR seeks to be impartial, accurate and non-offensive.
Consequently, an authorised editor rigorously checks material to ensure
content is compliant with these guidelines.

Novek also found that enabling North American prisoners to participate in the free press as active journalists enhances 'self-efficacy in
pro-social ways' (2005:5). However, she also found that setting up a
prisoner newspaper could amplify the controlling features of the prison
whilst paradoxically empowering prisoners. Novek discusses how prison
newspapers have conformed to institutional agendas and where they
have revealed contrary viewpoints these editorials have been censored
or withdrawn. In Novek's ethnography she describes the institutional
constraints of organising a prison newspaper, whereby the warden acts
as editor and makes a final decision on what makes the news (ibid.:12).
These kinds of decision-making were considered arbitrary for the female
prisoners who worked on the newspaper. However, the craft of writing
and producing stories that is to be shared was for many nurturing and
empowering.

The prison documentary is a popular programme for audiences. As
Jewkes (2011:194) suggests these set the prison up as an 'ethnography'
presenting the audiences with a feel for prison life and centring the
moral, ethical and painful consequences of doing time. Mason (2013
also adds that prison films (especially fictional) deliver material to satisfy voyeuristic needs, especially in relation to observing violence and
thus doing very little to broaden audiences' understanding of penal
reform. Capturing the 'real' side of prison life was something prisoners in this in-cell television study were sensitive to and often felt
disgruntled at the ways in which prison was depicted by programme
makers (see Section 7.3). In part, capturing truths about prison life may
also be hindered by institutional regulations to attempt to side line or

obscure prisoners' views of prison life. The timeliness of witnessing a serving prisoner talk about their experience is for many audiences compelling viewing whilst at the same time can be viewed as commercially exploitative. One departure from this is the work of Rex Bloomstein, a film-maker and producer of prison and crime documentaries. His style seeks to bring the voices of people in his art to the fore; not unlike an ethnographer, his films expose the natural and complex situations of people doing time (Bennett 2005). Juxtaposed with these cultural artefacts, the public's access to the prison is becoming increasingly obscured and distorted. Bloomstein's work is of historical significance and is situated with a landscape of penal reform, albeit fleetingly. More recently the 'poverty porn' documentaries such as *Benefits Street* have been criticised for using people's pain and discomfort as a source of pleasure for viewing audiences. The degrees to which these texts reflect the lived experiences is questionable, with many of this genre's critics claiming this as a barometer for modern political temperaments and thus giving all audiences something distasteful to comment on. Prison commentators like Wacquant worry that the disappearance of prison sociology means that our only points of reference come from the 'writings of journalists' (2002:385). Collectively then, these media products are bound up with organisational agendas linked acutely to economic and political priorities, thus signalling the 'end of the "inmate society"' (Simon 2000:296).

Summary

The analysis indicates that television is employed as a *package of care* which co-opts prisoners into a therapeutic relationship with television. This is *rationalised* through mechanisms like the IEP process, but also prisoners' active selection of television programmes. Television is *prescribed* (by staff and prisoners) to actively distract and minimise the harms of incarceration. Together staff and prisoners employ television to control social relations and the psychobiographies of prisoners. The situated culture of the prison has witnessed a shift in the ways social relations operate, with many prisoners preferring to stay behind their cell doors. As an instrument of control, television allows staff to deliver what they frame as caring practice. With few other resources to engage prisoners in purposeful activity, the care-giving features of television are routinely exploited, in particular providing time and space for prisoners to self-govern their own emotional lives (Bosworth 2007; Crewe 2009). Prisoners are vanishing from view and retreating into the most private enclaves of the prison, especially where television is. The paradox is that prisoners' behaviour has according to many accounts improved, yet this retreat to the cell means that staff fear that prisoners are increasingly disconnected from situated culture. Control is therefore beginning to transform and this is shared between staff, prisoner and television; it is therefore drawn from different 'contextual resources' (Layder 2004). The panoptic features of prison with in-cell television are benign but also acute. As a form of governance, the gaze is 'turned inwards' and also outwards with television (Jewkes 2011). Self-therapy is inculcated with television now in its place. The prison with television in place can fix and guarantee self-inspection, relinquishing and even limiting the need for direct and coercive interpersonal control. Finally the question of censorship and prisoners' communicative rights highlights the precarious nature in which access to mediated technologies is of concern to contemporary debates about the role of the prison.

8
Concluding Discussion

8.1 Introduction

The relevance of this research, using a unique body of data, has identified significant additions to prisoner audience research. This study has, by focusing on in-cell television, provided a unique perspective on the social relations within the prison setting. The analysis has identified that forms of governance (Rose 1999) and Layder's (2004) model of control (personal and interpersonal) provide a specific interpretation of the kinds of relationships prisoners have with television, between social agents and with the institution of the prison. There is a danger of viewing the role of television through a functionalist lens, and a risk of over-emphasising the qualities and direct impact of television in these ways: for example, the relationship between achieving personal control of emotion and watching television, and that television is a functional constant in the control of emotion. The problem of 'essentialism' as discussed by Morley (1997) is not easy to avoid and repeatedly throughout this book, the functionality of television for these audiences and this environment cannot be distinguishable from forms of control. More-over, uses and gratification models such as Lull's theory of the social uses of television (1990) have been validated and instrumental through-out the analysis. Oversimplifying this relationship, however, can also negate the diversity, richness, emotionality and complexity of every-day life in prison with television. This simplification can also lead to a fragmented view of social reality, resulting in a distancing between the personal (psychobiography and situated activity) and the impersonal (settings and contextual resources).

The dominant outcome of this research is that television is co-opted by prisoners in attempts to self-regulate and control their emotive responses to prison life. Neo-liberalist agendas have brought about governance of the social enterprise at a distance. This has culminated in prisoners taking care and control of themselves; hence viewing television enables prisoners, where possible, to achieve quasi-therapeutic control, as described by Rose (2000). Television in this particular setting directly assists prison services in caring for prisoners: television is a resource 'working' for the establishment and its people.

Television is adopted by prisoners as a quasi-therapeutic tool for assisting them with their pursuits to adapt and cope with incarceration. This is compounded and reinforced by staff, who perceive television in very similar ways to prisoners. Inadvertently, television is therefore contributing to the efforts to maintain control and assist in the delivery of care – television is put to work and thus contributes to what Crewe (2011) defines as a mechanism for 'soft-power', enabling services to govern at a distance. The introduction of 'in-cell' television has brought about additional opportunities for prisoners to interact with the social world which stretch beyond the direct setting of the prison. These changes to social relations are complex and contentious, where prisoners are, according to the testimonies that appear in this thesis, compelled to stay close to television inside their cells. Television has normalised the experience of the cell, in part replicating the comforting aspects of domestic life which result in legitimating the power structures which operate at a distance.

8.1.1   Domain theory: Inserting mediated action

The employment of Layder's (2004, 2006) theory of domains has enabled this study to explore the social uses of television in relation to prisoner emotion and governance. Layder's theory has provided the study with a renewed and important vocabulary to enable it to explore the emotionality of prisoner audiences and build upon the widely reported 'pains' of imprisonment (Sykes 1999). His theory of domains has been useful in demonstrating the kinds of 'psychological resilience' (2006:276) prisoners strive for (or fail at) by negotiating situated activity, the formal and informal mores of social settings and accessing and utilising a range of contextual resources, in this case via television. By employing Layder's view of social reality as four interrelated domains, a consideration of the linkages between and across the domains has been achieved using the concept of control. This is not to claim that control is always achievable; it is often precarious and sometimes lost. The psychobiographies of prisoners influence and are influenced by the setting and contextual resources that operate across the prison and the broader social enterprise. With television, prisoners are much more able to access a wider range of contextual resources in order to manage their emotionality. Accessing contextual resources via television can provide important respite from a range of harms that incarceration can bring about to prisoners' basic security system. Television is a 'gathering point' (Layder 2004:50) where prisoners can access settings (formal and informal) and contextual resources which are not solely restricted to the prison, they are stretched and extended (Moores 1995a). Social relations occur outside the setting in which they are placed, which is not fully extrapolated in Layder's theory. His model of situated activity also needs to acknowledge that social relations are also extended beyond face-to-face interaction. The value that prisoners place on avoiding situated activity and welcoming mediated activity outlines important features of control and his theory has allowed for interrogation of different levels and types of control:

- *personal* control or control of the self
- *situated* control within and across interaction in social settings
- *mediated* control within and across interaction with television

Most saliently, control from Layder's perspective on 'managing life situations' (2006) has amplified the dominant discourses in relation to the aims of incarceration: separation, deprivation, contamination and surveillance. In achieving personal control, prisoners demonstrate repeatedly that television is a significant medium in which they can accomplish self-regulation (Rose 1999). This includes the securing of content which enables opportunities for self-improvement, mechanisms to sustain their transition or reintegration back into society and maintaining social bonds, particularly with family. It is also pertinent that some prisoners exert or successfully accomplish 'self-control' with respect to their emotions. For others, these accomplishments of self-control either remain aspirational or are a source of anxiety, with some prisoner respondents reporting conflict and fear of their relationships with television. These responses are reinforced by the prison landscape encouraging and asserting emotional composure or 'feeling rules' (Hochschild 1983). Becoming a prisoner results in social agents learning which feelings are acceptable, which are reinforced by the formal and informal codes in the prison setting. Equally these rules of feelings also extend to watching television, where some respondents are sensitive to wider stigmas of watching too much television or programmes perceived as poor quality. Watching television is therefore conflicted, and for prisoner audiences this is accentuated by the process of incarceration. Staff are also significant in this enterprise, as they are instrumental in administering the aims of imprisonment. For example, using the IEP system, staff directly reward prisoners with communicative opportunities, such as in-cell television, visits, association, and use of the telephone to bring about control and order within the establishment. All stakeholders are therefore implicit in the project of 'rationalisation' (Garland 1991). The process of emotional composure is an underlying feature across all social domains and television assists in this endeavour, whether this is favourable or not.

This study has identified that staff adopted therapeutic roles by administering television as part of a package of care. Staff therefore used television to normalise the prison experience, as well as to standardise the treatment of prisoners. In essence, staff are instrumental in promoting self-governance in line with control, correction and regulation of social agents in their care (Rose 1999:188). Hence, prisoners and staff internalise the value and need for 'self-scrutiny' in order to fulfil mechanisms of rational control. Indeed, Garland's discussion of the rationalisation of punishment has facilitated a review of control, in particular the impact of the 'construction of sensibilities' to include perspectives from prisoners and staff (1991:213). In short, this study has provided important insights into what stakeholders do with emotion, and how rationalisation is actually practiced. Using the example of access to television in this setting, it was possible to address these concepts of governance and rationalisation from the elaboration of a range of concepts within domains, all of which are implicitly linked to techniques of control.

Alongside this, concepts of ontological security (Silverstone 1999a) and attachments to television have enabled the research to document more closely the nature of prisoners' relationships with television. Similar to the role of television in domestic households, in-cell television has rapidly become part of the prison's 'moral economy'. Here, television is highly valued by all stakeholders, and since it is framed under conditions of compliance and constraint, television has come to represent a reliable source of trust and security among prisoner audiences. Television's capacity to enable prisoners to 'reach' networks in a constrained environment further increases their reliance on television – it is dependable. Developing this, Moores's (1993a, 1995b) work has also been significant in providing helpful frameworks for considering mediated interaction in terms of reach, intimacy and the 'journeys' prisoners make with television. The study has enabled an understanding of the significance of emotionality and self-governance with respect to media use. These engagements with television are embodied since they are felt by the viewer. Locating viewing within this context of the prison has amplified and ratified these interpretations.

8.1.2 In-cell television at 'work'

Rose makes it clear that the advent of neo-liberalist practices and discourses can be traced in the shifting exercise of types of control and regulation.

> While there is an increasing monopolization of the legitimate use of force to constrain by the state machinery, there is a decreasing need to utilize such control as it becomes internalized within the structure of personality in the form of self-control... inducing self-scrutiny....
>
> (Rose 1999:225)

To control or to govern requires some intervention of the internal, personal and local features of mentality or psychobiography (Layder 2005). In-cell television is directly sought to assist in this enterprise. Prisoners' access to television, albeit conditional, allows them to access contextual resources, which can facilitate opportunities for self-regulation. Hence, television provides the prison with a resource which unwittingly distracts and occupies the prisoner in a number of ways. So much so that other opportunities have either been removed or declined in popularity. The removal of 'stage' newspapers (free daily newspapers for prisoners) from prisons in 2005 has been attributed by some commentators to the introduction of in-cell television (Erwin 2005). Before its introduction, policymakers and politicians made judgements of the value of in-cell television by anticipating its impact on calming or 'settling' of prisoners, assisting with loneliness and boredom and above all achieving control of the setting and its people. The placing of television in the cell, however, means that these 'benefits' have wider and diverse ramifications on prisoners and the prison and thus actually extend beyond the original aims of introducing in-cell television.

A major outcome in prisons has been the regulation of the 'emotional economy' (Rose 1999:225). As argued by Pratt (1999) and Garland (1991), the regulation of emotion has enabled and accompanied increased control of prisoner behaviour. The analysis in Chapters 6 and 7 argues that prisoners and staff are both encouraged and coerced into achieving emotional composure in line with prison's 'feeling rules' (Hochschild 1983; Crawley 2004). On the surface, emotions can become sanitised, constrained and even invisible. Sociological literature which reports in detail the 'pains' of imprisonment repeatedly fails in its efforts to record how these harms are felt or even managed by social agents. Thus these same influences of 'rationalisation' are also reflected in sociological discourses where social scientists are also complicit in the need to rein in emotive structures to everyday life. By including emotionality, a richer interpretation of everyday life can assist in the expansion of key debates in this field, for example pains of imprisonment and social uses of television. Chapter 6 forcefully argues that everyday life in prison is not rational; the interviews with prisoners were rich with description and expression of emotion. Television plays a crucial role in prisoners being able to actively manage their emotional lives by providing a platform to explore their emotionality. For some prisoners, television helps them to achieve a more rational or balanced experience; by countering frustration, tempering boredom and minimising fear. On other occasions, television can assist some prisoners to access and reach emotions like happiness and joy, but these outcomes are not always successfully achieved. Most prisoners want to achieve personal control and some staff want to help them achieve this.

Staff are tasked with maintaining good order and therefore their motivations to assist prisoners with personal control are not wholly altruistic. Television is actively used by staff to facilitate control, and as Rose suggests, objects such as television can help to 'direct all those emotional interests that would normally be directed towards their parents [the prison staff]' (1999:164). The theme of 'neo-paternalism' is increasing in relevance in current debates about staff-prisoner relationships (Crewe 2011). With the goal to make prisoners responsible for themselves, prisoners are routinely denied opportunities to take full control of their life situation. Television is therefore one of the few outlets for prisoners to direct and manage their emotionality with less direct contact from their keepers and thus not breach the culture's feelings rules. Television's place across social relations contributes to 'neo-paternalistic' agendas, where television is used to foster control either personal or interpersonal, with less direct intervention from staff.

If television did not deliver 'care-giving' qualities, prisoner audiences would be reluctant to use it (Silverstone 1999a). Given the deprivations prisoners endure, television has become an object which they regularly turn to in order to get through their daily lives. Being able to make object-relations or attachments is imperative in the exercise of governmentality (Rose 1999:168). This analysis highlighted significant levels of attachment to television, which were ratified by their intensity of use, their television routines and selection of programmes, that is, the diary entries showed that prisoners in this sample consumed over twice the national average of weekly television consumption. It was evident from the television diaries and the testimonies received from prisoners that television has become an integral and embedded feature of their everyday lives. The entrenched nature of television in this setting can point towards a 'dependent' relationship with television, whereby television becomes increasingly needed by prisoners (Vandebosch 2001). The uses and gratification tradition, informed by Lull (1990) and Jewkes (2002a), indicates that prisoners' motivations to consume television are adjusted to account for the conditions of incarceration. The impact of deprivation, separation and restricted autonomy results in television becoming increasingly trusted; thus this trust reinforces its presence in prisoners' coping repertoires. In particular, television can provide for some a route for emotion-focused coping (Harreveld et al. 2007). Incarceration demands, even for the most adjusted prison 'coper', constant attention to his 'need claims'. Consequently, prisoners are in relentless dialogue with their psychobiographical status (Layder 2004). Boredom is experienced and feared by all the prisoner respondents. Television can often provide reliable emotional respite or 'meaning' (Barbalet 1999:637). However, it does not always deliver the 'nourishment' they seek, which can then lead to frustration, fear, or anger. This raises important questions about the framing of television as 'care-giver', as suggested by Silverstone (1999a). There is a problem of 'care' in prison settings, which results in care being mostly self-directed and television is one functional mechanism to assist in this. It is observable that there is a dichotomous relationship between care and control. As Silverstone suggests, the experience of television is secured by attachments to it in the promise of achieving basic or ontological security. Instead, control, in both personal and interpersonal forms resembles care, most significantly care of the self. Tait (2011) has recently attempted to capture the nature and typologies of care among prison officers. The ambiguity of care is accentuated by the prevalence of control and this may result in care being difficult. Instead it is suggested that television is not necessarily 'care-giving', it is 'care-enabling' and that this is enabled by personal and interpersonal control.

The majority of prisoners become adept at using television in ways that benefit them and often seek to get the best they can from it, such as learning, sustaining citizenship and managing time. These also include guilty pleasures and resistant forms of engagement with television programmes, such as soaps, crime dramas and documentaries. Among the responses from prisoners, many directly attributed personal improvement to viewing television. For example, some were keen to learn about new topics and issues; some also felt that this supported their links with public and political life; in other instances viewing provided important temporal structures which helped them to psychologically manage their time. Some prisoners, however, struggle to trust what broadcasts offer, and are suspicious of its place in prison and the effects it has on themselves and other prisoners. For these prisoners, television is co-opted as a site for resistance and they seek to access contextual resources through television and other routes which help them to sustain their resistance, such as crime dramas and documentaries. Overall, television use can, in different ways, preserve their basic and ontological security; television is routinely co-opted as a 'protective device' (Silverstone 1999a; Layder 2004); as comforter, displacer or as a site for resistance.

Prisoners intensely stressed their need to achieve psychological and physical well-being and resist deterioration (Cohen and Taylor 1972). Television assists directly in personal control, with some prisoners more able to demonstrate self-knowledge than others (Rimke 2000:68). As we saw in Chapter 7, all prisoner respondents remarked on how they carefully selected programmes which they thought could help to get them through daily life. These features, correlate with what Rose describes as the proliferation 'psy' sciences across the social enterprise, have led to therapeutic forms of control. These are both interpersonal *and* personal, and thus the self becomes the 'object of knowledge'. Many prisoner respondents talked explicitly about how they had adopted techniques of self-scrutiny, where they review their ability to cope with prison and more broadly with their life situation. As Rose suggests, these techniques help to regulate and even modify behaviour in line with norms relating to responsibility and self-fulfilment (1998:182). Television, in this context, belongs to a range of 'civilising technologies' which aim to manage risk and dangerousness (Hannah-Moffat 1999). Such mechanisms represent forms of 'quasi-therapy' (Rose 1998:182), and television is not divorced from these representations, with staff and prisoners actively turning to television to achieve interpersonal and personal control. Television is adopted as 'techno-therapy', not necessarily to replace provision of limited and costly formal therapeutic interventions (such as cognitive behaviour therapy programmes or medical interventions), but to normalise the experience of prison and attempt to make the cell, especially, more palatable and attractive. According to Rose television and other media regularly communicate 'psychologized images of ourselves' (ibid.:182) which profess self-care and responsibility (Rose 1999:188).

Prisoners' exposure to these neo-hygienic discourses compound and reinforce the need for social agents to work on their psychobiographies or life situation. Television is therefore placed in the cell with unanticipated outcomes for therapeutic control, and inadvertently television is exploited to achieve personal and interpersonal control. This extends the remit originally intended by policymakers at the introduction of in-cell television to prison.

8.1.3   Extending social relations

Early prisoner research had observed changing dynamics of social relations since the introduction of mass communications, particularly broadcast media, to prison contexts (Jewkes 2002a; Gersch 2003; Bonini and Perrotta 2007). This research can corroborate these changes and offers significant additional insights relating to the impact of television on social relations in prison. The placing of television directly inside the prison cell has brought about a significant retreat from situated activity (i.e. face-to-face interaction) by prisoners. Earlier research by Jewkes (2002a) and Knight (2001) were unable to observe the medium-to-long-term impact of the introduction of in-cell television and thus did not offer an extended discussion of these dimensions. Rose (1999) says little about the role of situated activity or day-to-day relationships and the encounters individuals have with each other in relation to his thesis on governmentality.

Viewing television in the prison cell has not replaced situated activity but it has extended social relations; the kinds of interactions, relationships and encounters prisoners have with each other across media (Moores 2004). By including mediated activity in the process of interaction within the domains model, a richer appreciation of social relations can be included. The inclusion of this type of interaction using television-use diaries and interviews with male prisoners and staff has made it possible to trace the temporal and spatial movements of prisoners. Even when prisoners do not have to be in their cells, some prisoners preferred to stay behind their doors. This withdrawal has been facilitated, in part, by the presence of television inside the cell. With television, the prison cell can bring about 'at-homeness'; a closeness to features and routines that are familiar and private (Moores 2006:16). The benefits to the prisoner are wide reaching and viewing enables prisoners to personally manage their time and space, by offering additional temporal and spatial features which transcend their direct experiences. For example, prisoners could create their own temporal framework to mark and fill time, enable virtual movement away from the prison space and 'reach' encounters, particularly those that nourish their social ties and bring about mental stimulation (Moores 1995:330). These motivations were reported by prisoners because television provides opportunities to move out of prison time, such as the routine and their immediate spatial conditions. The prison cell is unattractive and can be claustrophobic, especially when most prisoners share a cell. Television viewing can therefore help prisoners to connect to other places that have personal significance: for example, watching programmes that they know their family are also watching. These kinds of features can also provide valuable meaning to the prison experience, by bringing opportunities to extend social relations beyond their immediate setting. The analysis, therefore, highlighted that these actions with television have emotive dimensions in preventing boredom and frustration relating to their inability to make their own choices and escape their incarceration. Television can offer important emotional respite with the benefits of providing purpose to social relations. But this is not always productive and fulfilling. In some instances, broadcasts can accentuate feelings of isolation, boredom and deprivation and thus some prisoners actively avoid some types of television. News programmes remind them of their loss of citizenship and of the punctuating nature of time, something to which prisoners are often acutely sensitive (Scannell 1996). Broadcast time provides material and shared experience of time, and that time is passing, yet prisoners feel that they are unable to move along with time in the same ways; thus their own subjective time or 'inside' time becomes challenged and disrupted. In some instances prisoners consider broadcast time to be counterproductive, as they feel 'frozen' in time (Zamble and Porporino 1988). Yet some programmes help to soothe these losses without necessarily amplifying isolation or deprivation; wildlife programmes and some documentaries were considered psychologically nourishing to counter psychological deterioration. These types of programme provide material to improve learning, increase knowledge and work towards self-improvement.

These factors can be aligned with some of Rose's thesis, in that social agents can achieve or at least strive for the 'good life' by the 'negotiation of a private life of personal relations rather than participation in a public life' (1999:220). Television enables a withdrawal from day-to-day situated encounters, thus securing privacy, and that engaging in public life becomes ancillary to the comfort of privacy. In the prison environment, privacy is in scarce supply, yet television permits, even in close proximity to others, a psychological and social disconnection from the prison and its people. This, for some, has the added benefit of working towards ontological security and providing a safer place to spend their time. As a consequence, these shifting patterns of social relations can assist in securing control of social agents. While prisoners are occupied with television in their cells, with some attempting to benefit from their viewing, certain guarantees of interpersonal control are protected: for example, minimising conflict and disorder, which is advantageous to managing secure prisons. When prisoners are occupied with television and have reduced contact with others, opportunities for conflict to manifest are reduced. This is not always effective and disruption and disorder still occur. Moreover, for those prisoners who struggle to cope, self-harm or attempt or commit suicide, television cannot always protect or direct them away from these vulnerabilities.

Prisoner and staff respondents in this study have repeatedly claimed that television has the capacity to provide therapeutic qualities. The early modern prison relied heavily on the capacity of faith to bring about control of the soul. The proliferation of 'psy' discourses in line with neo-liberalist agendas has therefore seen therapy as a replacement for these more spiritual doctrines. As Rose suggests, therapy 'is a method of learning how to endure the loneliness of a culture without faith' (ibid.:220). Television, for these male prisoners, is a resource they can reliably (under constraint) access to normalise their retreat into privacy and exercise 'reflexive scrutiny' in order to manage their own time and cope with prison deprivation; this permits prisons to manage prisoners at a distance. Techniques and technologies are adopted to control and subsequently care for prisoners. Television use in prison is distinguishable from the domestic sphere. Prisoners are more isolated than broader audiences and watching television can compensate for and also normalise the alienating experience of incarceration; these prisoner audiences adopt television in their lives to nourish and recompense these losses.

These viewing encounters are not, however, entirely neutral or without personal cost. Prisoners are not entirely at liberty to make active and independent viewing selections (Silverstone 1999a). A large proportion of prisoners are expected to share a cell, and at this research site it is the expected norm; unless risks have been identified through the CRSA. As wider ethnographic studies of family viewing have shown, dynamics of power based on age and gender feature as a significant factor in the ways in which family viewers are able to negotiate and experience their viewing. Using a case of cell-sharers, this research has offered insight into the modes of television consumption which takes into account cell-sharers' living arrangements. Few studies have provided insight into the social or even psychological impact of cell-sharing or the ways in which this space is experienced. This is methodologically challenging, as securing access to private space and private modes of consumption is a constant challenge for researchers. But as this research has shown, qualitative accounts from prisoners can illuminate the experience of the cell. For example, it has shown that television can assist and also hinder the ways in which cell-sharers relate to each other. The nature of television makes an individual's choices and modes of consumption public to their cell-mate and thus the visible and audible features of television make their private tastes public. As we saw in Chapter 7, their viewing choices do not always gain approval from fellow cell-sharers, and this can increase frustration and fear. However, even where tastes of television differ, some prisoners come to accept that compromise is necessary to secure their own 'basic security' (Layder 2004). Acts of resistance were commonplace amongst this sample of prisoners; in attempting to be 'entrepreneurs of themselves, shaping their own lives through the choices they make among the forms of life available to them' (Rose 1999:230), prisoners used television as much as they could to exercise choice and autonomy, even more so in conditions of claustrophobic incarceration.

One such example is that many of the prisoner respondents chose to watch crime and justice-related programmes (factual and fiction). Identification with their offender identities was significant, as Jewkes (2002a) and Vandebosch (2001) also found. Their role as a prisoner resulted in their motivation to use television to explore this identity and the context of their role across the social enterprise. In particular, their withdrawal from the public life of the prison in attempts to minimise harm, particularly from the threats of contamination by other prisoners and staff, did not mean their personal and direct experience of prison disappeared or was limited – in fact it was, for some prisoners, enhanced by television. Instead prisoners used television as a form of surveillance in order to keep abreast of crime and prison-related issues that they considered to be valuable to their current life situation. Viewing programmes that featured criminal-justice issues, especially those that featured prison, resulted in their ability to participate in the public life of the prison community, which extended beyond their immediate setting. Here some viewers actually 'reached' the prison through television. Television enabled access to contextual resources about prisons to enable them to ratify their own prisoner status. Moreover, the broadcast of these programmes, amongst other popular 'exciting' broadcasts like soaps and sports events, brought prisoners together as an audience. These shared events capture a sense of community, but this is limited. As Rose (2000:335) suggests, 'citizenship becomes conditional' and in the context of the prison setting this is dependent upon good and appropriate conduct.

The IEP system reasserts and disseminates a model of conduct which prisoners are expected to comply with, which is largely driven by incentives. To a degree, prisoners need to engage with the prison community to forge relations which in turn supply their basic needs. Other authors have suggested that technologies become entrenched in the 'moral economy' of households. Television is therefore employed to secure prisoner compliance, in much the same ways that parents employ television to manage their own children. Staff cannot directly control what prisoners watch, yet national prison policy has determined that that standard provision is now limited to pre-selected free-to-view television as a result of the digital switchover in 2011. Adult prisoners are free to select what they watch, taking account of cell-sharing, within the range of nine channels agreed by the Ministry of Justice. However the slow onset of digital technologies will see this evolve and change. These processes of paternalism clearly limit the ways in which prisoners can sustain an 'active' relationship with television. Access to television is never permanent or unconditional, as prisoners need to satisfy their keepers that their behaviour is acceptable in order to be rewarded by the services and opportunities entrenched in the IEP policy. Their access to television ratifies them as compliant prisoners. Given this conditional offer of television, the relief from boredom, frustration, isolation and sadness they may achieve from television viewing is at most temporary. While prisoners are occupied with television and focused on sustaining access to it, the prison is able to 'minimize the riskiness of the most risky' through mechanisms of surveillance, incapacitation and deprivation to achieve quasi-therapeutic control (Rose 1998:189). As Bosworth (2009:183) suggests, paternalism and care make deprivation and separation much 'more palatable', normal and less distasteful. Thus the benefits of placing television inside the cell have resulted in a system in which knowledge of the prisoner can be regulated and observed, without too much resistance from prisoners.

Most prisoners and staff are embroiled in a process of emotional composure or the process of 'rationalisation'. The benefits of this enable prison institutions to work towards a range of policy directives which align to neo-liberalist principles such as decency, safer custody and violence reduction, and thereby execute 'soft' rather than 'hard' power, which is a more palatable and less distasteful approach to imprisonment and punishment (Crewe 2011). Television allows prisoners to 'get on with' their time in prison without much direct intervention from prison staff. Prisoners become increasingly used to accessing the contextual resources television can offer, rather than seeking those made available through other mechanisms, such as use of libraries for information, seeking advice from staff and other prisoners. As Elias (2010:7) observed, these male prisoners had learnt how to 'exploit lifeless materials' to work on personal and interpersonal control. As rationalisation takes effect, social relations are directly modified to enable agents to deal with their emotionality away from public view: this withdrawal helps to disguise the abundance of emotions constantly evolving through one's life situation which in turn allows them to uphold rules of feeling. As a result there is an increasing danger that relations are no longer 'social', and as Garland (1991:187) suggests 'have become increasingly technical and professional', particularly in the landscape of punishment. The deployment of experts, systems and technologies to harness control are partly assisted by the prisoner watching television inside the cell. The television performs these tasks on behalf of the prison and often the prisoner is reasonably or reluctantly compliant with this process. The outcome is that many prisoners can 'conceal their emotional distress' (ibid.:242), which continues to qualify punishment discourses that are absent from the human-emotive experience. At the same time the harms of imprisonment also become hidden, until such time that distress and vulnerabilities appear as a complete loss of personal control. In-cell television has inadvertently perpetuated the disguise of emotions of everyday life, yet paradoxically it has also enabled prisoner viewers to manage access and stay in touch with emotions. Prisoners are encouraged to disregard their emotions and abandon them in favour of rationalist approaches. If emotions in this context are hidden, ethical and meaningful care of prisoners cannot be achieved. Punishment, in modern terms, now disguises valuable features of humanity. Television in prison assists the social enterprise in governance of souls, which would actually benefit from a system that is emotionally literate. In the meantime, television delivers care to large numbers of prisoner audiences at low cost. This form of care provides a mechanism for the prisoner to deal with themselves and social relations in the prison.

This research has contributed to a new understanding of the impact of in-cell television in the prison setting, achieved by capturing the voices of prisoners and prison staff and by analysis of television-use diaries by prisoners.

8.1.4 The digital landscape in prisons

This final section looks to the wider digital landscape and also to the evolving future of this in our prisons.[1] In doing it provides review of some of the developments that have taken place with respect to communication digital technologies and thus draws upon additional data collated from interviews with digital providers and key stakeholders from across the third sector relating to this topic. This goes some way to giving voice to 'security experts with the knowledge and skills to suggest how Internet use in prisons *could* be managed' (Jewkes 2013). Moreover, it reflects on the evolving nature of digital technologies and considers how prisons are managing these and the extent to which digital technologies are being embraced by prisons.

As described in Chapter 5 the introduction of in-cell television into prison was met with some anxiety and trepidation by both staff and prisoners. In similar ways, nervousness about introducing communication digital technologies into prisons is echoed once again and of course there are still routinely public outcries about prisoners having access to these kinds of devices and service. What sets communication digital technologies apart from television is that technologies like the internet, email and interactive television (iDTV) are interactive. What this fundamentally means in the context of the prison is that the prisoner can 'reach' the outside world and the world can also reach them. Despite these concerns for 'security', brought about by the permeability of digital technologies the prison services have been sensitive to the digital lag or gap brought about by such delays and stalling of introducing digital services across the sector. Overall provision is patchy across the estate in the UK and there is no definitive integrated ICT system like there is in countries like Belgium.

Overall, prisons are 'communication'-poor environments and therefore there is no surprise that prisons are places which enhance digital poverty and strengthen the digital divide (Champion and Edgar 2013). The Ministry of Justice's Digital Strategy (2012) sets out a national plan to boost and exploit digital technologies across the criminal justice sector in the UK. This is, however, limited and disjointed and makes no reference to the social uses of communication technologies with respect to prisoners and how they can use technologies to cope with everyday life. Others like Champion and Edgar (2013) have reviewed this enterprise and are collectively lobbying for a more synthesised approach to enable prisoners to learn and develop important digital skills for life. Other countries, however, like Belgium and the USA, have demonstrated a different approach to enabling provision. In Belgium the prison services have developed a coordinated approach to providing a whole package of digital capabilities and opportunities for prisoners. However, in the UK many prisons try to adapt current provision to communicate important messages to prisoners. Tony the Deputy Governor usefully captures the frustration of trying to use television like a computer.

Here we are restricted to a PowerPoint type presentation that just flicks over that would do my head in if I was waiting for one bit of information to come up, once they have got it flicks over and I have lost it and I have got to wait for another 100 pages for it to come back round. I don't think that side of it has been utilised to its full.

(Tony, Deputy Governor)

This review has identified that there are several challenges in relation to digital provision and access in prison. These include concerns about security, digital capability, cost to install and run the service, prisoners' rights and implications for staff workload. The evidence presented here outlines that despite obstacles 'technology can work well in a prison if it is managed' (digital industry interview 5). In addition there was a consensus across the interviews that digital technologies are 'a tool to look after themselves' (digital industry interview 5) – a theme iterated when prisoners and staff talk about the role of television with respect to self-care. Prison services readily highlight digital provision within pedagogic and resettlement discourses. Little is said about the social and emotional uses of such technology, as highlighted earlier in this book.

Email

In 2006 HMP Guys March was the first prison to introduce *emailaprisoner* in UK prisons. This was a service which allowed prisoners to receive an email from an approved sender instead of a letter. After a period of piloting, the provision was expanded across the prison estate in England, Wales and Scotland and now covers almost all prisons across this sector. Prisoners receive a printed version of the email that is downloaded by officers who examine incoming correspondence and censor the emails in the same way as they do letters (HMPS PSI06/2011). The advantage of having an email is there is no doubt that contraband will be concealed and since the message is printed there are no difficulties in deciphering hand-writing thus making it much easier for prison staff to manage. Moreover, costs are reduced for the sender and security concerns are mitigated much more efficiently for the prison. However, like in-cell television, its introduction and roll-out hasn't been seamless and a number of obstacles did slow down uptake by establishments. The next logical phase for *emailaprisoner* was to introduce a prisoner reply service and as a result a smaller number of prisons across the UK are using this system. Unlike conventional email where all transactions are done electronically the reply is undertaken by scanning in a handwritten letter from the prisoner and this reply is sent via a bar code that is attached to the originating letter. As a result the full email experience is not fulfilled. However the company that now owns *emailaprisoner*, Prison Technology Ltd, are supplying a number of prisons (predominantly private) with hardware such as kiosks and in-cell services linked to televisions and PC tablets which means prisoners are able to access a wider digital experience (see below), which includes sending approved and secure email replies. Prisons in Ireland are now also beginning to benefit from full email. A NOMS evaluation of this service in 2008 pointed towards revolving concerns about ICT security (NOMS 2008:4) but acknowledged how well its initial roll-out had been positively received. There has been no evaluation of the service since the reply functionality has been introduced in 2010.

In the USA, Trust Fund Limited Inmate Computer System (TRULINCS) has been providing an email service to all Bureau of Prisons (Federal State) prisons since 2007. This is a fee-based email service and prisoners are charged to send and read emails. Unlike the *emailaprisoner* the service in the USA is a complete electronic service where the prisoner accesses the email online. Emails are limited to 13,000 characters and they are not allowed to send or receive attachments. There is still a staff screening system. Access to the email system is not automatic. Prisoners have to have access approved and they have to provide a list of contacts which are then authorised. The prisoners' contacts are approached by the institution to check if they would like contact with the prisoner. As a result contacts can be barred from prisoners' lists of contacts.

One other example includes a coordinated initiative in Belgium called *PrisonCloud*. The prison service in Belgium has approached digital provision in a consolidated way and has ensured that digital services are networked together. Unlike the UK and US models, this approach means that *PrisonCloud* delivers a wide range of services from one single platform. This model is currently being developed in two mixed-sex adult prisons in Belgium and almost all of the prisoners there have access to basic services. A functioning and interactive email service is being developed to add to the cloud service. This will be managed under the same legislation as letters that prisoners receive and send. Prison staff can open letters to look for contraband but they are not, under statute, permitted to read the letters. As a result email is one of many services that prisoners can access with relative ease whilst in prison. This system is particularly useful for prisons to achieve control, surveillance and regulation with relative speed and accuracy and is described as being 'NATO certified' (digital industry interview 4). As a result, services can tailor access to different parts of the system according to the needs of the individual and the needs of the establishment.

Jewkes and Johnston (2009) highlight the constraining nature in which digital technologies are handled by prison services especially when prisoners are denied routine and regular access. They refer to these as 'modern' pains of incarceration which can be translated as feelings of loss. As Ron, a prisoner described,

> I have got a DAB radio in my cell, so I have got a bit more access to different radio stations...but we should be moving with the times...everything is going digital...so they have to make up their mind. If they don't it is like going back to the stone ages....
>
> (Ron, prisoner)

Thus Jewkes and Johnston, advocate access to 'computer-mediated communication' as part of 'normal rights of communication' (ibid.:135) and that limiting access is 'an example of technology being used as a strategy for social exclusion' (ibid.:137). As Champion and Edgar (2013) highlight, a disjointed service has amplified this digital poverty, particularly in relation to maintaining family ties. Belgium's *PrisonCloud* claimed to bring about a more 'individualised approach and is more humane' towards the treatment of prisoners (digital industry interview 4).

Internet: The World Wide Web

In the context of England and Wales most prisoners are denied the freedom to surf the Internet. This is regulated by PSO 9010 (HMP) which states that 'prisoners must not be allowed uncontrolled access'. As Champion and Edgar (2013) stress this may suggest that prisoners could have 'controlled' access but according to their review 'there is a blanket ban' (2013:5). This is because the UK model is not sufficiently coordinated. Their research found that there is controlled and restricted access in localised pockets of the prison sector, particularly in private prisons. This kind of access is only permitted to assist with prisoners' learning, resettlement plans and healthcare. Learning platforms like *Virtual Campus* (see section on e-learning) permit some prisoners to access restricted sites. However Champion and Edgar are critical of those kinds of provision as they fail to replicate the interactive features of using the Internet. They argue that there 'should be a clear national strategy and a Prison Service Order' (2013:3) that relates specifically to provision and access of digital technologies. Elsewhere, supporting access to online interaction has been challenging for services. For example *Virtual Campus* was intended to support and consolidate learning online, however many establishments have struggled to secure sufficient broadband speed and so services have been limited and disrupted (Turley and Webster 2010).

Concerns about prisoners' access to digital technologies have been best amplified by the media reporting how some prisoners have managed to gain unauthorised access to social networking sites. The development and speed in which mobile phones have become 'smart' and Internet ready has meant that access can no longer be strictly controlled by the prison. Prisoners' access to illicit mobile phones has seen the emergence of serving prisoners now developing their online profiles through sites like Twitter and Facebook, some of which have gained a large following. Other prisoners use third parties to set up websites on behalf of them. Charlie Bronson, a violent criminal who has famously spent long periods of time in segregation and secure hospitals, has his own website to promote his artwork (www.charliebronsonart.co.uk 2014). Moreover, in the USA there are a number of websites which supports a pen pal service. In these cases prisoners send their details (including a photo) to the provider. In these cases prisoners are using third parties to set up online identities. In the USA, it has been argued that denying prisoners access to these kinds of sites is an infringement of their rights to 'freedom of expression' (Holtz 2001). Provision in Belgium is geared towards providing a digital experience which is as close to the real world as possible and so 'normalization is huge without losing security is a priority' (digital industry interview 4).

Video conferencing

At present the use of video conferencing or virtual face-to-face contact across the UK is limited to court appearances and for meetings with their legal representatives (Champion and Edgar 2013). It was also noted that some prisons use this for foreign national prisoners to see their family and friends. There is a desire, as outlined by Champion and Edgar, for this to be extended to prison visits. Across parts of

Europe video conferencing is being developed to nurture family contact in Ireland and support for prisoners in the Netherlands (Europris 2013). These aspirations are a reality in the USA. Imprisonment can mean that many prisoners find themselves large distances away from their homes and family and therefore the logistics of family members travelling to encounter a face-to-face visit can be resource intensive, in terms of time and cost. Real time video conferencing was first introduced in the USA in the 1990s and a few years later this was extended for visiting arrangements. Phillips's (2012) review outlined that the cost of using this service varied across the prison estate. In some prisons they permitted two 25-minute video conferences at no cost to the prisoner or family member, whereas in other prisons there was a charge of $15 for a 30-minute conference. Reviews by Phillips (2012) and Doyle et al. (2011) outline that video conferencing helps assist more communication with families than if they just relied on face-to-face visits. Doyle et al. calculated that the return on investment for this service would be approximately six months since its introduction (2011:5). Virtual visits do enhance communicative opportunities by facilitating 'more meaningful relationships' between parents and their children (Welsh 2008:217). The *PrisonCloud* model in Belgium is also developing this facility within prisoners' cells, so instead of making a phone call they can make a video call. This is not intended to replace face-to-face visits but to enhance the quality of those interactions. Legislation in Belgium means that phone calls and also video calls cannot be recorded by the prison establishment for screening purposes as they are in the UK and USA.

E-learning and t-learning

Within the UK context there has been significant investment in the service *Virtual Campus*. This is a secure web-based learning environment managed by NOMS and the Department of Business Innovation and Skills and provides a through-the-gate capacity so learners can continue to use this facility during their resettlement back into the community. Like other initiatives, its roll-out was phased. The introduction of e-learning is considered a natural progression to assist education with prison settings and forms part of the 'normalising' of learning for prisoners (Turley and Webster 2010). Historically, supporting learning within the confines of prison, has meant prisoners have always had a limited educative experience, as Fong (2008) argues accessing materials, such as books and articles to support learning has been limited. As a result learning has always being at the mercy of the prison regime and security.

Compounding these issues, a significant proportion of prisoners have poor basic skills (Sparkes 1999) and learning disabilities (Loucks 2007); and thus come to education neither ready, supported nor motivated. Morgan and Kett (2003) found, for example, that many prisoners have a negative view of education, whilst the curriculum on offer within establishments may not be attractive (Hughes 2004). Prison teachers are also acutely sensitive to these challenges (Irwin 2008). The development of any new system to enhance educative experiences needed 'to ensure that prisoners themselves take ownership of their education' (House of Commons 2005:27). One interviewee remarked how some ICT lessons talked about the Internet and even showed videos of what it does and how it works, yet prison learners were denied the opportunity to try it out. This interviewee argued that 'it doesn't really take the prisoner as a responsible person' (digital industry interview 4). Thus the digital agendas purported by national strategies become limited.

With these issues in mind, an e-learning solution could have assisted in improving the prison education experience for both learners and teachers. The digital gateway is not without their constraints and capability still remains a problem. Birmingham City University conducted a review of the *Virtual Campus* network across the West Midlands in 2011 and found that most of the problems were considered organisational and technical (Birmingham City University 2011:6). For example, connectivity to the web was widely reported as problematic and some learners often found themselves frozen from their accounts due to log-in difficulties. Additionally, there is scepticism about its benefits for anything other than the most basic education (Pike and Adams 2012). There is no doubt that most research into this topic identifies that e-learning is an important tool for enriching learning. Here in the UK, Adams and Pike (2008) promote the concept that e-learning has transformative potential – enabling prisoners to reinvent themselves. Knight and Hine (2009) argue that e-learning and t-learning (learning using television rather than a computer) could boost the amount of time prisoners can learn in their own time, especially inside their cells. Belgium's *PrisonCloud* is one example where the transition from the classroom to the prison cell is seamless. Here learners can continue their learning in the cell with support from content that can be accessed via their in-cell television. In the USA, Gorgol and Sponsler (2011) advocate a move towards an IT mindset across prison services. Slow progress in this direction means that prison authorities are blocking educative progress of prisoners (Penal Affairs 2009). Europris's ICT Expert Group is one such initiative that is trying to support ICT capability across prisons in Europe. In Sweden they are developing a distance learning package for prisoners to ensure that they can access their teacher irrespective of location (Europris 2013). Here digital solutions are helping to overcome barriers to learning.

Digital kiosks, handheld devices and in-cell communications

Developments are always evolving but as outlined in this section the speed in which introducing digital technologies takes place is slow. There are a number of prisoners across the UK estate that are benefiting from electronic interactive services. Private prisons especially are moving at a much faster speed than state prisons. Digital industry experts explain that private prisons 'are more open' to installing these kinds of services as they want to ensure that their contracts offer a number of 'selling points' (digital industry interview 5). As a result kiosks, handheld devices, interactive televisions and in-cell telephones are becoming a feature of prison life for some prisoners. With this kind of hardware, establishments across the UK are beginning to pull together a number of services which resemble the likes of *PrisonCloud* currently available in Belgium. What this means for prison services is that 'having advancements in technology does open avenues for education bodies and health bodies too' (digital industry interview 5) and thus services can be directed and channelled to individual prisoners depending on their needs and profile. For example a prisoner who smokes can be exposed to advice about quitting through their digital accounts. As a result this technology can assist services to ensure prisoners are being targeted with the right support and interventions. Moreover, the availability of digital platforms outside the traditional learning environments such as classrooms means that availability and usage encourage wider use. Currently just over 20 prisons have implemented these devices and two prisons are currently trialling in-cell provision (one based in London and one based in the North of England). Belgium's *PrisonCloud* provides a valuable portal which also attracts use by prisoners. Here prisoners can access details about the prison regime and have their own personalised timetable, get judicial advice, access their own judicial files and send requests across the prison to make applications for appointments and apply for jobs both inside and (in preparation for release) outside prison. A move towards a paperless environment is claimed to enhance transparency and allow prisoners to take control and 'get their life back' (digital industry interview 4).

Kiosks operate using a touch screen function and prisoners access their accounts using pins or biometrics. From here prisoners can access and directly manage a wealth of detail including their own money, order their meals, email approved contacts, make appointments to see health-care, apply for prison jobs and access their learning portfolios. Currently these kiosks appear in landings and public spaces across the prison. One digital provider confirmed that there are '8 million transactions on kiosks in a year' (digital industry interview 5) and thus are well used by those prisoners who have access to them. This kind of usage data can help unlock knowledge about the behaviour of users in this environment. Instead of challenging security, industry experts believe it can tighten security controls. Surveillance data on the use of digital prisoner accounts can provide important data on aspects relating to safer custody such as bullying, data to support purposeful activity and spotting opportunities for family contact. Moreover, setting up electronic systems for prisoners' pay and finances, ordering their canteen and meals is claimed to assist with efficiency. In Northern Ireland digital technologies are assisting in prison work with developments to move towards a tablet platform to help officers keep up with paperwork. Moreover, surveillance systems like cell cameras and microphones activating when officers approach the cell are also being developed. There is some anxiety amongst staff that these kinds of systems could mean staffing levels are cut. Currently this is a reality and since 2010 many prisons have seen in some cases a 40% reduction in staffing (Howard League 2014). Fears of machines taking over the work and input of people are not new, but in the light of current sector reviews the introduction of digital services which reduce workloads can arouse resistance and suspicion, especially from staff.

In-cell digital provision is revolutionary and is a far cry from the old and decaying cells that once had no in-cell sanitation and in-cell electrics. However not all cells are digitally ready, but where they are these prisoners can enjoy digital access to their prison accounts via their in-cell television. This is supported not only by a remote control but also a keyboard. This kind of hardware is claimed to be tamper proof and there are no back-doors to gaining access to the Internet. Additional services include in-cell telephone, in which telephone calls can be made in the privacy of their own cells instead of the public prison landings. Calls are monitored by the establishment in exactly the same ways. In Belgium the in-cell provision is advancing and in the same ways the *PrisonCloud* platform is accessible via the television. Significant investment is being made to ensure cells are digitally capable. However, a move to more mobile devices like tablets means that services might not need to wire up cells as they are currently doing. In Belgium the service is exploring the use of 4G in place of Wi-Fi to ensure there is a secure bandwidth. Other discussions include some solution to develop a social networking site that provides prisoners with a sense of community, albeit located only within the prison setting. Other considerations include designing a system which is suitable for people with learning disabilities and also for different languages. *PrisonCloud* is developing a translator application to ensure all of its population can access information. Countries like Norway, Sweden and the Netherlands are keen to move towards the *PrisonCloud* model and investment in digital solutions is now an important development.

This in-cell provision will have some important effects, still yet to be observed and evaluated. However, this research into in-cell television can highlight some anticipated outcomes. In particular the withdrawal of prisoners from the public landscape of the prisoners will undoubtedly see a decline in situated activity and a rise in mediated activity. The attractiveness of these facilities means again the use of the cell becomes normalised and thus can assist with current government drives to reduce costs. Whilst prisoners are 'busy' in their cells, there is no need to invest in additional services to enhance treatment and infrastructure. However, the enriching benefits of prisoners taking control of their own lives, however small, can nourish the social and emotional responses to modern imprisonment.

Appendix 1: Prisoner Interview Respondent Portraits

Carlton was aged 32 years when I met him and of white and black Caribbean origin. He worked full-time in the prison as a cleaner and was on Enhanced IEP status when I met him. He was sentenced to two and half years and this was his first experience of prison. He shared a cell and they both had in-cell TV and Freeview and he owned a radio and CD player. He regularly bought phone credits and stamps for letters. Carlton completed a TV diary before I interviewed him. He was coming to the end of his sentence and he told me of his plans to get back into work and provide for his family. I had met Carlton several times through the work I do for the IMB. He enjoyed reggae and dancehall music and his current cell-mate introduced him to Spanish reggae called reggaeton, which he enjoyed. He also enjoyed sport and spin off sports programmes. Carlton avoided watching news.

Sunny was of Indian origin and was employed in the prison and was on Enhanced IEP status. He was sentenced to eight years and this was his first sentence. He shared a cell where they had and in-cell TV, Freeview, a DVD player and in-cell radio. Sunny bought phone credits and postage stamps. Sunny completed a TV diary after I interviewed him. He enjoyed news and documentaries.

Stuart was of white British origin, was employed and was on Enhanced IEP status. Stuart was sentenced to one year and he thinks this was approximately his seventh prison sentence. He shared a cell where they had TV with Freeview and a DVD player. Stuart enjoyed accessing radio via the Freeview facility. He didn't bother with phone credits as he didn't really have anybody to contact, instead he relied on buying stamps for letters and enjoyed swapping newspapers with other prisoners. He also enjoyed using the library and watching wildlife documentaries. He completed a TV diary after I interviewed him. Stuart was not looking forward to being transferred out to another prison, which he had been to before. I happened to visit this prison on IMB business and bumped into him on one of their landings, he looked down and explained he had too much unstructured time, he preferred the regime at the prison where I had first met him.

Malcolm was 63 years old and of white British origin. He was employed as a cleaner and was on Standard IEP status. He was sentenced to three years, but this was his second time in prison on the same sentence, he was released and then recalled; he said he was happier to see his sentence through in prison rather than in the community. I had met Malcolm several times through IMB business and he was curious about the diaries I was trying to get completed. He offered to fill one in. At the time of interview Malcolm lived on a vulnerable prisoner unit where prisoners are kept separate from mainstream prisoners in order to offer them protection. I interviewed him in his cell where I enjoyed several cups of tea and the opportunity to watch some day time television with him. Malcolm had completed the TV diary before the interview while he was housed in the healthcare section of the prison recovering from ill health. Malcolm was a sociable person and everyone on his unit knew him. He shared his cell and at the time of interview only had in-cell TV. He liked to access free newspapers and buy phone credits and stamps. Malcolm was the proud owner of a remote control and he showed me where he hid it. He insisted that they were contraband in the prison and he found that other prisoners would offer him tobacco for a loan of the remote for an evening.

Bill, 66 years old of white British origin, was employed and was on Enhanced IEP status. This was his first sentence and he was serving a 'long time'. Bill was experiencing ill health and lived permanently in the healthcare facility in the prison. He didn't share a cell with anybody else. Bill tried to complete the TV diary but his health meant that it proved too difficult. He was however happy to be interviewed. Bill benefitted from access to in-cell TV, Freeview, a DVD player and CD player. He bought lots of magazines and newspapers as well as phone credits and stamps. I interviewed Bill in his cell and spent several hours talking with him off the record. When I arrived another prisoner was with him watching television, he explained who I was and how much he was looking forward to the interview. Bill turned off the television. He missed his family and found prison a big shock. He explained how he became involved in Christian worship and believed this gave him strength. Bill described himself as a caring individual and was employed as a mentor to assist new prisoners with their induction to prison life. Bill was also keen to learn and wanted to find time to improve his spelling. He especially enjoyed history and political programmes and also enjoyed sport, particularly football.

Mick was 37 years old of white British origin. He was unemployed and was on Standard IEP status. Mick was in a single cell due to his 'high-risk' status. He was sentenced to six years and he estimated that this was his eighth prison sentence. Mick had in-cell TV, Freeview and a CD player and bought phone credits and postage stamps. He didn't complete a TV diary. Mick talked a lot about the kinds of crimes he had committed, mostly fraud and robbery and the neighbourhood in which he lived. He had experienced prison without in-cell televisions.

Pete was 43 years old and of white British origin. He was employed as a cleaner on the First Night Centre and was also a Listener. This meant he shared a cell with another Listener and they enjoyed a large cell, with nice furniture including a settee. The Listener cells were intended to be welcoming and this was where I interviewed him. He was on Enhanced IEP status and sentenced to life. This was his fourth time in prison, with three 'short' sentences and this 'long' sentence. He was due to be released on licence but wasn't looking forward to this, because he didn't know how he would cope with a bail hostel. I saw Pete a few months later returning to prison after a short time in the community. Pete's cell was well equipped with media, TV, DVD, CD and radio players. Due to the location, Freeview reception was not achievable. He bought phone credits and stamps to stay in contact with his family. Pete had experienced prison without in-cell television many years ago. He completed his diary before the interview.

Shaun was 22 years old and of white British origin. He was unemployed and was on Basic IEP status because he had received three 'strikes'. The last strike was for calling an officer a 'nob'. He shared a cell with another interviewee, Lee, who he knew from coming to jail and also from out in the community. Shaun was currently remanded in custody and was likely to receive a life sentence. This was his fourth time in prison, beginning his first prison term when he was 16 years old. Shaun was in care from a very young age and was in and out of foster homes and residential care homes most of his life. He devoured books and was a keen learner; on every occasion I bumped into him in the prison he was eager to share with me what he had read. On one occasion he showed me a psychology text book he was reading and we talked about the famous 'Stanford Prison Experiment'. Shaun completed a TV diary some time after our interview, at which point he had managed to secure Enhanced IEP status. At the time of interview Shaun and Lee didn't have an in-cell TV as a consequence of their bad behaviour. They had a stereo with a radio and Shaun liked to buy phone credits and stamps.

Lee was 22 years old and of white British origin. He was unemployed and was on Basic IEP status due to an incident at another prison involving barricading and flooding a cell. He also explained that he had problems controlling his temper. Lee was sentenced to two years and this was his 22nd sentence, first coming to prison at the age of 15. Lee shared a cell with Shaun and therefore had no in-cell television, but they did have a stereo. He bought phone credits and postage stamps. Lee explained he was trying to overcome drug addiction.

Leon was 30 years old and of mixed race. He was employed in the prison and also was a Listener. He was on Enhanced IEP status and currently in a single cell. He was sentenced to seven and a half years on IPP, so his release date was unknown. This was Leon's first time in prison and he was just at the beginning of his sentence. He was trying to appeal his sentence and we talked extensively off the record about his case. I was with Leon when the Freeview boxes were removed from the landing. He had a TV and DVD player. I interviewed Leon in his cell where he shared his family photographs and also certificates for various courses he attended in prison. He also showed me a hand-written exercise schedule he mounted on the wall, which he followed every day either at the prison's gym or in his cell. Leon missed his family and was keen to show them he was doing well and saw prison as an opportunity to enhance his skills and CV. Leon liked to buy music magazines, phone credits and stamps.

Alan was 28 years old of and white British origin and employed in the prison as a cleaner. He was on Standard IEP status and remanded in custody. This was his 12th time in prison. He shared a cell with Ryan, another interviewee. I interviewed Alan in his cell whilst the television was on and we watched a bit of *Jeremy Kyle* broadcast on ITV1. Alan wouldn't sit down for the interview and kept moving around while I sat at a small desk and table in his cell. Ryan kept coming in and then leaving during the interview. They both just had a TV in their cell. The interview was relatively short, probably because of interruptions and the distraction of the television.

Ryan's age was not disclosed and was white British and employed in the prison. He was on Standard IEP status and sentenced to 13 years in prison. This was his fifth time in prison. Ryan shared a cell with Alan and they just had a television. Ryan lay on his bed for the interview watching ITV1 and Alan left the cell, but nipped in occasionally. Ryan liked to buy phone credits and postage stamps. This was a short interview as bang-up time was approaching and I had to leave the cell before that time.

Simon was 42 years old and of black Caribbean origin. He was currently unemployed and on Standard IEP status. Simon was currently remanded but had served eight prison sentences. He explained that he had spent most of his adult life in prison, with only small periods of time in the community during this time. I was introduced to Simon via the officers on the landing. He was in prison when his mother died and explained he had only spent one birthday with his daughter, she was 19 years old when this occurred. It appeared that Simon had just had his cell searched and the officers were still removing items as I entered his cell. The television was on but Simon turned the sound down. Simon shared a cell and his cell-mate popped in from time to time. He had a TV but officially nothing else; he hinted he might have other things but wasn't prepared to divulge. Simon seemed irritable and continued to challenge the purpose of the interview and also the consent form and process. In justification of my credentials I offered to bring him one of my published articles on in-cell TV. When I returned to the prison some days later I slipped the article in a sealed envelope under his cell door, with a short note thanking him for his time. He was, however, very willing to tell me what he thought and agreed for me to record (hand written) the interview. Eventually the interview broke down and he began to interview me, towards the end his cell-mate and other prisoners filed into the cell and I began to feel uncomfortable. He became increasingly more vocal as an audience began to gather. Simon was obviously very well known and 'respected' by other prisoners as they continued to pay Simon lots of compliments. Officers came to the door and said I was needed elsewhere. I took this opportunity to leave.

Barry was 36 years old and of white British origin. He was unemployed but unusually was still on Enhanced status; he explained he was 'between' jobs for the moment. He was currently remanded for a violent crime which he suggested I looked up on the Internet when I got home. I refrained from doing this. He had previously been in prison for one sentence and during that sentence was recalled to prison to serve his sentence there rather than in the community. I interviewed Barry in his cell where he explained his television had broken; the sound had 'gone'. Soon into the interview an officer brought a replacement with a remote control. Barry shared a cell with Will, whom I also met and agreed to interview at another time. With their TV they also had a DVD player, in-cell radio and CD player. He liked to buy a newspaper at the weekend for the TV guide and also bought phone credits and postage stamps. He explained he spoke to his mother every day. Barry showed me lots of photos of his family and several girlfriends. He also talked about how he got on well with staff, and offered opinions about female staff in other prisons he had been to.

Will was 25 years old and of white British origin. He was on Enhanced IEP status and had been remanded for five months at the point I had met him. This was his third time in prison. He shared a cell with Barry where I met him. We arranged an interview for another day and he explained where he would be. He worked as a DVD orderly, booking out DVDs to other enhanced prisoners. I interviewed him in the office where he worked; there were no interruptions. Will had access to a TV, DVD player and CD player. He enjoyed bringing back several DVD movies each day from his job. Will liked to buy broadsheet newspapers and magazines and also phone credits and stamps. He was worried about his relationship with his partner and step-children as a result of his incarceration; he hinted that his crime was related to them. Will was also a big sports fan and enjoyed watching sport on television. At the time, an athletics championship was being broadcast as well as football and cricket. After getting their new television and remote control, Will explained they had two remote controls, which he considered to be a luxury.

Ned was of white and black Caribbean origin, employed and was currently on Enhanced IEP status. He was currently remanded and had been in prison for the last five months when I met him. This was his third time in prison and he had been to other prisons. Ned was in a single cell, not sharing with anybody; he had a TV and DVD player (Freeview had been removed) by the time I met him. Ned had been in prison before in-cell TVs were introduced. He really enjoyed wildlife documentaries and reading true life stories. He was also worried about his heavily pregnant partner. I interviewed Ned on the landing where he was working, in a small but private interview room. The conversation was tape recorded.

Ron was of Caribbean origin and was employed on the same landing as Ned. He was on Standard IEP status and coming to the end of a seven-year sentence. Throughout this time he had been in many jails and moved around the estate quite a lot. This was Ron's third time in prison and he was currently a single-cell prisoner. In his cell he had a TV and CD player with a radio. He liked to buy phone credits and postage stamps. He also liked to access newspapers to follow sport, but never bought these. He spoke at length about his love for sport. The interview was tape recorded.

Joshua's age was not disclosed and was of Caribbean origin and currently employed in the prison. He was on Enhanced IEP status and currently serving an 11-and-a-half-year sentence. This was his third time in prison. He only had a TV in his cell, which he did not currently share with anyone. He liked to buy magazines and newspapers as well as phone credits and stamps. I interviewed Joshua in an interview room that was located on the landing where he worked. The interview was tape recorded. He had experienced prison before the introduction of in-cell televisions. Joshua enjoyed watching news and documentaries including crime-related and wildlife programmes. Joshua spoke about his family a lot and how he maintained relationships with them. The interview was tape recorded.

Maalik was 28 years old and was of Indian origin. He was employed as a race relations representative and worked in the staff tea room and was also a Listener. He was on Enhanced IEP status and shared a cell with another Listener. Maalik was on remand and awaiting sentence; this was his first time in prison. I was introduced to Maalik through the Race Relations Officer, Fran, whom I also interviewed. Maalik and I enjoyed a hot drink in Fran's office whilst the interview took place. Fran was not in the room and we had no interruptions. Maalik liked to keep himself busy and enjoyed the benefits of in-cell television and also watching Indian films on the DVD player. Sometime after our interview I met Maalik again in the prison and he told me he had set up a prison magazine with support from staff. He told me that this was as a result of the interview he had with me, and he explained that the topic of media in prison had ignited this idea. Maalik invited me to write a small contribution about my research for their publication. The interview was tape recorded.

Appendix 2: Staff Interview Sample

Interviewee	Length of service	Current position	Duties	Gender	Ethnicity
Paul	22 years	Residential PO	Manage SMU, VPU, L3 & L4 Staff 4 SO and 30 Staff	Male	White British
Claire	14 years	The Governor	Leadership and management of local prison, accountable to Dom	Female	White British
Tony	30 years	Deputy Governor	Operational running of jail, security, residential, safer custody	Male	White British
Fran	20 years	REO and landing officer	Promoting and implementing race equality	Female	White Irish
Ann	3.5 years	Co-ordinating Chaplain	Pastoral care of prisoners and staff	Female	White British
Steve	2 years	Residential officer, landing	Constant contact with prisoners, personal officer, well-being of prisoners	Male	White British
Tim	13 years	Segregation and landing officer	Residential care of prisoners, discipline	Male	White British
Brian	17 years	Senior officer	Orderly officer	Male	White British

Appendix 3: Comparison of Average Television Viewing for Prison Site and UK National Average (BARB)

Total hours of TV	Prison site	Total hours of TV	UK national average
61.39	Overall average per week (Mon–Sun)	26.63	Average weekly viewing in UK households
8.77	Overall average per week day (Mon–Fri)	3.8	Average per day viewing in UK households
9.1	Overall average per day at weekends (Sat & Sun)		
18.22	Overall average per weekend (Sat & Sun)		

Source: BARB 2008.

Appendix 4: Example of Number of Hours of Television Watched Each Day for Diarist C

Diarist C					Diary day									
	1	2	3	4	5	6	7	8	9	10	11	12	13	14
Hours of TV per day	7	6	7	0	2	0	1	2	2	2	2	2	0	1
Location	Research prison site- local category B			Transferred out	Category B closed training prison									

Glossary

Association: a designated period and space for prisoners to associate with other prisoners at leisure, access showers and use the telephone

Bang-up *also* **lock-up:** prisoners locked in their cells

Basic: lowest tier of privileges for prisoners in line with the Incentives and Earned Privilege system

Cabbaged: slang term meaning to become braindead and to psychologically deteriorate

Cell-mate: the person with whom a prisoner shares his/her cell

CSRA: Cell Sharing Risk Assessment (PSO 2750)

Double cell: a cell a prisoner shares with another prisoner

Enhanced: highest tier of privileges for prisoners in line with the Incentives and Earned Privilege system

Freeview: the generic term for the free-to-view digital television channels available through digital receivers or digitally ready television sets in the UK

IEP: Incentives and Earned Privilege system based on the PSI 11/2011

Lock-up *also* **bang-up:** prisoners locked in their cells

PSO: Prison Service Order, instructions and guidance for prison staff

Purposeful Activity: a key performance target to engage prisoners in activity such as work, training, education or exercise

Safer Custody: to assess and manage vulnerable prisoners, especially those at risk of self-harm and suicide (PSO 2700)

Screw: slang term for prison officer

Single cell: a cell a prisoner does not share with another prisoner. This is usually based on a risk assessment (*Cell Sharing Risk Assessment- CSRA* PSO 2750). This contributes to the Violence Reduction strategy.

Slash up: slang term for self-harm or attack using a knife or sharp instrument

Standard: middle tier of privileges for prisoners in line with the Incentives and Earned Privilege system

Time-shifting: a term to describe how broadcast media, usually television, can be stored or recorded to be consumed outside broadcast time. For example, using a video recorder to record a programme that can be watched at another time

Unlock: prisoners unlocked from their cells to engage in work, training, education, visits, treatments and association

Violence Reduction: a strategy to reduce violence in prisons across England and Wales. The PSO 2750 states: 'To reduce violence, promote a safe and healthy prison environment and foster a culture of non-violence among all staff and prisoners.'

Notes

1 Research Foundations

1. Through conversation, interviews and letters received from prisoners in 2000 and 2010.
2. From May 2007 the Ministry of Justice was established, taking responsibility for justice. Previously, the Home Office led in this area. Throughout this book I will refer to this government organisation as the Ministry of Justice. However, where sources and references come from the Home Office, this term will be adopted.
3. Directly influenced by Willis's (1977) ethnography of school leavers' transition from school to the workplace.
4. Access to prisons proved difficult. I decided to approach the governor at the local, adult male prison establishment where I volunteer as a member of the Independent Monitoring Board and access was permitted. I was 'embedded' (Harvey 2008:489) in the culture of this particular establishment as a result of making regular visits to monitor the prison.[1] Access to the site was also facilitated by the fact that I have permission to draw keys and I was therefore not a burden to staff. This meant I could enter freely without escort or supervision. A 'come and go as you like' agreement was made after I outlined the research to prison governors and principal staff. I was already security cleared and up to date with security protocol. As a member of the IMB, visiting and behaving responsibly in prison was familiar practice. I continued to be a member of the IMB as well as carrying out the fieldwork. Strategies to manage 'distance' were adopted.
5. This deviates from Laing's discussion on the contrasts between 'ontologically secure' and 'ontologically insecure' people in his text *The Divided Self* (1990).

2 Perspectives on Prison

1. In Britain the last public execution was in 1868 and the last 'private' execution took place in 1964, followed by the abolition of hanging in 1965. Populist perceptions largely disseminated through the press remarked on the distasteful nature of executions. Most saliently, miscarriages of justice had occurred, and famously Derek Bentley, who was hanged in 1953, signalled a campaign to end punishment of this kind.
2. The 'growing welfare expectations' (Pratt 1999:283) saw changes and improvements to the quality and quantity of prison food for example and in the same ways prison had 'a duty to provide diet which preserves health' (ibid.:283). These improvements did not however marry directly to welfarism experienced in mainstream society, 'reductions in suffering occurred steadily and in a piecemeal manner rather than dramatically' (ibid.:283). Within

the prison itself the employment of separation can also be traced by the emergence of communal eating (ibid.:283) and in the 1950s evidence of the use of plates and cutlery first began to appear (ibid.:284).

3. For instance the introduction of the contemporary category system in England and Wales by Mountbatten in 1966 could also illustrate this.

4. Despite the abolishment of slopping out it was reported in 2011 that 2000 prison cells across England and Wales still do not have in-cell sanitation (*Guardian* 2011a).

5. Bentham's philosophy is underpinned by utilitarian principles, achieving good and morality for the greatest number of people. This can only be achieved, according to Bentham's philosophy if the observed know they are being observed. The Panopticon was never realised in Britain.

6. See 'Caring for the Suicidal in Custody', 1994.

7. Some prisons in England and Wales are owned privately, currently this stands at 14 prisons, while 123 prisons belong to the public sector. Prisons were privatised from the early 1990s under the Conservative government. The government still sets these prisons performance targets and if they fail to meet these, financial penalties are imposed.

8. For example, Charles Dickens regularly documented his prison visits in newspapers and periodicals and made reference to this in much of his literature (see Wilson 2002). Moreover, prison reformers like John Howard and Elizabeth Fry still capture the imagination of the public today.

9. Current and even daily prison population figures are reproduced by the Prison Service in the UK and are accessible on their website, along with news bulletins, policy documents and prison rules and orders. Other initiatives like Her Majesty's Prison Inspectorate, Ministry of Justice, Prisons and Probation Ombudsman, Independent Monitoring Board all produce 'public' documents that report on the social aspects of prison life.

10. Historical public records tracing the introduction and related policy for mass communications are difficult to access. The 30-year rule for public records results in early and key policy documents still being locked into this clause and difficult to access. Significant changes to broadcast media occurred during the late 1970s and 1980s in England and Wales and therefore any policies are unavailable for public consumption. No historical record of mass communication is available.

11. Prisoners enter prison as a standard prisoner, now called entry level. This is reviewed to ensure they can maintain a standard status.

4 Audiences of Television

1. As a result, key debates which appear across media studies are excluded from this section i.e. 'effects' research.

5 Making Room for In-Cell Television: Access, Availability and Points of Use

1. Personal contact was made with the Offender Safety, Rights & Responsibilities Group at the Ministry of Justice who lead and coordinate in-cell TV as part of their remit.

2. Despite political rhetoric during 1998 that this would be 'closely monitored' (Hansard 1998) no formal evaluations commissioned by the Home Office or Ministry of Justice of the in-cell television programme have taken place to date. However a small evaluation at HMP Stocken by McClymont (1993) began to suggest that in-cell television might impact on prisoners' willingness to come out of their cells, limit staff and prisoner relationships and impact on regimes such as increased lock-up periods.

3. Personal correspondence with the MoJ (2011) confirms that there are restrictions on the provision of digital technologies including Freeview and satellite TV. The digital switchover has enabled service through in-cell TV revenue has updated prisons to receive nine Freeview channels. This project was due to be completed by the end of 2011 to comply with national switchover. Prisons Minister Maria Eagle in 2009 announced that satellite TV was available in-cell to a small raft of contracted prisons, which permitted approximately 4070 prisoners to access this additional facility in line with IEP targets. At present the MoJ confirm this provision is no longer permitted.

4. All the prisoners I spoke to have an in-cell television, except Shaun and Lee who were on the 'basic' regime as a result of poor conduct, a breach of prison rules and the contract.

5. Deviations from this are very rare. If this does change it is usually associated with general alarms as a result of incidents or staffing detail. This often means prisoners are locked-up whilst situations are resolved. Unlock periods are never extended

6. Not all prisoners are entitled to association every day and this is organised according to their IEP status. Basic prisoners will have one to two association sessions, standard prisoners will have three and enhanced prisoners can have five to six association sessions per week.

7. Prisoners will only be unlocked if they have a planned visit or are entitled to association for this period at weekends. If this is not applicable they are expected to be locked behind their doors.

8. Freeview and DVD players are predominantly an incentive, at no extra cost for enhanced prisoners only.

9. At the time of data collection proportions of status are typically 60% standard, 30% enhanced and 10% were basic. As a result the findings here may actually underestimate the amount of time spent viewing television.

10. During this year seasonal variations occurred with the range of viewing hours varying from 22.5 hours (lowest) to 30.72 (highest) (BARB 2011). Demographic variations across the UK are also evident with older people (65+) beginning to watch more broadcast television than ever before and younger people (16–24) are watching less broadcast television as well as listening to less radio. All prisoners in this sample are classed as adults at 21 years or older. Younger people are however consuming more diverse interactive media particularly non-linear content like downloads and using on-demand facilities (OFCOM 2010) and other media hardware like handheld devices and computers. However, these are not permitted in prison.

11. Freeview was made available to enhanced prisoners when I started the fieldwork. However this was withdrawn from the prison during the time I was carrying out the study. In 2010 the prison switched to digital and some

Freeview channels were made available. I had completed data collection by this time.

12. There is some discrepancy here with some staff describing to me that material was often recorded using a VCR prior to the provision of in-cell television and played during evening association periods in the communal television areas.

13. There is a limited regime in this part of the prison site and as a result prisoners are compensated by the provision of DVD players and Freeview in some instances.

14. Training prisons are different from local prisons and are generally intended to serve medium to long-term prisoners and offer a variety of rehabilitative programmes. Time out of cells in training prisons is generally longer than in local closed prisons.

15. There were no diary entries made after 1am in this sample, although some interviewees talked about staying up to watch TV late into the night, with some preferring to do this and sleep in the day as a mechanism for avoiding the prison routine and its people. All but one of the diarists were employed and were generally expected to work, which meant that late night viewing was not necessarily a feasible option. Achieving enhanced status requires prisoners to work during the day and standard prisoners are encouraged to work. The unemployed prisoners consistently watched television later than most other respondents, but only usually by one hour per day. The other prisoners were potentially moderating late viewing of television in order to incorporate sleep and rest into their routines.

6   Personal Control: Television, Emotion and Prison Life

1. This chapter also appears as a published article: Knight, V. (2015) Television, Emotion and Prison Life: Achieving Personal Control, *Participations*, 12:1.

2. Freeview was therefore withdrawn but 18 months later the prison switched to digital reception and this meant that a selection of Freeview channels were reintroduced as 'standard' provision for to all television sets in the prison. This featured as part of the MoJ digital regeneration programme (2011).

3. Parts of this section appear in a published article: Knight, V. (2014) A Modus Vivendi – In-cell Television, Social Relations, Emotion and Safer Custody, *Prison Service Journal*, November 2014, No. 215, pp. 19–23.

4. Barry was interviewed first and whilst I was in his cell Will came in. We arranged another time to meet as he wanted to be interviewed too. Will left the cell to allow Barry to continue with the interview in private.

5. My experiences in the field were diverse, and I can recall many instances of laughter within and outside the interviews with prisoners and also staff. I routinely observed 'banter' within the prison and often found that this lifted the mood. On other occasions the atmosphere could be austere and tense.

6. With variation from one to 12 hours per day across the 14-day period. This is over three hours less than the overall average of the diary sample at 8.77 hours per day.

7   Situated and Mediated Control: Managing Souls with In-Cell Television

1. Purposeful activity refers to PSO 7101 which can include up to 27 different activities e.g. education, work opportunities, tackling substance misuse, maintaining family ties, Offending Behaviour Programmes and other resettlement activities.
2. Whannel's (1995:187) definition of game or quiz shows relates to this idea with demands on knowledge, winning prizes, playing games and the featuring of ordinary people in these programmes.
3. As a visitor I was aware I was in constant view of both prisoners and staff, even when I interviewed prisoners in their cells I was completely aware that this space was not wholly private and interruptions occurred all of the time from staff and prisoners. Surveillance is not necessarily constant but it is tacit. Prison cells are therefore not excluded from this and I witnessed on occasion the liberated access staff had to prison cells.
4. In fact prisoners continue to campaign against the costs of goods and services they are permitted to access, for example the rate of telephone calls (BBC 2008). Also prisoners in England and Wales do not have the right to vote, although the European Court of Human Rights have indicated prisoners have a right to vote, politicians to date have voted against this idea and are still deliberating about how to satisfy this court ruling (BBC 2011).
5. Prison Rule 45 is intended to segregate prisoners from mainstream populations in order to protect them and others in the prison establishment. As a result these prisoners are prevented from associating with mainstream populations and are often housed in separate and discrete units, wings or landings. The prisoner or the prison may request removal from association for their protection.
6. Constant watches are when a prisoner is observed continually by a member of staff. This is a culmination of safer custody procedures including ACCT where senior managers and health professionals agree that this prisoner will benefit from constant observation to ensure that the prisoner does not harm themselves.
7. According to PSI11/2011 nine free-to-view channels are available: BBC1, BBC2, ITV1, Channel 4, Channel 5, Sky News Sports (E4 in female prisons), ITV, VIVA and Film 4. Subscription channels are not permitted in public sector prisons (HMPS 2011:16).

8   Concluding Discussion

1. Knight, V. (2015) Some Observations on the Digital Landscape of Prisons Today, *Prison Service Journal*, July 2015 No. 220.

References

Adams, K. (1992) Adjusting to Prison Life, *Crime and Justice*, 16, pp. 275–359.

Adams, A., & Pike, A. (2008). Evaluating empowerment and control of HE e-learning in a secure environment.

Alasuutari, P. (1999) *Rethinking the Media Audience*. London, Sage.

All-Party Parliamentary Group on Penal Affairs (2009) Prisoners' Education: Are We Doing Enough? http://www.open.ac.uk/cetl-workspace/cetlcontent/documents/4a8293cab678c.pdf

Anderson, B. (2004) Time-stilled Space-slowed: How Boredom Matters, *Geoform*, 35:6, pp. 739–754.

Anderson, D.R., Collins, P.A., Schmitt, K.L. and Smith Jacobvitz, R. (1996) Stressful Life Events and Television Viewing, *Communication Research*, 23:3, pp. 243–260.

Ang, I. (1991) *Desperately Seeking the Audience*. London, Routledge.

Ang, I. (1993) *Watching Dallas: Soap Opera and the Melodramatic Imagination*. London, Routledge.

Ang, I. and Hermes, J. (1991) Gender and/in Media Consumption, in Curran, J. and Gurevitch, M. (eds.) *Mass Media and Society*. London, Edward Arnold.

Atkin, C., Greenberg, B. Korzenny, F. and McDermott, S. (1979) Selective Exposure to Televised Violence, *Journal of Broadcasting*, 23:1, pp. 5–13.

Bandura, A. and Huston, A.C. (1961) Identification as a Process of Incidental Learning, *Journal of Abnormal and Social Psychology*, 63:2, pp. 311–318.

Barbalet, J.M. (1999) Boredom and Social Meaning, *British Journal of Sociology*, 50:4, pp. 631–649.

Barbalet, J.M. (2004) Consciousness, emotions, and science, *Advances in Group Processes*, 21, 245–272.

Baumeister, R.F. (1991) *Escaping the Self: Alcoholism, Spirituality, Masochism, and Other Flights from the Burden of Selfhood*. New York, Basic Books.

BBC News (2008) Row Over Prison Phone, Calls Costs, 23/06/08, http://news.bbc.co.uk/1/hi/7470051.stm accessed 19/10/11.

BBC News (2011) Jack Straw and David Davis Secure Prison Vote Debate, 18/01/11 http://www.bbc.co.uk/news/uk-politics-12214988 accessed 19/10/11.

BBC News (2014) Grayling's Letter to Laureate in Full 29.3.14 http://www.bbc.co.uk/news/uk-26806541 accessed 23/9/15.

Becker, G. (1997) *Disrupted Lives*. Berkeley, University of California Press.

Bennett, J. (2005) Undermining the Simplicities: The Films of Rex Bloomstein, *Captured by the Media*, pp. 122–136.

Berker, T., Hartmann, M., & Punie, Y. (2005). Domestication of media and technology. London McGraw-Hill Education (UK).

Berker, T., Hartmann, M., Punie, Y. and Ward, K. (eds.) (2006) *Domestication of Media and Technology*. Maidenhead, Open University Press.

Bird, S.E. (2003) *The Audience in Everyday Life: Living in a Media World*. New York, Routledge.

Birmingham City University (2011) Working with the Prison Virtual Campus – End of Project Report p6, http://archive.excellencegateway.org.uk/page.aspx?o= accessed 16/02/15.

Blumler, H. (1969) *Symbolic Interactionism: Perspectives and Methods*. New Jersey, Prentice Hall.

Blumler, J.G. (1979) The Role of Theory in Uses and Gratifications Studies. *Communication Research*, 6:1, pp. 9–36.

Blumler, J.G. and Katz, E. (eds.) (1974) *The Uses of Mass Communications: Current Perspectives on Gratifications Research*. London, Sage.

Bonini, T. and Perrotta, M. (2007) On and Off the Air: Radio Listening Experiences in the San Vittore Prison, *Media, Culture and Society*, 29:2, pp. 179–193.

Bosworth, M. (2007) Creating the Responsible Prisoner, *Punishment and Society*, 9:1, pp. 67–85.

Bosworth, M. (2009) Governing the Responsible Prisoner: A Comparative Analysis, in Sørensen, E. and Triantafillou, P. (eds.) *The Politics of Self-Governance*. Farnham, Ashgate.

Bosworth, M., Campbell, D., Demby, B., Ferranti, S.M. and Santos, M. (2005) Doing Prison Research: Views From Inside, *Qualitative Inquiry*, 11:2, pp. 249–264.

Bottoms, A.E. (1990) The aims of imprisonment, in Garland, D. (ed.) *Justice, Guilt and Forgiveness in the Penal System*. Occasional Paper No. 18, Edinburgh, Edinburgh University Press.

Bottoms, A.E. (1995) The Philosophy and Politics of Punishment and Sentencing, in Clarkson, C. and Morgan, R. (eds.) *The Politics of Sentencing Reform*. Oxford, Clarendon Press.

Bourdieu, P. (1977) *Outline of a Theory of Practice*. Cambridge, Cambridge University Press.

Boyanowsky, E.O. (1977) Film Preferences Under Conditions of Threat: Whetting the Appetite for Violence, Information or Excitement?, *Communication Research*, 4:2, pp. 133–144.

Broadcast Audience Research Board (2008) Average Weekly Viewing http://www.barb.co.uk/trendspotting/data/average-weekly-viewing?data_series%5B%5D=2008&button_submit=View+graph accessed 26/11/15.

Broadcasters' Audience Research Board (BARB) (2011) Viewing Figures, http://www.barb.co.uk/report/weekly-viewing?_s=4 accessed 19/10/11.

Brunsdon, C. (1981) Crossroads: Notes of a Soap-Opera, *Screen*, 22:4, pp. 32–37.

Brunsdon, C. (1986) Women Watching Television, *MedieKultur: Journal of Media and Communication Research*, http://ojs.statsbiblioteket.dk/index.php/mediekultur/article/view/737 accessed 12/09/11.

Bryant, J. and Zillman, D. (1984) Using Television to Alleviate Boredom and Stress: Selective Exposure as a Function of Induced Excitational States, *Journal of Broadcasting*, 28:1, pp. 1–20.

Caplan, R.D., Cobb, S., French, R., van Harrison, R. and Pinneau, S.R. (1975) *Job Demands and Worker Health*. Washington, DC, Department of Health Education and Welfare, http://babel.hathitrust.org/cgi/pt?id=mdp.39015071884410;view=1up;seq=3 accessed 21/10/15.

Carlen, P. (2002) Carceral Clawback: The Case of Women's Imprisonment in Canada, *Punishment Society*, 4:1, pp. 115–121.

Castel, R. (1991) From Dangerousness to Risk, in Burchell, G., Gordon, C. and Miller, P. (eds.) *The Foucault Effect: Studies in Governmentality*. Chicago, University of Chicago Press.

Champion, N. and Edgar, K. (2013) Through the Gateway: How Computers Transform Rehabilitation London, Prison Reform Trust, http://www.prisonreformtrust.org.uk/Portals/0/Documents/Through%20the%20gateway.pdf accessed 16/02/15.

Clemmer, D. (1958) *The Prison Community*. New York, Rinehart.

Cohen, S. (2007) *Visions of Control*. Cambridge, Polity Press.

Cohen, S. and Taylor, L. (1972) *Psychological Survival: The Experience of Long-Term Imprisonment*. Middlesex, Pelican.

Cohen, S. and Taylor, L. (1975) *Escape Attempts*. London, Allen Lane.

Cope, N. (2003) 'It's No Time or High Time': Young Offenders' Experience of Time and Drug Use in Prison, *The Howard Journal*, 42:2, pp. 158–175.

Corneo, G. (2005) Work and Television, *European Journal of Political Economy*, 21: 1, pp. 99–113.

Corti, L. (1993) *Using Diaries in Social Research Social Research Update 2*. Guildford, University of Surrey.

Couldry, N. and McCarthy, A. (eds.) *MediaSpace: Place, Scale and Culture in a Media Age*. London, Routledge.

Crawley, E. (2004) *Doing Prison Work: The Public and Private Lives of Prison Officers*. Cullompton, Willan.

Crewe, B. (2005) Codes and Conventions: The Terms and Conditions of Contemporary Inmate Values, in Liebling, A. and Maruna, S. (eds.) *The Effects of Imprisonment*. Cullompton, Willan.

Crewe, B. (2006) Prison Drug Dealing and the Ethnographic Lens, *The Howard Journal*, 45:4, pp. 347–368.

Crewe, B. (2009) *The Prisoner Society: Power, Adaptation and Social Life in an English Prison*. Oxford, Oxford University Press.

Crewe, B. (2011) Soft Power in Prison: Implications for Staff-Prisoner Relationships, Liberty and Legitimacy, *European Journal of Criminology*, 8:6, pp. 455–468.

Crewe, B., Warr, J., Bennett, P. and Smith, A. (2013) The Emotional Geography of Prison Life, *Theoretical Criminology*, 18:1, pp. 56–74.

Csikszentmihalyi, M. (1999) If We Are So Rich, Why Aren't We Happy?, *American Psychologist*, 54:10, pp. 821–827.

de Viggiani, N. (2007) Unhealthy Prisons: Exploring Structural Determinants of Prison Health, *Sociology of Health and Illness*, 29:1, pp. 115–135.

DeLisi, M., Berg, M.T. and Hochstetler, A. (2004) Gang Members, Career Criminals and Prison Violence: Further Specification of the Importation Model of Inmate Behavior. *Criminal Justice Studies*, 17:4, pp. 369–383.

Dhami, M.K., Ayton, P. and Loewenstein, G. (2007) Adaptation to Imprisonment: Indigenous or Imported, *Criminal Justice and Behavior*, 34:8, pp. 1085–1100.

Dilulio, J.J. (1987) *Governing Prisons*. New York, Free Press.

Doyle, P., Fordy, C. & Haight, A. (2011) Prison Video Conferencing The University of Vermont http://www.uvm.edu/~vlrs/CriminalJusticeandCorrections/prison%20video%20conferencing.pdf accessed 20/1/15.

Easton, S., & Piper, C. (2008). *Sentencing and punishment: The quest for justice*. Oxford, Oxford University Press.

Easton, S. and Piper, C. (2012) *Sentencing and Punishment: The Quest for Justice*. Oxford, Oxford University Press.

Elias, N. (2010) *The Civilizing Process*. Oxford, Blackwell.

Elliott, P. (1974) Uses and Gratifications Research: A Critique and a Sociological Alternative, in Blumler, J.G. and Katz, E. (eds.) *The Uses of Mass Communications: Current Perspectives on Gratifications Research*. London, Sage.

Ellis, J. (2000) *Seeing Things: Television in the Age of Uncertainty*. London, I.B. Tauris.

Erwin, J. (2005) Never a Luxury, *The Guardian*, 14/06/05, http://www.guardian.co.uk/society/2005/jun/14/prisonsandprobation.erwinjames accessed 12/09/11.

Europris (2013) ICT Expert Group Meeting 12–13 December 2013, Europris Netherlands, http://www.europris.org/resources_package/report-ict-workshop-2014/ accessed 07/07/15.

Ferrell, J. (2004) Boredom, Crime and Criminology, *Theoretical Criminology*, 8:3, pp. 287–302.

Festinger, L. (1957) *A Theory of Cognitive Dissonance*. Stanford, Stanford University Press.

Fiddler, M. (2010) Four Walls and What Lies Within: The Meaning of Space and Place in Prisons, *Prison Service Journal*, 187, pp. 3–8.

Finn, S. and Gorr, M.B. (1988) Social Isolation and Social Support as Correlates of Television Viewing Motivation, *Communication Research*, 15:2, pp. 135–158.

Fong, J. (2008) Facilitating Education in Prisons, in *Advances in Blended Learning*. Berlin Heidelberg, Springer, pp. 1–15.

Forsythe, B. (2004) Loneliness and Cellular Confinement in English Prisons 1878–1921, *British Journal of Criminology*, 44:5, pp. 759–770.

Foucault, M. (1991) *Discipline and Punish: The Birth of the Prison*. London, Penguin.

Foucault, M. (2009) Alternative to the Prison: Dissemination or Decline of Social Control?, *Theory, Culture, Society*, 26, pp. 12–24.

Frazier, C. and Meisenhelder, T. (1985) Exploratory Notes on Criminality and Emotional Ambivalence, *Qualitative Sociology*, 8:3, pp. 266–284.

Frey, B.S., Benesch, C. and Stutzer, A. (2007) Does Watching TV Make Us Happy?, *Journal of Economic Psychology*, 28:3, pp. 283–313.

Garfinkel, H. (1967) *Studies in Ethnomethodology*. Englewood Cliffs, Prentice Hall.

Garland, D. (1991) *Punishment and Modern Society: A Study in Social Theory*. Oxford, Clarendon.

Genders, E. and Player, E. (1995) *Grendon: A Study of a Therapeutic Prison*. Oxford, Oxford University Press.

Gersch, B. (2003) *Dis/connected: Media Use among Inmates*. Unpublished PhD Oregon, University of Oregon, USA.

Gersch, B. (2004) *Race, Television, and Power Dynamics in Correctional Facilities*. Paper Presented at International Communication Association, New Orleans 27 May 2004, http://www.allacademic.com/meta/p113310_index.html accessed 06/06/11.

Gersch, B. (2007) *Keeping Up and Shutting Out: Media Use among Female Inmates*. Paper Presented at International Communication Association, San Francisco 24 May 2007, http://citation.allacademic.com/meta/p_mla_apa_research_citation/1/7/3/0/4/pages173043/p173043-1.php accessed 06/06/11.

Gershuny, J. and Sullivan, O. (1998) The Sociological Uses of Time-use Diary Analysis, *European Sociological Review*, 14:1, pp. 69–85.

Giddens, A. (2009) *The Consequences of Modernity*. Cambridge, Polity Press.

Goffman, E. (1990) *The Presentation of Self in Everyday Life*. London, Penguin.

Goffman, E. (1991) *Asylums: Essays on the Social Situation of Mental Patients and Other Inmates*. London, Penguin.

Gorgol, L. and Sponsler, B. (2011) Unlocking Potential: Results of a National Survey of Postsecondary Education in State Prisons Washington, DC, IHEP, http://www.ihep.org/sites/default/files/uploads/docs/pubs/unlocking_potential-psce_final_report_may_2011.pdf accessed 26/11/15.

Gorton, K. (2009) *Media Audiences: Television, Meaning and Emotion*. Edinburgh, Edinburgh University Press.

Gramsci, A. (1971) *Selections from Prison Notebooks*. New York, Columbia University Press.

Gray, A. (1987) Behind Closed Doors: Video Recorders in the Home, in Baeur, H. and Dyer, G. (eds.) *Boxed In: Women and Television*. London, Pandora Press.

Gray, A. (1992) *Video Playtime: The Gendering of a Leisure Technology*. London, Routledge.

Greer, K. (2002) Walking an Emotional Tightrope: Managing Emotions in a Women's Prison, *Symbolic Interaction*, 25:1, pp. 117–139.

Guardian (2011a) Prison 'slopping out' Case Goes to High Court, 26/9/11, http://www.guardian.co.uk/society/2011/sep/26/prison-slopping-out-high-court-case accessed 01/10/11.

Guardian (2011b) http://www.theguardian.com/technology/2012/mar/02/censorship-inseperable-from-surveillance accessed 09/06/15.

Gullone, E., Jones, T. and Cummins, R. (2000) Coping Styles and Prison Experience as Predictors of Psychological Well-Being in Male Prisoners, *Psychiatry, Psychology and Law*, 7:1, pp. 170–181.

Habermas, J., Lennox, S. and Lennox, F. (1974), The Public Sphere: An Encyclopedia Article (1964), *New German Critique*, 3, 49–55.

Hall, S. (1980) Encoding/Decoding, in Hall, S., Hobson, D., Lowe., A. and Willis, P. (eds.) *Culture, Media, Language*. London, Hutchinson.

Hall, S., Hobson, D., Lowe., A. and Willis, P. (eds.) (1980) *Culture, Media, Language*. London, Hutchinson.

Hajjar, W.J. (1998) *Television in the Nursing Home: A Case Study of the Media Consumption Routines and Strategies of Nursing Home Residents*. New York, The Haworth Press.

Hammersley, M. and Atkinson, P. (2007) *Ethnography: Principles in Practice*. London, Routledge.

Hammersley, M. and Atkinson, P. (2010) *Ethnography*. London, Routledge.

Hannah-Moffat, K. (1999) Moral Agent or Actuarial Subject: Risk and Canadian Women's Imprisonment, *Theoretical Criminology*, 3:1, pp. 71–94.

Hansard – House of Commons Debates (1998) Vol. 314, Session 1997–1998, http://www.publications.parliament.uk/pa/cm/cmvo314.htm accessed 03/03/11.

Harreveld, F.V., Pligt, J.V., Claassen, L. and Van Dijk, W.W. (2007) Inmate Emotion Coping and Psychological and Physical Well-Being: The Use of Crying Over Spilled Milk, *Criminal Justice and Behavior*, 34:5, pp. 697–708.

Harrison, J., Harrison, O. and Martin, E. (2004) In-cell Television: A Study to Identify the Positive Impact of In-cell TV, *Prison Service Journal*, (158), 12–16.

Harvey, J. (2008) An Embedded Multimethod Approach to Prison Research, in King, R.D. and Wincup, E. (eds.) *Doing Research on Crime and Justice*. Oxford, Oxford University Press.

Healy, S.D. (1984) *Boredom, Self and Culture*. Cranbury NJ, Associated University Press.

Her Majesty's Prison Service:

- Prison Service Order 4000 (2000) Incentives and Earned Privileges, http://www.justice.gov.uk/offenders/psos accessed 13/11/11.
- Prison Service Order 0550 (2005) Prisoner Induction, http://www.justice.gov.uk/offenders/psos accessed 13/11/11.
- Prison Service Order 2800 (2006) Race Equality, http://www.justice.gov.uk/offenders/psos accessed 13/11/11.
- Prison Service Instruction 49/2011 https://www.justice.gov.uk/offenders/psis/prison-service-instructions-2011 accessed 21.10.15.
- Prison Service Instruction 11/2011 (2011) Incentive and Earned Privilege, https://view.officeapps.live.com/op/view.aspx?src=http%3A%2F%2Fwww.justice.gov.uk%2Fdownloads%2Foffenders%2Fpsipso%2Fpsi-2011%2Fpsi_2011_11_incentives_and_earned_privileges.doc accessed 13/11/11.

Her Majesty's Prison Service (1991) *Prison Rules*. London, HM Prison Service.
Her Majesty's Prison Service (2008) Statement of Purpose HM Prison Service, http://www.hmprisonservice.gov.uk/abouttheservice/statementofpurpose/ accessed 13/11/11.
Hobson, D. (1980) Housewives and Mass Media, *Culture, Media and Language*.
Hobson, D. (1982) *Crossroads: The Drama of a Soap Opera*. London, Methuen.
Hochschild, A. (1983) *The Managed Heart*. Berkeley, University of California Press.
Holstien, J.A. and Gubrium, J.F. (1995) *The Active Interview*. Thousand Oaks, Sage.
Holtz, T.A. (2001) Reaching Out from Behind Bars: The Constitutionality of Laws Barring Prisoners from the Internet, *Brooklyn Law Review*, 67, p. 855.
Home Office (2004) Reducing Re-Offending National Action Plan. London: Home Office.
Horton, D. and Wohl, R. (1956) Mass Communication and Para-Social Interaction: Observations on Intimacy at a Distance, *Psychiatry*, 19, pp. 215–229.
House of Commons (2005) Select Committee on Education and Skills: Seventh Report 31.3.05, p. 27 http://www.publications.parliament.uk/pa/cm200405/cmselect/cmeduski/114/11407.htm accessed 20/01/15.
House of Commons (2006) *Report for the Zahid Mubarek Inquiry*. London, Stationery Office.
Howard League (2014) http://www.howardleague.org/prison-officer-numbers/ accessed 21/10/14.
Hughes, E. (2004) *Free to Learn?* Mitcham, Prisoners' Education Trust.
Illich, I. (1985) *Limits to Medicine – Medical Nemesis*. Harmondsworth, Penguin.
Irwin, J. (1970) *The Felon*. Englewood Cliffs, Prentice-Hall.
Irwin, J. and Cressey, D.R. (1962) Thieves, Convicts and the Inmate Culture, *Social Problems*, 10:2, pp. 142–155.
Irwin, J. and Owen, B. (2005) Harm and the Contemporary Prison, in Liebling, A. and Maruna, S. (eds.) *The Effects of Imprisonment*. Cullompton, Willan.
Irwin, T. (2008) The 'Inside' Story: Practitioner Perspectives on Teaching in Prison. *The Howard Journal of Criminal Justice*, 47:5, pp. 512–528.
Jacobs, J.B. (1962) Street Gangs Behind Bars, *Social Problems*, 21:3, pp. 395–409.
Jacobs, J.B. (1974) Participant Observation in Prison, *Urban Life and Culture*, 3:2, pp. 221–240.

Jefferson, A.M. (2003) Therapeutic Discipline? Reflections on the Penetration of Sites of Control by Therapeutic Discourse, *Outlines*, 1, pp. 55–73.

Jewkes, Y. (2002a) *Captive Audience: Media, Masculinity and Power in Prison.* Collumpton, Willan.

Jewkes, Y. (2002b) The Use of Media in Constructing Identities in the Masculine Environment of Men's Prisons, *European Journal of Communication*, 17:2, pp. 205–225.

Jewkes, Y. (2005a) Men Behind Bars: 'Doing' Masculinity as an Adaptation to Imprisonment, *Men and Masculinities*, 8:1, pp. 44–63.

Jewkes, Y. (2005b) Loss, Liminality and the Life Sentence: Managing Identity Through a Disrupted Lifecourse, in Liebling, A. and Maruna, S. (eds.) *The Effects of Imprisonment*. Cullompton, Willan.

Jewkes, Y. (2010) Penal Aesthetics and the Architecture of Incarceration, *Prison Service Journal*, 187, pp. 23–28.

Jewkes, Y. (2011) *Media and Crime*. Los Angeles, Sage.

Jewkes, Y. (2013) What has Prison Ethnography to Offer in an Age of Mass Incarceration? Yvonne Jewkes Considers the Importance of Research in Understanding the Prison. *Criminal Justice Matters*, 91:1, pp. 14–15

Jewkes, Y. and Johnston, H. (eds.) (2006) *Prison Readings: A Critical Introduction to Prisons and Imprisonment*. Cullompton, Willan.

Jewkes, Y. and Johnston, H. (2009) 'Cavemen in an Era of Speed-of-Light Technology': Historical and Contemporary Perspectives on Communication within Prisons, *The Howard Journal*, 48:2, pp. 132–143.

Johnson, R. and Toch, H. (1982) *Pains of Imprisonment*. California, Thousand Oaks, Sage.

Jones, R.S. and Schmid, T.J. (2000) *Doing Time: Prison Experience and Identity Among First Time Inmates*. Stanford, JAI Press.

Kagan, J. and Rosman, B.L. (1964) Cardiac and Respiratory Correlates of Attention and an Analytic Attitude, *Journal of Experimental Child Psychology*, 1, pp. 50–63.

Karp, D.R. (2010) Unlocking Men, Unmasking Masculinities: Doing Men's Work in Prison, *The Journal of Men's Studies*, 18:1, pp. 63–83.

Katz, E. and Lazarsfeld, P. (1955) *Personal Influence*. New York, Free Press.

King, R.D. and Liebling, A. (2008) Doing Research in Prison, in King, R.D. and Wincup, E. (eds.) *Doing Research on Crime and Justice*. Oxford, Oxford University Press.

King, R.D. and Wincup, E. (eds.) (2008) *Doing Research on Crime and Justice*. Oxford, Oxford University Press.

Klapp, O.E. (1986) *Overload and Boredom*. New York, Greenwood Press.

Knight, V. (2000) *An Investigation into Mass Communication Consumption in a Closed Young Offenders' Institution*, Unpublished Masters Thesis, Leicester, De Montfort University.

Knight, V. (2001) *An Investigation into the Mass Communication Consumption in a Male Young Offenders' Institution*. Unpublished MA thesis, Leicester UK, De Montfort University.

Knight, V. (2005a) The Potency of In-Cell Television: The Appropriateness and Usefulness, *Prison Service Journal*, 161, November 2005, pp. 53–58.

Knight, V. (2005b) An Investigation into Mass Communication Consumption in a Closed Young Offenders' Institution, *Particip@tions Journal*, 2:1, http://www.participations.org/volume%202/issue%201/2_01_knight.htm accessed 10/01/11.

Knight, V. (2005c) Remote Control: The Role of TV in Prison, *Criminal Justice Matters* No. 59. London: The Centre for Crime and Justice Studies.

Knight, V. (2012) *The Role of in-cell Television in a Male Adult Prison. Governing Souls with Television*, PhD thesis. De Montfort University, Leicester.

Knight, V. (2014) A Modus Vivendi – In-cell Television, Social Relations, Emotion and Safer Custody, *Prison Service Journal*, 215, November 2014, pp. 19–23.

Knight, V. (2015a) Television, Emotion and Prison Life: Achieving Personal Control, *Particip@tions*, 12:1, http://www.participations.org/Volume%2012/Issue%201/3.pdf accessed 10/06/15.

Knight, V. (2015b) Some Observations on the Digital Landscape of Prisons Today, *Prison Service Journal*, pp. 3–9.

Knight, V. and Hine, J. (2009) Learning their Lesson: T-Learning as a Vehicle for In-Cell Learning by Prisoners, *The International Journal of Learning*, 16:10, pp. 51–61.

Kubey, R. (1986) Television Use in Everyday Life, *Journal of Communication*, 36:3, pp. 108–123.

Kubey, R. (1990) Television and the Quality of Family Life, *Communication Quarterly*, 38:4, pp. 312–324.

Kubey, R. (1994) Television Use in Everyday Life, *Communication*, summer 1986.

Kubey, R. and Csikszentmihalyi, M. (1990) Television as Escape: Subjective Experience Before an Evening of Heavy Viewing, *Communication Reports*, 3, pp. 92–100.

Laing, R.D. (1990) *The Divided Self*. London, Penguin.

Layder, D. (2004) *Emotion in Social Life: The Lost Heart of Society*. London, Sage.

Layder, D. (2005) *Sociological Practice: Linking Theory and Social Research*. London, Sage.

Layder, D. (2006) *Understanding Social Theory*. London, Sage.

Lazarus, R. and Folkman, S. (1984) *Stress, Appraisal and Coping*. New York, Springer.

Lemish, D. (1982) The Rules of Viewing Television in Public Places, *Journal of Broadcasting*, 26:4, pp. 757–781.

Levin, B.H. and Brown, W.E. (1975) Susceptibility to Boredom of Jailers and Law Enforcement Officers, *Psychological Review*, 36, p. 190.

Liebling, A. (1991) *Suicide and Self-Injury Amongst Young Offenders in Custody*. Unpublished PhD thesis Cambridge University.

Liebling, A. (1999a) Prison Suicide and Prisoner Coping, *Crime and Justice*, 26, pp. 283–359.

Liebling, A. (1999b) Doing Research in Prison: Breaking the silence?, *Theoretical Criminology*, 3:2, pp. 147–173.

Liebling, A. (2002) Suicides in Prison and the Safer Prisons Agenda, *Probation Journal*, 49, pp. 140–150.

Liebling, A. (2004) The Late Modern Prison and the Question of Values, *Current Issues in Criminal Justice*, 16:2, pp. 202–219.

Liebling, A., Crewe, B., Hulley, S. and McLean, C. (2010) *Values, Practices and Outcomes in Public and Private Sector Corrections*. ESRC End of Award Report Swindon ESRC.

Liebling, A., Elliott, C. and Arnold, H. (2001) Transforming the Prison: Romantic Optimism or Appreciative Realism, *Criminology and Criminal Justice*, 1:2, pp. 161–180.

Liebling, A. and Krarup, H. (1993) *Suicide Attempts and Self-Injury in Male Prisons. Report for the Home Office Research Planning Unit.* London, Home Office.

Liebling, A. and Maruna, S. (eds.) (2005) *The Effects of Imprisonment.* Cullompton, Willan.

Liebling, A., Muir, G., Rose, G. and Bottoms, A. (1999) *Incentives and Earned Privileges for Prisoners: An Evaluation.* Research Findings No. 87, London, Home Office, http://www.homeoffice.gov.uk/rds/pdfs/r87.pdf accessed 05/08/08.

Liebling, A., Price, D. and Elliott, C. (1999) Appreciative Inquiry and Relationships in Prison, *Punishment and Society*, 1:1, pp. 71–98.

Liebling, A., Price, D. and Shefer, G. (2011) *The Prison Officer.* Oxford, Willan.

Lindlof, T.R. (1986) Social and Structural Constraints on Media Use in Incarceration, *Journal of Broadcasting and Electronic Media*, 30:3, pp. 341–355.

Lindlof, T.R. (1987a) *Natural Audiences: Qualitative Research of Media Uses and Effects.* New Jersey, Ablex.

Lindlof, T.R. (1987b) Ideology and Pragmatics of Media Access in Prison, in Lindlof, T.R. (ed.) *Natural Audiences: Qualitative Research of Media Uses and Effects.* New Jersey: Ablex.

Lindquist, C.H. (2000) Social Integration and Mental Well-Being among Jail Inmates, *Sociological Forum*, 15:3, pp. 431–455.

Livingstone, S. (1990) *Making Sense of Television: The Psychology of Audience Interpretation.* Oxford, Pergamon.

London Evening Standard (2011) *Offenders 'Sleep Through Sentences'.* London Evening Standard 09/03/11, http://www.standard.co.uk/newsheadlines/offenders-sleep-through-sentences-6575755.html accessed 12/08/11.

Loucks, N. (2007) *No One Knows: Offenders with Learning Difficulties and Learning Disabilities–review of Prevalence and Associated Needs.* London, Prison Reform Trust.

Lull, J. (1988) *World Families Watch Television.* London, Sage.

Lull, J. (1990) *Inside Family Viewing: Ethnographic Research on Television Audiences.* London, Routledge.

Mason, P. (Ed.). (2013). Captured by the Media. CollumptonWillan.

McBain, W.N. (1970) Arousal, Monotony and Accidents in Line Driving, *Journal of Applied Psychology*, 54:6, pp. 509–519.

McCarthy, A. (2003) *Ambient Television.* Durham, Duke University Press.

McClymont, K. (1993) *In Cell Television at HMP Stocken: An Initial Evaluation.* HMP Stocken, HM Prison Service.

McConville, S. (1995) *The Use of Punishment.* Cullompton, Willan.

McDermott, K. and King, R. (1988) Mind Games: Where the Action Is in Prisons, *British Journal of Criminology*, 28:3, pp. 357–378.

McIlwraith, R.D. (1998) 'I'm addicted to television': The Personality, Imagination and TV Watching Patterns of Self-identified Addicts, *Journal of Broadcasting and Electronic Media*, 42:3, pp. 371–386.

McLuhan, M. (1964) *Understanding Media.* London, Routledge & Kegan Paul.

McQuail, D., Blumler, J.G. and Brown, J.R. (1972) The Television Audience: A Revised Perspective, in McQuail, D. (ed.) *Sociology of Mass Communications.* Harmondsworth, Penguin.

Martel, J. (2006) To Be, One Has To Be Somewhere: Spatio-temporality in Prison Segregation, *British Journal of Criminology*, 46:4, pp. 587–612.

Martinson, R. (1974) What Works?–Questions and Answers about Prison Reform, *Public Interest*, 35, pp. 22–54.

Maruna, S. and Roy, K. (2007) Amputation or Reconstruction/ Notes on the Concept of 'Knifing Off' and Desistance Crime, *Journal of Contemporary Criminal Justice*, 231, pp. 104–124.

Mason, P. (Ed.). (2013). *Captured by the Media*. Collumpton, Willan.

Matthews, R. (1999) *Doing Time*. Basingstoke, Macmillan.

Medrich, E. (1979) Constant Television: A Background to Daily Life, *Journal of Communication*, 29:3, pp. 171–176.

Meyrowitz, J. (1985) *No Sense of Place: The Impact of Electronic Media on Social Behaviour*. Oxford, Oxford University Press.

Miller, P. and Rose, N. (2008) *Governing the Present*. Cambridge, Polity Press.

Ministry of Justice (2011) *Breaking the Cycle: Government Response*. London, Stationery Office.

Ministry of Justice (2012) Digital Strategy, https://www.gov.uk/government/publications/ministry-of-justice-digital-strategy

Mohino, S., Kirchner, T. and Forns, M. (2004) Coping Strategies in Young Male Prisoners, *Journal of Youth and Adolescence*, 33:1, pp. 41–49.

Moores, S. (1995) TV Discourse and 'Time-Space Distanciation': On Mediated Interaction in Modern Society Time and Society, 4:3, pp. 329–344.

Moores, S. (1988) 'The box on the dresser': Memories of Early Radio and Everyday Life, *Media, Culture & Society*, 10:1, pp. 23–40.

Moores, S. (1993a) *Interpreting Audiences: The Ethnography of Media Consumption*. London, Sage.

Moores, S. (1993b) Television, Geography and 'Mobile Privatization', *European Journal of Communication*, 8:3, pp. 365–379.

Moores, S. (1995a) TV Discourse and 'Time-Space Distanciation': On Mediated Interaction in Modern Society, *Time and Society*, 4:3, pp. 329–344.

Moores, S. (1995b) *Satellite TV in Everyday Life*. Luton, University of Luton Press.

Moores, S. (2000) Media and Everyday Life in Modern Society Edinburgh: Edinburgh University Press.

Moores, S. (2004) Doubling of Place: Electronic Media, Time-Space Arrangements and Social Relationships, in Couldry, N. and McCarthy, A. (eds.) *Media Space: Place, Scale and Culture in a Media Age*. London, Routledge.

Moores, S. (2006) Media Uses & Everyday Environmental Experiences: A Positive Critique of Phenomenological Geography, *Particip@tions*, 3:2, http://www.participations.org/volume%203/issue%202%20-%20special/3_02_moores.htm accessed 01/07/11.

Morgan, M. and Kett, M. (2003) The Prison Adult Literacy Survey. Results and Implications. Irish Prison Service, http://www.iprt.ie/files/adult_literacy_survey.pdf accessed 20/01/15.

Morley, D. (1980) *The 'Nationwide' Audience*. London, British Film Institute.

Morley, D. (1986) *Family Television: Culture, Power and Domestic Leisure*. London, Comedia.

Morley, D. (1992) Television, Audiences and Cultural Studies London: Routledge.

Morley, D. (1997) *Television, Audiences and Cultural Studies*. London, Routledge.

Moskalenko, S. and Heine, S.J. (2003) Watching Your Troubles Away: Television Viewing as a Stimulus for Subjective Self-Awareness, *Personality and Social Psychology*, 29:1, pp. 76–85.

Mulvey, L. (1975) Visual Pleasure and Narrative Cinema, *Screen*, 16:3, pp. 6–18.

NOMS (2008) Evaluation Report Following Survey of Prisoners on use of emaila prisoner.com, http://www.prison-technology-services.com/NOMS_Report.pdf

NOMS (2014) Prison Radio Requirements & Editorial Guidelines, London, NOMS personal correspondence November 2014.

Novek, E.M. (2005) Heaven, Hell, and Here: Understanding the Impact of Incarceration Through a Prison Newspaper, *Critical Studies in Media Communication*, 22:4, pp. 281–301.

O'Connor, P.E. (2003) Telling Bits: Silencing and the Narratives Behind Prison Walls, in Thiesmeyer, L. (ed.) *Discourse and Silencing.* Amsterdam, John Benjamins.

O'Hanlon, J.F. (1981) Boredom: Practical Consequences and a Theory, *Acta Psychologica*, 49, pp. 53–82.

O'Sullivan, T. (1991) Television Memories and Cultures of Viewing 1950–65, in Corner, J. (ed.) *Popular Television in Britain.* London, BFI.

OFCOM (2010) Viewing Patterns on Weekends, by Day Part and by Age, http://www.ofcom.org.uk/static/cmr-10/UKCM-2.71.html accessed 15/01/11.

Padfield, N. and Maruna, S. (2006) The Revolving Door at the Prison Gate: Exploring the Dramatic Increase in Recalls to Prison, *Criminology & Criminal Justice*, 6:3, pp. 329–352.

Parliament UK (2014) HC Deb, 5 November 2014, cW, http://www.parliament. uk/business/publications/written-questions-answers-statements/written-question/Commons/2014-10-31/212857/ accessed 09/06/15.

Peck, J. (1995) TV Talk Shows as Therapeutic Discourse: The Ideological Labor of the Televised Talking Cure, *Communication Theory*, 5:1, pp. 58–81.

Perse, E.M. and Rubin, A.M. (1990) Chronic Loneliness and Television Use, *Journal of Broadcasting and Electronic Media*, 34:1, pp. 37–53.

Phillips, S.D., Sentencing Project, & United States of America. (2012). Video Visits for Children Whose Parents Are Incarcerated: In Whose Best Interest? Washington, DC: The Sentencing Project, http://sentencingproject.org/doc/publications/cc_Video_Visitation_White_Paper.pdf

Pike, A. and Adams, A. (2012) Digital Exclusion or Learning Exclusion? An Ethnographic Study of Adult Male Distance Learners in English Prisons, *Research in Teaching and Learning*, 20:4, pp. 363–376.

Potts, R. and Sanchez, D. (1994) Television Viewing and Depression: No News is Good News, *Journal of Broadcasting and Electronic Media*, 38:1, pp. 79–90.

Pratt, J. (1999) Norbert Elias and the Civilized Prison, *British Journal of Sociology*, 50:2, pp. 271–296.

Pratt, J. (2000) The Return of the Wheelbarrow Men; or, the Arrival of Postmodern Penality?, *British Journal of Criminology*, 40:1, pp. 127–145.

Prison Commission (1954) Imparting of News to Prisoners: Termination of News Reading in Chapel: Use of Radio, Newspapers and Periodicals, Prison Commission PCOM9/1703, http://www.nationalarchives.gov.uk/catalogue/displaycataloguedetails.asp?CATID=10296&CATLN=3&FullDetails=True accessed 03/06/11.

Prison Reform Trust (2009) *Bromley Briefings*. London, Prison Reform Trust.

Prison Reform Trust (2010) *Bromley Briefings*. London, Prison Reform Trust.

Pryor, S. (2001) *The Responsible Prisoner*. London, Home Office.

Putnam, R. (2000) *Bowling Alone. The Collapse and Revival of American Community*. New York, Simon & Schuster.

Radway, J. (1984) *Reading the Romance*. Chapel Hill, University of North Carolina Press.

Raine, J.W. and Willson, M.J. (1997) Beyond Managerialism in Criminal Justice, *The Howard Journal of Criminal Justice*, 36, pp. 80–95.

Reuss, A. (1999). Prison (er) education. The Howard Journal of Criminal Justice, 38:2, 113–127.

Ribbens, W. and Malliet, S. (2015) Exploring the Appeal of Digital Games to Male Prisoners, *Poetics*, 48, pp. 1–20.

Rimke, H.M. (2000) Governing Citizens Through Self-Help Literature Cultural Studies 14:1 61–78.

Robinson, W.P. (1975) Boredom at School, *British Journal of Educational Psychology*, 45:2, pp. 141–152.

Rokach, A. (1997) Loneliness in Jail: Coping Strategies, *International Journal of Offender Therapy and Comparative Criminology*, 41:3, pp. 260–271.

Rose, N. (1998) Governing Risky Individuals: The Role of Psychiatry in New Regimes of Control, *Psychiatry, Psychology and Law*, 5:2, pp. 177–195.

Rose, N. (1999) *Governing the Soul: The Shaping of the Private Self*. London, Routledge.

Rose, N. (2000) Government and Control, *British Journal of Criminology*, 40:2, pp. 321–339.

Roth, J. (1963) *Timetables: Structuring the Passage of Time in Hospital Treatment and Other Careers*. Indianapolis, Bobbs-Merrill Co. Inc.

Rotter, J. (1954) *Social Learning and Clinical Psychology*. Englewood Cliffs, Prentice-Hall Inc.

Roy, D. (1960) Banana Time: Job Satisfaction and Informal Interaction, *Human Organization*, 18:4, pp. 158–168.

Rubin, A.M. (1993) The Effect of Locus Control on Communication Motivation, Anxiety, and Satisfaction, *Communication Quarterly*, 41:2, pp. 161–171.

Sapsford, R.J. (1978) Life-Sentence Prisoners: Psychological Changes during Sentence, *British Journal of Criminology*, 18:2, pp. 128–145.

Scannell, P. (1996) *Radio, Television and Modern Life*. Oxford, Blackwell.

Scheff, T.J. (1988) Shame and Conformity: The Deference-Emotion System, *American Sociological Review*, 53:3, pp. 395–406.

Schwartz, B. (1971) Pre-Institutional vs. Situational Influence in a Correctional Community Prison, *Criminological Law, Criminology & Police Science Journal*, 62:4, pp. 532–542.

Scott, D. and Codd, H. (2010) *Controversial Issues in Prison*. Maidenhead, Open University Press.

Scott, D. and Flynn, N. (2014) *Prisons & Punishment: The Essentials*. London, Sage.

Seeman, T. E. (1996). Social ties and health: The benefits of social integration. *Annals of epidemiology*, 6:5, 442–451.

Serge, V. (1978) *Men in Prison*. London, Pluto Press.

Shattuc, J.M. (1997) *The Talking Cure: TV, Talk Shows and Women*. New York, Routledge.

Silverstone, R. (1994) Television and Everyday Life London: Routledge.

Silverstone, R. (1999a) *Television and Everyday Life.* London, Routledge.

Silverstone, R. (1999b) *Why Study the Media?* London, Sage.

Silverstone, R., Hirsch, E. and Morley, D. (1991) Listening to a Long Conversation: An Ethnographic Approach to the Study of Information and Communication Technologies in the Home, *Cultural Studies*, 5:2, pp. 204–227.

Sim, J. (1994) Tougher than the Rest? Men in Prison, in Newburn, T. and Stanko, E. (eds.) *Just Boys Doing Business Men, Masculinities and Crime.* London, Routledge.

Simon, J. (1993) *Poor Discipline.* Chicago, University of Chicago Press.

Simon, J. (2000) The 'Society of Captives' in the Era of Hyper-Incarceration, *Theoretical Criminology*, 4:3, pp. 285–308.

Sirgy, M.J., Lee, D., Kosenko, R., Meadow, L., Rahtz, D., Cicic, M., Xi Jin, G., Yarsuvat, D., Blenkhorn, D. and Wright, N. (1998) Does Television Viewership Play a Role in the Perception of Quality of Life?, *Journal of Advertising*, 27:1, pp. 125–142.

Smart, U. (2001) *Grendon Tales: Stories from a Therapeutic Community.* Waterside Press, Winchester.

Smith, R.P. (1981) Boredom: A Review, *Human Factors*, 23:3, pp. 329–340.

Sørensen, E. and Triantafillou, P. (eds.) (2009) *The Politics of Self-Governance* Farnham, Ashgate.

Snacken, S. (2005) Forms of Violence and Regimes in Prison: Report of Research in Belgian Prisons, in Liebling, A. and Maruna, S. (eds.) *The Effects of Imprisonment.* Cullompton, Willan.

Sparkes, R. (1999) *Schools, Education and Social Exclusion Centre for Analysis of Social Exclusion.* London, London School of Economics.

Sparks, R. (1994) Can Prisons be Legitimate? Penal Politics, Privatization and the Timeliness of an Old Idea, *British Journal of Criminology*, 34:SPI, pp. 14–28.

Sparks, R. and Bottoms, A.E. (1995) Legitimacy and Order in Prisons, *British Journal of Sociology*, 46:1, pp. 45–62.

Sparks, R., Bottoms, A. and Hay, W. (1996) *Prisons and the Problem of Order.* Oxford, Clarendon Press.

Spigel, L. (1992) *Make Room for TV.* Chicago, University of Chicago Press.

Stockdale, E. (1983) A Short History of Prison Inspection in England, *British Journal Criminology*, 23:3, pp. 209–228.

Sykes, G. (1958) *The Society of Captives: A Study of A Maximum Security Prison.* Princeton, NJ, Princeton University Press.

Sykes, G. (1999) *The Society of Captives: A Study of A Maximum Security Prison.* Princeton, NJ, Princeton University Press.

Tait, S. (2011) A Typology of Prison Officer Approaches to Care, *European Journal of Criminology*, 8:6, pp. 440–454.

Tester, K. (1998) Bored and Blasé Television, the emotions and Georg Simmel, in Bendelow, G. and Williams, S.J. (eds.) *Emotions in Social Life: Critical Themes and Contemporary Issues.* London, Routledge.

The Lifer (2015) @Prison_Diaries (Twitter) https://twitter.com/Prison_Diaries accessed 21/10/15.

Thiesmeyer, L. (2003) *Discourse and Silencing.* Amsterdam: John Benjamins.

Thomas, C.W. (1977) Theoretical Perspectives on Prisonization: A Comparison of the Importation and Deprivation Models, *The Journal of Criminal Law and Criminology*, 68:1, pp. 135–145.

Thompson, J. (2005) The New Visibility, *Theory, Culture & Society*, 22:6, pp. 31–51.

Thompson, J. (2011) *The Media and Modernity: A Social Theory of Media*. Stanford, Stanford University Press.

Toch, H. (1977) *Living in Prison*. New York, Free Press.

Toch, H. and Adams, K. (1986) Pathology and Disruptiveness among Prison Inmates, *Journal of Research in Crime and Delinquency*, 23:1, pp. 7–21.

Turley, C. and Webster, S. (2010) Implementation and Delivery of the Test Beds Virtual Campus Case Study. National Centre for Social Research, https://www.gov.uk/government/uploads/system/uploads/attachment_data/file/32322/11-827-implementation-of-test-beds-virtual-campus.pdf accessed 20/01/15.

UK Parliament (2014) Prisons: Mobile Phones:Written question – 212857 http://www.parliament.uk/business/publications/written-questions-answers-statements/written-question/Commons/2014-10-31/212857/ accessed 26/11/15.

Vandebosch, H. (2000) Research Note: A Captive Audience? The Media Use of Prisoners, *European Journal of Communication*, 15:4, pp. 529–544.

Vandebosch, H. (2001) Criminal Involvement and Media Use, *Deviant Behavior*, 22:6, pp. 541–570.

Wacquant, L. (2002) The Curious Eclipse of Prison Ethnography in the Age of Mass Incarceration, *Ethnography*, 3:4, pp. 371–397.

Wahidin, A. (2004) *Older Women in the Criminal Justice System: Running Out of Time*. London, Jessica Kingsley.

Whannel, G. (1995) The Price is Right But the Moments are Sticky, in Strinati, D. and Wagg, S. (eds.) (1992) *Come on Down? Popular Media Culture in Post-War Britain*. London, Routledge.

Welsh, D. (2008) Virtual Parents: How Virtual Visitation Legislation is Shaping the Future of Custody Law, *Journal of Law & Family Studies*, 11, pp. 215–225.

Williams, B. (2002) The Victim's Charter: Citizens as Consumers of Criminal Justice Services, *Howard Journal of Criminal Justice*, 38:4, pp. 384–396.

Williams, R. (1974) *Television: Technology and Cultural Form*. Hanover, Wesleyan University Press.

Williams, S. (2001) *Emotion and Social Theory: Corporeal Reflections on the (Ir)Rational*. London, Sage.

Willis, P. (1977) *Learning to Labour*. Aldershot, Gower.

Wilson, D. (2002) Millbank, the Panopticon and Their Victorian Audiences, *The Howard Journal*, 41:4, pp. 364–381.

Wilson, D. and McCabe, S. (2002) How HMP Grendon 'Works' in the Words of Those Undergoing Therapy, *Howard Journal of Criminal Justice*, 1:3, pp. 229–291.

Wood, H. (2005) Texting the Subject: Women, Television and Modern Self-Reflexivity, *The Communication Review*, 8:2, pp. 115–135.

Wood, H. (2009) *Talking with Television Women, Television and Modern Self-Reflexivity*. Urbana, University of Illinois Press.

Wooldredge, J.D. (1999) Inmate Experiences and Psychological Well-Being, *Criminal Justice and Behavior*, 26:2, pp. 235–250.

Woolf, L.J. (1991) Prison Disturbances April 1990: Report of an Inquiry by the Rt. Hon Lord Justice Woolf (Parts I and II) and His Honour Judge Stephen Tumin (Part II).

Woolf, J. and Tumin, S. (1991) *Prison Disturbances*. Norwich, Her Majesty's Stationery Office.

Zamble, E. and Porporino, F.J. (1988) *Coping, Behaviour and Adaptation in Prison Inmates*. New York, Springer-Verlag.

Zamble, E. and Porporino, F.J. (2013) *Coping, Behavior, and Adaptation in Prison Inmates*. Springer Science & Business Media, New York.

Zillman, D. (1988) Mood Management through Communication Choices, *The American Behavioral Scientist*, 31:3, pp. 327–340.

Zimmerman, D. and Wieder, D. (1977) The Diary, *Journal of Contemporary Ethnography*, 5:4, pp. 479–498.

Zuckerman, M. (1979) *Sensation Seeking; Arousal (Physiology); Testing*. Hillsdale, Lawrence Earlbaum Associates.

Index

Lightning Source UK Ltd.
Milton Keynes UK
UKOW06n0637121116
287347UK00005B/29/P